M.I.9

M.I.9

AN OFFICIAL HISTORY OF THE SECRET ESCAPE AND EVASION ORGANISATION

AN OFFICIAL HISTORY

FRONTLINE
BOOKS

M.I.9
An Official History of the Secret Escape and Evasion Organisation

This edition published in 2024 by Frontline Books,
an imprint of Pen & Sword Books Ltd,
47 Church Street, Barnsley, S. Yorkshire, S70 2AS,

This book is based on file reference WO 208-3242 which is held at The National Archives, Kew, and is licensed under the Open Government Licence v3.0.

Text alterations and additions © Frontline Books

ISBN: 978-1-39907-955-6

Pen & Sword Books Ltd incorporates the imprints of Air World Books, Pen & Sword Archaeology, Atlas, Aviation, Battleground, Discovery, Family History, History, Maritime, Military, Naval, Politics, Social History, Transport, True Crime, Claymore Press, Frontline Books, Praetorian Press, Seaforth Publishing and White Owl.

For a complete list of Pen & Sword titles please contact:

PEN & SWORD BOOKS LTD
47 Church Street, Barnsley, South Yorkshire, S70 2AS, UK.
E-mail: enquiries@pen-and-sword.co.uk
Website: www.pen-and-sword.co.uk

Or

PEN AND SWORD BOOKS,
1950 Lawrence Road, Havertown, PA 19083, USA
E-mail: uspen-and-sword@casematepublishers.com
Website: www.penandswordbooks.com

CONTENTS

PUBLISHER'S NOTE

This official history is based on original archive material, and, as far as possible, is reproduced in the form and format it was originally written in the relevant documents. Aside from correcting obvious spelling mistakes or typographical errors, we have strived to keep the edits and alterations to the absolute minimum.

INTRODUCTION

Before the outbreak of war conferences of ex-prisoners of war escapers of the 1914-18 war were held under the auspices of M.I.1, the Air Ministry also being involved. In Nov-Dec 39 G.H.Q. British Expeditionary Force recommended to the Director of Military Intelligence that an organisation should be set up in the War Office to facilitate escapes of British prisoners of war from enemy prison camps. The matter was considered by Military Intelligence Research who advised agreement. The D.M.I. then took up the question with the Director of Naval Intelligence at the Admiralty and the Director of Intelligence at the Air Ministry, and as a result M.I.9 was established as an inter-service section consisting in the first instance of a G.S.O.1, a G.S.O.2, a G.S.O.3 and officers attached from the Admiralty and the Air Ministry:

Conduct of Work No. 48.
M.I.9
1. A new section of the Intelligence Directorate at the War Office has been formed. It will be called M.I.9. It will work in close connection with and act as agent for the Admiralty and Air Ministry.
2. The Section is responsible for:
    (a) The preparation and execution of plans for facilitating the escape of British Prisoners of War of all three Services in Germany or elsewhere.
    (b) Arranging instructions in connection with above.
    (c) Making other advance provision, as considered necessary.
    (d) Collection and dissemination of information obtained from British Prisoners of War.
    (e) Advising on counter-escape measures for German Prisoners of War in Great Britain, if requested to do so.
3. M.I.9 will be accommodated in Room 424, Metropole Hotel.

(Sgd.) J. Spencer.
Col. G.S. for D.M.I.

23.12.39.

Resulting from further consultation with selected escapers of the 1914-18 war, it was decided to carry out immediately a programme of lectures by the latter in order to teach service personnel how to behave in the event of capture, emphasis being laid on the duty not to be taken prisoner and to escape if captured. It was decided that the best way to get escape material into prison camps in the early stages of the war was on the man, and these lectures were also designed to give instruction on the use of escape gadgets. In addition, a code was taught to selected personnel.

At the same time a secret M.I.9 fund was authorised, and a technical officer brought in to experiment and advise upon escape material.

PART I

M.I.9 FORMATION AND STRUCTURE

Chapter 1

HISTORICAL BACKGROUND

In April 1940, M.I.9 took over that part of M.I.1(a) which was responsible for Intelligence work connected with enemy prisoners of war and internees. (This element of M.I.1(a) had been working on these problems since June 1939 and on the outbreak of war, had established in the Tower of London a small Combined Services Detailed Interrogation Centre.) The side which dealt with enemy prisoners of war and internees in the U.K. was incorporated in M.I.9 as M.I.9(a), the side which dealt with British prisoners of war and internees in enemy and neutral countries being thenceforward known as M.I.9(b), which as a further commitment was responsible for intelligence aspects of persons arriving in the U.K. on repatriation from enemy countries.

During 1940 and 1941 work on both the enemy and British sides expanded to an extent which resulted in the establishment, at the end of 1941, of a Deputy Directorate of Military Intelligence (Prisoners of War), M.I.9(b) becoming M.I.9 (British Prisoners of War Intelligence) and M.I9(a) becoming M.I.19 (Enemy Prisoners of War Intelligence); and a new unit, Intelligence School 9, being created to take over the executive work of M.I.9. The Intelligence aspects of aliens, repatriated persons and internees came under M.I.19.

Objectives of M.I.9

    (a) To facilitate escapes of British prisoners of war, thereby getting back service personnel and containing additional enemy manpower on guard duties.
    (b) To facilitate the return to the United Kingdom of those who succeeded in evading capture in enemy occupied territory.
    (c) To collect and distribute information.

(d) To assist in the denial of information to the enemy.
(e) To maintain morale of British prisoners of war in enemy prison camps.

Methods
Methods of facilitating escapes and evasion were:

i.   Preliminary training (pre-capture) by lectures and instruction in code.
ii. Preparation and issue of the M.I.9 Bulletin.
iii. Technical research and production of Escape Aids (including special maps).
iv. The issue of Escape Aids, either in conjunction with pre-capture training or by post to Prisoner of War Camps.
v.   The issue of 'Blood Chits' in conjunction with pre-capture training.
vi. The preparation of plans for escape and evasion.

(It should be noted that rescue work in connection with aircraft flying over friendly territory or sea is the responsibility of the Air Sea Rescue Service. M.I.9 is responsible for escapes from or evasion in enemy territory.)

Information was obtained by the following methods:

i.   Through code correspondence with Prisoner of War Camps.
ii. Through the interrogation of escapers and evaders (British Service Personnel), infiltrators (Allied) and of civilians (British).

Information so obtained was embodied in reports and transmitted to all three services and other government departments. (It must be noted that as P/W were forbidden by A.C.I. to make public broadcasts after capture this method of transmitting code messages was rejected.)

Methods of maintaining morale
The high morale of British prisoners was sustained by the receipt of news letters and by the realisation that the War Office, evidenced through its correspondence and wireless contacts with P/W Camps, was concerned with the prisoners welfare. Obviously M.I.9 cannot claim entire credit for what is a native British characteristic, but the morale value of these contacts was admitted by the P/W themselves to have been considerable. That British prisoners' morale was incredibly high is proved by the translation of an SS Report on Questions of

Internal Security (12 Aug 43). It was possible through this method of communication to ginger up those few Senior Officers who were known to be weak in relation to the Germans by sending strongly worded messages from the British Government.

Although classified as Military Intelligence, M.I.9 work is in fact a mixture of M.O., M.I., M.T. and Q. Escape planning is Military Operations (sometimes on quite a large scale – e.g. in Italy after the Italian armistice); the collection of information by code communication with P/W Camps and by interrogation of escapers and evaders is Military Intelligence; preventive training is Military Training and the supply of escape and evasion material can be regarded as Q.

Organisation

On 1 January 1942 M.I.9 was re-organised into two sub-sections, M.I.9(b) and M.I.9(d), the former dealing with general questions, co-ordination, distribution of information and liaison with other services and government departments and overseas commands, the latter, M.I.9(d), being responsible for organising preventive training (instruction in evasion and escape) to combatant personnel of the three services in the United Kingdom and for the issue of evasion and escape equipment and information to units at home and M.I.9 organisations overseas.

In order to centralise the collection and distribution of "Intelligence" available from M.I.9 sources a sub-section – exclusively responsible for this task – M.I.9(f) was formed in April 1944.

M.I.9(b)

The sub-section consisted in January 1942 of the following:

> One G.S.O.2.
> Two G.S.O.3s.
> One 2/O W.R.N.S.

The work of M.I.9(b) in January 1942 consisted of the following:

i.   General correspondence, co-ordination and Secretariat.
ii.   Official cover and correspondence for I.S.9.
iii.   Distribution of information externally and internally.
iv.   Liaison with the Directorate of Prisoners of War on Policy, Geneva Convention, intelligence and security questions affecting British prisoners.
v.   Liaison with Security Service on special cases arising in Camps.

vi.   Press and Publicity questions affecting escapers and evaders.

vii.   Intelligence and Security questions affecting prisoners. Correspondence in collaboration with M.I.12(P/W).

viii.   Liaison with Military Attachés abroad.

ix.   Liaison with M.I.9 organisations abroad, A.F.H.Q., M.E., India.

x.   Liaison with Casualty Branches of all three Services, Dominion, Colonial and India Offices.

xi.   Liaison with Finance Sections on questions of expenses and allowances of escapers and evaders.

xii.   Liaison with Admiralty, Air Ministry, M.I.5, and other departments in regard to arrival in U.K. of escapers and evaders.

xiii.   Organising and carrying out interviews with, and preparation of reports of, escapers and evaders of all three Services and distribution of the ensuing reports. (Up to February 1943 when I.S.9(W) was formed).

xiv.   Grading of recommendations for awards and keeping records. (Until a separate sub-section directly under D.D.M.I.(P/W) was formed).

xv.   Collection and collation of information for M.I.9 Bulletin for use of all three Services. (Taken over by M.I.9(d) in November 1942).

xvi.   Posting of personnel to I.S.9 and exchanges of personnel between M.I.9 organisations abroad.

xvii.   Annotations and distribution of information obtained from M.I.9 sources regarding camp locations in Germany.

xviii. Distribution of maps and overlay of German P/W camps.

M.I.9(d)

The sub-section was inter-Service in composition and in Jan 42 the organising staff consisted of:

R.A.F.:
> One S/Ldr. (attached) O i/c.

R.N.:
> One Lt. Cdr. (attached) and later: One 2/O W.R.N.S. (attached)

Army:
> One G.S.O.3 (upgraded to G.S.O.2) and later: One Captain I.O.
> With an instructional staff of:
> Two S/Ldrs (attached)   }
> One F/Lt. (attached)   } All escapers in the war
>   of 1914-1918.
> Four civilian part-time lecturers (ex-officers) }
> and additional Naval and Army instructional staff at later dates.

During the period 1940-1941, instruction in Escape had been organised by M.I.9(b) in addition to the other duties performed by that sub-section, and was given chiefly by travelling lecturers who visited operational units of the three Services in the United Kingdom and certain Army formations of the B.E.F. Owing to the large number of personnel (principally R.A.F.) who found themselves cut off behind the enemy lines, it was decided to expand the teaching to include evasion of capture as well as escape. On the formation of the Deputy Directorate of Military Intelligence (Prisoners of War) in Jan 42 and the consequent re-organisation of M.I.9, M.I.9(d) was formed with the specific duties of organising and co-ordinating the training of Evasion and Escape of combatant personnel of the Royal Navy, Army and Royal Air Force in the United Kingdom, and for the issue of Evasion and Escape Equipment to units at home and M.I.9 organisations overseas.

Training

Lectures given to all three Services were divided into two categories.

General lectures. These were given to all Officers, Warrant Officers and Sergeants. The object of the lectures was:

(a) to emphasise the undesirability of being captured.
(b) to give instruction in evasion of capture.
(c) to give instruction on conduct in the event of capture.
(d) to demonstrate certain "aids to escape" with which units were equipped by M.I.9 prior to going overseas.

Officers and N.C.O.s were expected to pass on the subject matter of these lectures to the troops (while making no mention of the "aids to escape", as they were available for issue only to limited numbers) but stressing the necessity for secrecy.

As it was desirable that a uniform lecture should be given to units, a general outline of the lecture and a draft specimen lecture for the guidance of officers concerned was circulated amongst units.

The lecture took the form of an informal secret talk, and it was recommended that the audience at each lecture should not exceed 200 persons.

As conditions were constantly changing, modifications to the lecture needed continually to be made. These modifications were published in the form of the "M.I.9 Bulletin", which gave up to date information on the subject and was distributed to H.Q.s of all commands and armies.

A supply of aids for demonstration purposes was given to G.S. (I) commands and armies.

Special Instruction
This was a lecture of a Top Secret character and dealt with a system of code communication which could be used in normal correspondence. For reasons of security, it was sometimes given the title of "Camp Conditions" and was always restricted to a very limited number of officers and W.O.s. A small number of staff officers and all Intelligence officers on H.Q.s of formations received this instruction.

It was recommended that no attempt should be made to instruct more than ten persons at a time and only those capable of grasping details readily.

Lecturers were instructed to satisfy themselves by checking practice letters that personnel who attended the lecture understood the system, and their capabilities were further checked by M.I.9 before their registration with M.I.9 as potential "users".

Early difficulties
During the early months of 1942 preventive training was carried out under a considerable handicap.

Lecturers at this time were not available to cover the vast number of operational units then in Great Britain, and members of the instructional staff were worked to the limit. Units visited were scattered all over the country from the Orkneys to the South of England, including Northern Ireland. These purely instructional lectures were augmented whenever possible by talks given by returned evaders and escapers.

Endeavours were made to obtain the full-time services of officers who had recently escaped from enemy hands to supplement the instructional staff, but this proved difficult owing to the shortage of manpower, and it was not until October 1942 that an Army officer who had made an outstanding escape from German hands was made available. Subsequently the services of one Naval officer who had escaped in the war of 1914-1918 and two Naval officers who had made brilliant escapes from a German Prisoner of War Camp in the present war were obtained, to be followed by one Army officer who had escaped from Japanese hands after the fall of Hong Kong and an R.A.F. officer who had made his escape from Singapore after its capitulation.

R.A.F. Intelligence Course 'B'
This initial difficulty in obtaining a sufficient quantity of trained lecturers was appreciated at an early stage and in January 1942, on the suggestion of the Air Ministry, a special intelligence course was opened at R.A.F. Station "X", Harrow, which was administered by

the Air Ministry, the training policy being controlled by M.I.9. This course dealt exclusively with matters relating to Evasion and Escape and was originally formed for the purpose of training R.A.F. Station Intelligence officers who, in turn, would brief operational personnel on these subjects. Not long after its inception it became R.A.F. Intelligence Course 'B', by which name it was known throughout its further existence. Later it was expanded to include Intelligence officers of the Royal Navy and the Army and eventually Intelligence officers of the American forces and moved to more suitable premises at Highgate.

With the increased instructional staff and the number of officers available as a result of this course within Army and R.A.F. commands and Naval establishments and ships, it was possible in October 1944 to dispense with the services of the civilian lecturers.

Development and Expansion of Training

Royal Navy

Before the formation of M.I.9(d) a very limited number of lectures on evasion and escape had been given to Naval personnel, but no definite system had been established to deal with this form of training.

The officer responsible for the Naval side of M.I.9(d) immediately made the following contacts:

> D.N.I. (for backing only).
> A.G.R.M. (for Royal Marines personnel).
> N.A.D. (later D.A.W.T.) (for Aircraft Carriers).
> D.D.O.C.(C) (for Coastal Forces).
> D.T.S.D. (Officers training).
> D.D.O.D.(M) (for Minelayers)
> F.O.N.A.S. (for Naval Air Stations).
> F.O.S. (for submarine personnel).
> A.C.O. (later C.C.O.) (for Naval personnel engaged in Combined Operations).

In every case the response was favourable except that F.O.S. directed that preventive training be confined to special operations only, as he thought that the morale of ordinary S/M crews might be adversely affected if stress were laid on the possibility of capture. D.T.S.D. also ruled that no M.I.9 lectures could be given to ratings under training owing to their very full syllabus.

Until the middle of 1942 no directive on M.I.9 training had been issued by the Admiralty, but on 12 March 1942 an Admiralty letter, drafted by M.I.9(d), was issued. This letter legalised the whole position and after its publication the organisation of lecture tours was much simplified.

Preventive training at Coastal Forces, Submarine and Combined Operations Bases and in the Fleet Air Arm was supplemented by instruction given by local officers who had qualified at R.A.F. Intelligence Course 'B'. In the last named, as no Intelligence Staff existed up till 1945, Meteorological officers and C.B.A.L. officers dealt with M.I.9 matters. Subsequently (in 1945) Naval Air Intelligence officers were appointed, and these officers passed through R.A.F. Intelligence Course 'B' before taking up their duties.

It should be mentioned here that during the period 1943-1944 considerable assistance was given by N.I.D. Lecture Section giving talks on the will to escape and prisoner of war security to all ranks at Naval establishments which M.I.9, with the limited number of lecturers available, could not cover.

On the whole, since the early months of 1942 the Naval side was adequately catered for, but the chief handicap was the insufficient warning given to M.I.9 of impending operations. In fact, it was largely due to the personal contacts of the officer responsible for the Naval side in M.I.9(d) that prior notice of the smaller operations at any rate was obtained.

Army

As has already been stated, preventive training had been given, previous to 1942, to certain Army formations at home and in the B.E.F., but this had been necessarily of an improvised and sketchy nature and although arrangements had been made with Army Commands at home for instruction to be given by visiting lecturers from M.I.9, the matter had not been legalised with G.H.Q., Home Forces.

This state of affairs made it possible for commanders of formations to refuse to have M.I.9 instruction given to units under their command. Generally speaking, few objections were raised, but one or two senior officers were very much opposed to the ideas, as they considered that the possibility of capture should not be discussed on the grounds that it was bad for morale, ("The British soldier fights to the death"). These doubters were eventually persuaded that circumstances arise when soldiers do get cut off and cannot fight to the death, and it was emphasised that all lectures began by stressing that the soldier's duty was not to be captured.

Early in 1942 the question was taken up with G.H.Q., Home Forces, with the result that a directive was issued by G.H.Q. to Army

Commands in the United Kingdom. Similar arrangements were made with Canadian Military Headquarters, Northern Ireland District and Combined Operations Headquarters.

It was agreed that M.I.9 should deal directly with formations down to Divisions on all matters of routine, but that questions of policy should be referred to higher authorities concerned.

Briefly, the directive laid down that M.I.9 would be responsible for the necessary instruction being given to:

(a)
    i.   Armoured, Airborne and Infantry Divisions.
    ii.   Formations and units of the Canadian Army in England.
    iii. A.A. units likely to go overseas.
    iv. Units of the Special Service Brigade.
    v.   Units of the Royal Marines operating under Army Command.
    vi. Units on special operational role operating under C.C.O.
    vii. Training Establishments and Schools.

Commands and Armies were to be responsible for instruction being given to:

(b)
    i.   Army and Corps Troops.
    ii.   Independent Brigades and Independent Units.

Only troops liable to go overseas or to be in close contact with the enemy were to be given M.I.9 instruction.

Formations and units at (a) above were covered by M.I.9 as a matter of routine with the exception of vi. which were instructed at the request of C.C.O. prior to an operation taking place. Training establishments and Schools were covered at three-monthly intervals, the programmes being arranged by M.T.(L) with whom a close liaison was kept.

Formations and units at (b) above were normally covered by Army Commands when requested by M.I.9 who, on receipt of Mobilisation Preparatory Orders from the S.D. Section concerned, reminded the appropriate command. The instruction was then given by an officer who had qualified at R.A.F. Intelligence Course 'B'.

When a sufficient number of officers within Army Commands had passed through R.A.F. Intelligence Course 'B' vacancies were allotted to Armoured and Infantry Divisions and certain lower formations likely to take part in the expected operations in Western Europe. By May

44 all Armoured and Infantry Divisions had from three to four such officers on their strength. This enabled M.I.9 instruction to be given to personnel who had been unable to attend the lectures arranged by M.I.9 which had by this time been given to all formations of 21 Army Group.

The organisation of training described above may be said to have worked extremely well, although, owing to commitments of various kinds on the part of units, it was impossible to cover 100% of personnel.

Royal Air Force

Here also preventive training had been carried out prior to 1942 almost entirely by visiting lecturers from M.I.9(d). This method was continued but, owing to the limited number of lecturers available, it soon became obvious that only a limited number of aircrew could be covered. It was at this stage that R.A.F. Intelligence Course 'B' was formed, and in due course every operational R.A.F. station and O.T.U. in the United Kingdom possessed at least one Intelligence Officer qualified to instruct in M.I.9 subjects.

This instruction was supplemented by lectures from officers on the staff of M.I.9(d), who visited Groups, etc., as required and by visits from recent evaders and escapers.

By these means all aircrew were thoroughly briefed on evasion and escape before taking part in operations.

Statistics

A summary of preventive training lectures given by officers on the staff of M.I.9(d) during the period 1 January 1942 to 25 August 1945 is shown below:

Service	No. of lectures	Estimated number of personnel who attended
Royal Navy	608	90,000
Royal Marines	102	20,000
Army	1,090	346,000
Royal Air Force	1,450	290,000

The above figures are conservative and are exclusive of lectures given under local arrangements by officers who qualified at R.A.F. Intelligence Course 'B'.

Evasion and Escape Equipment
Control and Specification. Except in the case of P/W Camps, the control of issue of Evasion and Escape equipment, which was devised and produced by I.S.9(Z), was vested in M.I.9(d) and issued by I.S.9(Z) on indent. This equipment consisted of:

1. Purses: Containing normally about £12 in notes of the currency of the country or countries in which the recipient might find himself cut off, appropriate silk maps, a small compass and hacksaw.
2. Aids Boxes: Containing compressed food, chewing gum, Halazone, Benzedrine, matches, safety razor and soap, needle and thread, surgical tape, fishing line and hook, water bottle and small compass. These Aids Boxes were designed to give the evader sufficient nourishment for 48 hours and so enable him to lie up or move from his original location without the necessity of obtaining food.
3. Supplementary Aids Boxes: These were designed to meet the needs of flying personnel forced down in Germany where no help could be expected from the inhabitants and were carried in addition to the Aids Box and provided sufficient nourishment for seven days.
4. Far East Aids Boxes: These were specially designed for tropical climates.
5. Special Aids Boxes: Far East
6. Silk Maps: For enclosure in Purses or Wallets or for issue separately; these maps were specially prepared for evasion and escape purposes and covered territories in European and Far East Theatres.
7. Compasses: Of various small types suitable for concealment.

Issue

Royal Navy:
Evasion and Escape Equipment was issued to the authorities and establishments concerned for distribution, as necessary, to operational personnel of:

Fleet Air Arm (including Aircraft Carriers).
Coastal Forces.
Submarines (special operations).
Midget Submarines.
Combined Operations (Naval Parties).

Stocks were held by Chatham, Portsmouth and Plymouth Divisions of the Royal Marines for distribution to ships' detachments before embarkation.

Army:

After instruction had been given to formations and units proceeding overseas, or on special operations from the United Kingdom, the necessary "Aids" were issued by M.I.9(d) for distribution on the following scale:

Airborne units.   }
Commandos.   }   All ranks.
Armoured units. Officers and senior N.C.O.s and crews of A.F.V.s.
All others. Officers and senior N.C.O.s.

Special parties operating under Combined Headquarters were equipped as desired by C.O.H.Q.

Troops taking part in the landings in N. Africa, Italy and France were equipped on the scales shown above, special maps and additional "Aids" having been produced for the purpose.

Royal Air Force:

Evasion and Escape Equipment was issued to all Operational Groups etc., in the United Kingdom, for distribution to flying personnel on 100% scale.

Overseas:

A continuous supply of M.I.9 equipment was maintained to "E" Group, S.E.A. and I Commands, and consignments were forwarded as required to I.S.9(M.E.), I.S.9(C.M.F.), I.S.9(W.E.A.) and the M.I.9 organisation in Australia. Supplies were also sent to War Dept., Washington, prior to their own technical section getting into production.

Summary of Evasion and Escape Equipment issued
During the period 1 January 1942 to 25 August 1945 the following principal items of equipment were issued on M.I.9(d) indent:

Items.	European Theatres, N. Africa and M.E. R.N., Army, R.A.F. and M.I.9 organisation overseas.	Far Eastern Theatre 'E' Group S.E.A. & I Commands.	M.I.S. X Sec. S.W.P.A.
Aids Boxes.	423,075	145,770*	-
Purses.	275,407	-	-
Silk Maps.	760,757	454,678	3,424
Compasses and Devices.	1,700,241	635,823	116,798
Miscellaneous.	434,104	329,123	126,482

*These included European type Aids Boxes.

Blood Chits

To serve the dual purpose of (a) overcoming the language difficulty so that a flyer forced down in enemy occupied territory could explain himself to the natives and (b) to act as a pledge (or promise to pay) redeemable when the enemy was ejected from the country, "Blood Chits" were prepared in a number of languages by M.I.9(d) and issued in conjunction with escape and evasion equipment.

Blood Chits were not issued for Europe because of the ease with which they could be forged but phrase books in many European and Asiatic languages were compiled and issued.

Publications

Various publications were issued by M.I.9(d), the principal being:

(a) "The M.I.9 Bulletin". This document was the "Bible" of Evasion and Escape and contained everything that could be of assistance to service personnel who might find themselves cut off in enemy occupied territory or captured by the enemy. It was devised as a textbook and guide to Intelligence officers who were called upon to give instruction in evasion and escape.

Information on conditions in Europe, escape routes, etc., was mainly collected and supplied by I.S.9, who also provided maps and other material.

It will be appreciated that for efficient and up-to-date preventive training intimate relations with the executive body,

I.S.9 were vital as teaching was frequently changed radically as the underground organisations changed.

To overcome the delay often caused by the insertion of frequent amendments, "Advice Memos" were instituted. These contained the latest long-term information available for ultimate inclusion in the "Bulletin".

Short term or transitory information was sent out under the title of "Mercury" on the day of receipt. The "Mercury" series was issued only to recipients to whom the information would be of immediate value. This series proved of considerable value during the campaign in Western Europe, for which it was originated.

(b) "The M.I.9 Bulletin, Far East". A similar publication to the "M.I.9 Bulletin" but dealing only with the Far East and largely devoted to survival in jungle etc.

Owing to the difficulty of obtaining material for this document it was unfortunately not available for issue until Jun 45 when it was most favourably received by the three Services.

(c) Specimen Lectures. These, with stories of actual escapes, were issued for the guidance of Intelligence Officers.

(d) Pamphlets. Various pamphlets directly or indirectly associated with evasion in the Far East were published by M.I.9(d), the principal being Far Eastern Survival, Land and Sea, for which there was a large demand, and the Malay Language. These pamphlets were printed on silk.

Security

Although security instruction was not a part of the M.I.9 charter, P/W security was so closely linked up with the teaching of M.I.9 that the closest liaison had to be maintained with M.I.11 and the equivalent sections in the Admiralty and Air Ministry. For instance, when it became apparent that a continuation of the rule of "Name, Rank and Number only" would probably have repercussions inimical to the interests and safety of British and Dominion prisoners in Japanese hands, it was largely through the efforts of M.I.9 that the rule was modified. After agreement had been reached the War Office pamphlet "Precautions to be taken by British personnel in the event of capture 1942" was re-written for the Far East by M.I.9(d), as was also the Admiralty equivalent publication.

Difficulties

The chief difficulty encountered in the early days was the lack of interest shown in M.I.9 activities by certain elements of the Royal Navy and Army, and it was only after a considerable number of personal contacts had been made that this state of affairs improved. Even so, there were instances, right up to the spring of 1944, of senior officers refusing to have anything to do with it.

As far as the Army was eventually concerned, however, practically all Commanding Officers of units mobilising for overseas were keen that their troops should have a knowledge of what to do if cut off or captured and should be escape-minded, and excellent co-operation was given by formation Commanders of 21 Army Group.

Another difficulty experienced was the insufficient warning frequently given of impending operations. This applied particularly to Combined Operations.

Allied Naval Commander Expeditionary Force in February 1944 directed that pre-capture training should not be given in general to Naval personnel training for operation "Overlord". His reason was that the time was limited and that, as R.N. and R.M. personnel would be operating off beaches already in our hands or to be occupied by our forces as a result of the operation, the possibility of their capture was a remote one. In actual fact, through the co-operation of G.O.C. Royal Marines, a large number of R.M. crews of minor landing craft were covered by M.I.9(d) before joining their vessels.

Except in Force 'J' which had been in existence for some considerable time, and Coastal Forces, no M.I.9 training was given to R.N. personnel who took part in the invasion of France.

It is felt that if there had been earlier and closer liaison with A.N.C.X.F. better results would have been achieved.

It can be noted that Preventive Training can be overdone, e.g., a case is recorded of certain American crews who would not fly because purses and Aids Boxes were not available!

Statistics

The total of British Commonwealth escapers is 21,533, and of British Commonwealth evaders is 4,657 making a grand total of 26,190. Of these 4,916 were interned in Switzerland, but the rest were available for further service. It can be fairly claimed that of these 90% of evaders and 33% of escapers were brought out as a result of M.I.9 organisation and activities.

Chapter 2

LECTURE FOR ARMY UNITS ON CONDUCT IF CUT OFF FROM UNIT OR CAPTURED: EUROPEAN THEATRE

The following lecture was prepared for all ranks and all arms of the service. It was to be given by Intelligence Officers.

Introduction
How many of you I wonder, have thought what you would do if you were captured, if you were isolated from your own troops. What conditions would you find – what treatment would you receive – what chances have you of escaping, and if you do – how would you move about the countryside. I hope to answer these and other questions in the course of my talk.

The real answer is – do not be captured. Only as a last resort should you be in the position of being captured. Your job is to fight – and only through wounds, lack of ammunition or food should you ever allow yourself to be captured. Should you be captured, it must be your firm and constant determination to escape at the earliest opportunity – to bring back information to our people – to be a nuisance to the enemy. Every German soldier occupied in guarding you – every German soldier occupied in searching the countryside for you is one less in Germany's war machine. The manpower situation there is not likely to improve as time goes on.

In 1939 the German authorities produced a fairly lengthy document for consumption by the German people dealing with the question of Escape in the last war. In it was pointed out to the Germans the vital

18

part our escapes had played in bringing about the collapse of Civilian Morale. By propaganda – by taking back information to our people – by the very fact that they were abroad in the country – all these aspects had their effect. The Document warns the German people against this danger and pleads with them to resist any attempts at bribery – to stand firm in 'mutual confidence' and to do all in their power to assist in the capture of evaders and re-capture of escapers. What went for the last war goes equally well for this. Be a nuisance to the enemy – keep him 'on the hop' – sow the insidious seeds of propaganda – seek out information – you can help to make their collapse the more complete.

I propose to give you a General Background of the situation in Europe as it has existed up to the present – we shall then consider how this is likely to be affected on the opening of a Second Front.

Evasion and Escape
Evasion and Escape – what is the difference between these two. It is important. Evasion? You are evading capture – you have not been in the hands of the enemy at all – you have been cut off from your own people. Escape – you have been in the hands of the enemy – even if only for 10 minutes – and have escaped. The important point is this: as an evader – if you reach a Neutral Country, you will be interned – as an escaper you will be repatriated to this country. There is then only one answer – if you are an Evader and reach a Neutral Country you must say that you are an escaper. Have a simple story ready – the simpler the better – you have been in the hands of the enemy – if only for half an hour – and escaped. Keep it simple, and if there are two of you – have the same story. The Authorities will not check-up – they are friendly towards us. I'll deal later with the legal aspects of Evasion and Escape.

An example of neutral friendliness occurred when an American plane was flying over Switzerland – the pilot had deviated from his course on a raid over Italy. Ground troops wirelessed to the plane "You are flying over Swiss territory". Back went the reply from the American "We know". "If you don't turn back we shall open fire" came the next message. "We know" replied the American. The Swiss guns opened up – wireless message from plane to guns "Your A.A. fire is about 500 yds short". From the Swiss gunners came the reply "We know!".

Evasion
Let us deal with evasion first. What does it imply? It means moving about undetected by the enemy – in the occupied countries, moving

about a countryside where most of the inhabitants are friendly towards you. In France, Holland, Denmark, about 90% of the people are willing to help an Allied evader – in Belgium the people are practically 100% helpful. Of all the European countries – no people are more eager to help then the people of Belgium. Anything they can do against the Germans they will do.

First Steps

The first steps in successful Evasion are all important. Approach a lonely farm during the day – lie up in hiding – watch the movement in and about it – watch out for Germans near it or billeted in it. If all is well, approach the farmer in the evening – choose your opportunity. See that he is alone – get him when he is pottering about the yard – make it known to him who you are – in most cases he will help you. This question of approaching a helper alone is all important. The people of the occupied countries cannot tell with certainty who are their friends – who are their enemies. If you approach a crowd, they will refuse help – they do not know who amongst them may be a German Agent – who amongst them may report them to the Gestapo. You must make your contact when your prospective helper is alone. They have to be constantly on the alert against enemy agents – they will help you – help them to help you by contacting them alone.

There is the story of an American pilot – an evader. He had been told that a café was a good place to make a contact. It is, but he went the wrong way about it. Entering the café he made it known to everyone, in rather a loud voice, just who and what he was and asked for help. People looked at him in some alarm and all quickly left the café. The proprietor himself told him to leave at once.

The pilot left feeling very disgruntled – feeling that all he had heard about helpers had been greatly exaggerated. But he hadn't gone 200 yds along the road when a figure hurried alongside him and slipped a note into his hand. The note contained instructions to make for a wood just out of the village where he was to wait until nightfall. That night many of the people who had been in the café came to him, bringing food, clothing and money and helped him on his way, but not before having told him he was nearer to being shot than helped. He was shown the absolute stupidity of his behaviour in the café – when no one could tell who among those there might be an informant or enemy agent.

In most of the villages the school teacher and the doctor speak English. They may be brought to you – it will help you over the language difficulty. The Village Priest is another good contact. Confessionals are usually held on Saturday evenings or Sunday mornings. Take your place with the others – make it known to the Priest who you are – he will help you. With all these people be honest – answer their questions – unless in regard to military operations – remember they do not know that you are genuine – they have to be careful.

General Behaviour

Remain hidden with your host as long as may seem desirable – but don't overdo it – no matter how attractive the daughter may be! Keep in mind your job is to get back to your own lines. One evader in France, staying with a farmer found life very comfortable – the daughter was attractive – he married her – the old man is dead – he now owns the farm and has a family of two! But we have that man 'taped' and he will find that he will have to answer some very awkward questions at his court martial.

Do all you can to assist your helpers – they have little – yet they will give it to you. Be courteous – respectful – especially to women. Be careful of the odd case you may find – of a farmer holding on to you because he finds you useful about the farm. Generally speaking – if at the end of 14 days say, he has made no move to put you on your way – you should suggest that you should move on. This will generally elicit information as to whether he can put you in touch with further helpers. He may tell you to wait for another day or so, as he has someone coming to see you. Otherwise move on – if your first contact does not give you all the help you expected – your next one most likely will. Above all, do not ask to be put in touch with further helpers – the approach will come from them.

Do not let anything detract from your intention to get away.

A Sgt. Pilot in the R.A.F. came down in France close to a Convent. He had not been on the ground for more than a few minutes when several Nuns rushed out and hustled him into the Convent. He was given civilian clothes and in due course was allowed into the grounds of the Convent where he posed as a gardener.

On his first day in the grounds, he caught sight of an exceptionally pretty Nun walking about the garden. All thoughts of Evasion and Escape departed, and the Sgt. envisaged many happy days in front of him if he could but win himself into the good graces of this most attractive young lady. With this purpose in view, he made tentative advances towards her, but was rather dismayed at the complete lack of response. Refusing to give up, however, he continued his efforts in rather a clumsy mixture of French and English, until at last she turned to him with an angry grunt and said in perfect English, "Don't be a damned fool – I've been here since Dunkirk!"

Helpers
This question of helpers – what does that imply? For you it implies a planned and assisted journey to a neutral country; being supplied with food, clothing, papers, money. For those helping you it implies their risking their lives every hour of the day. You must be absolutely honest and answer their questions truthfully. Remember they are always on their guard against enemy agents. You must obey their instructions implicitly – if you are told to stay hidden – stay hidden. If someone accompanies you on your journey, obey him without question – watch what he does – if you are told to follow at 200 yds, he means 200 and not 20.

Never write down anything but remember everything. Write nothing – one address written on a scrap of paper can result in the tracing of many helpers. Never discuss your previous helpers with those with whom you find yourself. Security must be of the highest order. Remember if you are caught it only means that you will be sent to a P/W Camp. If your helpers are caught it means death for them and their families. Do nothing which can endanger their lives. They do this without thought of reward. All they ask is that you do not talk. They trust their lives to your hands – do not betray that trust.

There have actually been cases where evaders and escapers have sent post cards back to the helpers "thanking them for everything". The motive may have been good, but the supreme stupidity of their actions is almost incredible. Write nothing and do not talk. Only to the official interrogators should names and addresses of helpers be given.

Working Alone
It may be that you will move about alone – by that I mean from one helper to another without any of them necessarily accompanying you. Your individual helpers will give you food, clothing and money. They will help you with routes – buy railway tickets for you or rehearse you in what to say. The difficulties of language are not so great as you might imagine. One escaper travelled through Germany posing as a Norwegian businessman. The only Norwegian he knew was "I am sorry I have no tobacco". While this would undoubtedly conserve his supply of tobacco – it wasn't a great foundation to go on! Yet he got through. Another man got through Germany only knowing "Auf Wiedersehen" which he used on all and sundry occasions. Better to be thought an idiot than an evader!

The question of travel I shall deal with later – let us now turn to the escaper. Once escaped you become an evader and we shall therefore leave the evader for the moment, and link up again when our escaper is free.

Escape

Let me emphasise again that capture is a last resort – if you are so unfortunate as to be captured it should be your firm determination to escape at the earliest opportunity. The first 48 hours are very important. Once you are in a P/W Camp your chances of escaping are greatly diminished. Resort to any means to delay your arrival at a P/W Camp. Malinger – feign sickness – anything but get away soon. Keep your eyes open for every opportunity to escape. You will find yourselves in transit camps – hospitals – local jails. Look about you – let no opportunity escape you. You will travel by rail – opportunities will present themselves. Guarding cannot be so strict as at a P/W Camp. Determine to get away before you reach there. It can be done – many have done so already.

A Commando Sgt. found himself in a small local jail. A small window in his cell gave access to the street but an escape that way would have been impossible. He soon devised a simple plan – smashing the window with a stool, he waited for the rush of a sentry to his cell. As soon as the door was thrown open, he hid behind it, the sentry seeing the cell apparently empty rushed out again leaving the door open and gave the alarm. In the ensuing confusion, the Sgt. walked out of the cell; out of the jail; and made a successful escape.

One party on their way by rail to a P/W Camp, made a successful escape by sawing through the floor of the cattle truck in which they were travelling, and dropping through whenever the train stopped for any reason.

P/W Security

If you find yourself at a camp or interrogation centre – you will of course be questioned. Generally, the procedure is a period of solitary confinement lasting up to 14 days before interrogation. There is only one answer to all interrogation. Name, Rank and Number. There is no alternative. You may feel depressed – tired – hungry – dispirited – that is the state the enemy want you to be in. That is the state when the relief of hearing the voice of the interrogator speaking English is so great that you want to open out. Do not be misled by apparent kindness – remember he is the enemy – his show of kindness has only one purpose – to get you to talk. Don't be tricked by apparently innocent conversation about your family affairs, into giving information. There is only one answer Name, Rank and Number. Don't lie – don't try to be clever – they will find you out – it helps nobody – don't be insubordinate – look straight ahead. Answer you Name, Rank and Number – nothing else. "I am sorry I cannot answer that" or "you would not answer that in my position", will gain respect for you as a British soldier. If you are kept for an unduly long period at an interrogation centre, you are being useful to them either willingly or unwillingly – stop talking.

Beware the bogus Red X form – the genuine one contains only Name, Rank and Number and next of kin. Do not answer or be tricked into answering any other questions that may appear. Don't be fooled by an apparently vast amount of information in the hands of the enemy. Don't feel that the little you can tell him "won't make any difference". They may know much but they don't know all – remember they would not be questioning you if they knew all the answers.

Watch out for microphones – they are concealed – and because you find one it does not mean you are safe. Even in the open be careful – trees no less than walls have ears.

Beware the stool pigeon – agents planted as British prisoners to get you to talk. Talk to no one you didn't know before you were taken prisoner.

Don't be taken in by "threats". They will make their threats seem very real – but they will not be carried out. You will not broadcast to your people at home even though tempted. It encourages our people to listen to German propaganda and in any case your broadcast will be distorted to suit their purposes. There is an Army Order on this subject, which expressly forbids broadcasting by P/Ws.

Five British prisoners were being interrogated – they were marched into a room where the whole atmosphere was made very threatening. A tough looking German Officer sat behind the desk on which lay a revolver – round the room were Nazi thugs armed to the teeth.

The first man to be interrogated refused to give anything but his Name, Rank and Number. At a sign from the Officer a sentry came forward and roughly hustled him outside. A few minutes later there was the sound of firing from the direction in which they had gone.

The second man also refused to give any information, and the same procedure was repeated. When it came to the turn of the third man, he broke down under the strain and told what he knew. Shortly afterwards all five prisoners were together again. No shooting had, of course, taken place – but the trick had had its success.

At Final Camp

At your final camp the Senior British Officer or Senior Warrant Officer will keep you right. He is responsible to the Camp Authorities for the discipline of the men under him. He will warn you as to your behaviour.

Through him you can contact the Escape Committees which exist at P/W Camps. Approach the committee and register as a would-be escaper. They co-ordinate and control escapes. They will help you with plans – they will give you routes – they will assist you to acquire money, maps, papers, food, clothing. They have access to gadgets, compasses etc., and to the services of tradesmen – tailors – cobblers – locksmiths – and such valuable professional men as amateur forgers.

Morale at a P/W Camp is not maintained solely by Concerts and Gramophone Records. Real morale comes from the maintenance of a determination to escape. Watch and plan – don't be content to abandon yourself to the situation. That way lies depression – the destruction of initiative and a feeling of dull hopelessness – the effects may well be permanent. Maintence of the Offensive Spirit – a constant determination to escape – therein lies the way to high morale. Keep fit – you will require to be fit to escape successfully – it will help you to be on the alert.

Escaping

Obviously, I cannot tell you how to escape – you will find ways. O.R's have opportunities on Working Parties – fatigue squads etc. officers may have more difficulties. But seemingly insurmountable difficulties can be overcome – they have been overcome.

One man escaped by concealing himself in a barrow of refuse and, being dumped in the refuse dump outside the camp, made good his escape at nightfall.

An R.A.F. Officer, by the name of Snooks, after many attempts at escape found himself at a P/W Camp in Germany. The camp had the record, for about two years, of never having had a successful escape from it. It was exceptionally well guarded and the only way of getting out was by tunnelling. Successful tunnelling, however, seemed impossible as in all about 90 tunnels had been started over a period of 2 years but all were discovered by the sentries at various stages of construction.

Along with another R.A.F Officer, however, Snooks devised a plan which eventually brought them a successful escape. With the help of other prisoners in the camp, they constructed a wooden vaulting horse, capable of holding two men inside it. Soon the plan was put into operation – a P.T. period was inaugurated, and the horse was carried outside and placed as near as possible to the outside fence which ran alongside the road outside the camp. Willing helpers threw themselves backwards and forwards over the horse while the two men who had been carried out inside the horse began to sink a vertical shaft.

It is not necessary to dwell on the difficulties they met with – earth had to be disposed of – the period they could work in the tunnel each day was limited – the horse had to be carried in and out of the hut where it was stored – with men concealed inside it. The opening of the tunnel had to be cleverly and strongly covered so that when the horse was removed after P.T. each day, no evidence of the activity going on underneath it would be apparent. But patience, determination, and hard work had their reward and at the end of two months a tunnel 90 ft. long and 1½ ft. square had been completed. The exit was calculated to come out on the grass verge alongside the road outside the camp, and on the other side of which was a wood which would give cover for a get-away.

Meantime, Snooks and his companion had collected civilian clothes, money, maps and so on and finally the day arrived for the attempted escape. With the help of others, they entered the tunnel, the entrance was closed, and the horse removed. At nightfall they broke the exit which, to their joy, was in a position in accordance with their calculations. Quickly they crossed the road and made the cover of the woods.

Their adventures before reaching this country were many and varied, but both men did eventually return safely to this country, via a neutral country.

Remember German morale will go – as it did in the last war – and you will find that more help will become available. Sentries can be bought – generally by cigarettes – and in the rather belated hope that their lot may be easier for helping you, that help will come to be more readily given.

General

A few general points. Unless you have a good knowledge of Germany and the language, it is inadvisable to represent yourself as a German. Adopt the characteristics and appearance of a foreign worker of which there are thousands in Germany. In other countries adopt the obvious characteristics of the Nationals. Avoid that 'hunted' look – don't imagine that everyone is looking at you with suspicion. A confident bearing without overdoing it. Don't march along with a military bearing – but don't overdo the slouching. Keep reasonably clean and tidy – don't wear rings or watches and don't smoke British cigarettes. Keep your wits about you – be ready to take advantage of every circumstance which will help you. Don't get panicky when you get into trouble. Be on the alert – fit in with your background. Don't worry if your clothes and appearance seem a little odd in your eyes – they won't seem so in the eyes of the people you mix with.

An O.R. escaping through Holland found he had to cross a bridge over a canal. On the opposite side was a sentry. Afraid that his appearance should arouse suspicion, he paused to consider what he should do. Just then a Dutch girl approached pushing a perambulator with a baby in it. He made up his mind quickly and went up to the girl and while pretending to play with the baby indicated to the girl who he was and that he wanted to cross the bridge. The girl played up magnificently – put the perambulator in his hands and taking his arm they crossed the bridge together and passed the sentry without incident.

An evader making his way through France was waiting at a railway station. The train was late and during the rather long wait he somehow aroused the suspicion of a German Officer who was on the station platform. The man became rather nervous, and his nervousness increased when the Officer beckoned to a German soldier standing by. Just then, however, a group of French peasant women entered the station – without hesitation he hurried over to them and with the greeting "I am English – speak to me in French" embraced the foremost one with some fervour. Without hesitation she responded and in the ensuing babble of greetings and embraces, the suspicions of the German Officer were dispelled.

One escaper who made a difficult but successful escape obtained a bicycle to travel on. He remembered to keep to the right-hand side of the road, but when he came to a roundabout, for some reason, he swung round to the left. A policeman standing by stopped him – not because he suspected him as an escaper – but simply because of the fact that he had gone round the roundabout the wrong way. Unfortunately, the man didn't realise that fully – and in the next few minutes gave himself away. He was arrested and taken back to a P/W Camp. He has since successfully escaped, having learnt his lesson.

Legal Aspects

I think this might be the time to deal with the legal aspect. Escapers are covered by the Geneva Convention – the position of evaders is not so clear. So far in this war, however, evaders and escapers have been treated similarly so long as the evader is able to prove identity as a soldier, sailor or airman. It is permissible to assist in escapes, to adopt disguises – enemy uniform or civilian clothes. When in civilian clothes avoid violence – don't carry arms – and don't commit acts of sabotage. You render yourself liable to be shot as a franc tireur or spy and may also interfere with the work of people specially trained for the job. In uniform carry on the war – keep your arms and equipment and behave like soldiers.

If you are re-captured the maximum penalty for attempted escape is 30 days solitary confinement, but if you have committed other offences, e.g., violence, rape, murder, robbery etc., you will have to stand the consequences by trial.

Travel

Let us now deal with the question of travel – rather briefly as the position is likely to alter considerably.

By road in Germany – there is only one way and that is not to be seen. Hide by day – walk by night. In summer you can live off the land to some extent – obviously you won't be given help from farms. You must discipline yourself to remain hidden by day – progress may seem slow – but your success depends on not being seen. That aspect won't alter! Many a man, just by that eagerness to reach the safety he sees, has been captured as he crossed the frontier by day. Be careful at weekends – beware the Hitler Youth – let loose about the countryside when the presence of an evader is suspected.

In the occupied countries the position at present is easier. You will get help. Walk or cycle – if you cycle don't steal your cycle – offer to pay for it – you can move by day – villages can be passed through – though they must be avoided by night as a curfew operates during the hours of darkness. The roads are fairly well signposted.

By rail in Germany – papers are required. The main one is the *Ausweis* – but there are other various permits operating in particular localities. Travel must be by 3rd class – in the corridor for preference. Travel by goods train is possible at present – with the help of foreign railway workers – this is changing now as German railway workers are presently being moved into the big marshalling yards to take over from the foreign workers. At present, control is less strict in slow local trains than on express trains.

In occupied countries – again this goes for the present – the position is somewhat easier. The language difficulty is not so acute – helpers buy tickets or travel with the evader. I'll deal with crossing the frontiers later.

The Second Front

I think I have said enough to give you a general idea of conditions at present. How far is all this likely to be altered on the opening of a Second Front? The future is of course unknown and problematical – much will depend on events themselves – and special briefing will be necessary depending on the Theatre of Operations. But much of what I have told you will still be applicable.

There is this big difference – Allied forces will be in the country and your job therefore either as an escaper or evader is to regain your own lines. You must appreciate the vital importance of this. We want back every possible man with his arms and equipment. Only as a last resort make for neutral countries – especially Switzerland where the difficulties of getting out are great. In occupied countries, if it is judged to be at the time the best means by which capture or re-capture can be avoided you may, as a temporary measure join up with Guerillas or local Partisans. In so doing, however, an escaper or evader runs the customary risks of being treated on capture or re-capture as a franc-tireur or saboteur if he or other members of the band do not observe strictly the laws of legitimate warfare in regard to the wearing of uniform.

If you are forced to join up with Guerillas, emphasise to the leader that you want to get back to your own lines. It may not be possible at the time – abide by his instructions implicitly. But keep at him – your job is to regain your own lines. Retain your arms and uniform as long as possible.

The value of remaining in a hide-out – in a position likely to be over-run by our own forces – is to be considered. Lie up and keep your eyes and ears open. Remember our people want information – every scrap that you can get. But don't write anything down – if you are in civilian clothes, you're likely to be shot as a spy if you're caught with written information. Memorise everything.

New Difficulties – New Advantages

Now, what new difficulties are we likely to find? So far as we know the German plan is to round up all able-bodied men between 16 and 60 in the occupied countries, and herd them into concentration camps. Few able-bodied youths, therefore, out of uniform will be evident. It is possible – almost probable – that there will be no civilian travel by road or rail. There will most certainly be a curfew in the battle zone and probably hundreds of miles to the rear.

What then are the chances of successful evasion. If there are new difficulties – so also will there be new advantages. A stream of refugees from the battle zone will add to the Germans' confusion – careful checking of papers will be made more difficult. If the people are willing to help now, they will be even more willing to help when we invade. That help may be more limited, but it will still be forthcoming. Valuable information as to enemy lines – where best to get through – which roads and bridges are most carefully guarded – routes and so on. Remember what I have told you regarding the procedure in contacting helpers.

Present Instructions

Your present instructions are to rejoin your own forces at the earliest opportunity. In many cases this will only involve one- or two-days march. You will have to cross the enemy lines – but experience in Italy has shown that this is not as difficult as you may imagine. Where the front is fluid, it does not present any great difficulty provided the ordinary rules of reconnaissance and patrol are observed. Travelling should be done by dark – and certainly the front must be crossed at night. Keep your eyes and ears open.

Keep in mind this point too – if you are cut off or captured – you are not forgotten – go on – never give up. When we do go over there let's finish it off as soon as we can. You can help – every man who comes back is important – every scrap of information you can bring back – everything you can do to bring the collapse of German morale.

Neutral Countries – Frontiers

It may be that circumstances make it impossible for you to regain your own lines and your only alternative is to make for a neutral country. Generally speaking, if you find yourself in N.E. Germany you should make for the Baltic Ports – Swedish boats leave from Danzig frequently. If in Northern Germany, make for Holland or Denmark. Boat ferries leave from Denmark to Sweden frequently. Otherwise make for Belgium or get inland and make your way to Spain. This will entail crossing the Pyrenees – which must be done with the aid of a guide. Helpers will arrange this.

Crossing frontiers should be done at night – careful reconnaissance being made by day. Avoid crossing frontiers in woods. They give excellent cover – but that is just the point – because of that woods and copses on the frontier are generally wired with trip wires, booby traps etc., and there is generally a forest patrol – men extremely well camouflaged with police dogs. Don't be put off with tales of electrified fences – mines and so on. There is little evidence of these.

Having crossed the frontier travel as far as you can before (in the case of Spain and Switzerland) giving yourself up, or in the case of the occupied countries, contacting a helper. It avoids the chance of being handed back to the frontier police. In Spain let your guide approach the Consul for you – you will be sent for. Generally speaking, it is inadvisable to discuss your experience with the British Consul – wait till you reach the military attaché.

Conclusion

That is all I have to say. Let me emphasise the main points again. Firstly – capture itself is the last resort – if captured a firm and constant determination to escape – to bring back information – to be a nuisance to the enemy.

If captured – P/W Security – there is only one answer, Name, Rank and Number. There is no other.

Finally – security in regard to your helpers. For no reward they risk their lives and those of their families to help you. The only repayment they ask is that you do not tell anyone they helped you. That is little. Do not talk – write nothing – remember everything. You have these peoples' lives in your hands.

A last word in security generally. You must not discuss the subject I have dealt with outside – in mess – pubs – or at home. The information I have given you is most or top secret – regard it as such. Do not talk. You will endanger the lives of these helpers – you lessen your own chances of successful evasion later on if you talk now.

Aids to Escape

These were to be demonstrate to Officers, W.O.s and Sgts., only unless otherwise instructed.

Chapter 3

NO.9 INTELLIGENCE SCHOOL

No. 9 Intelligence School, which was formed in Jan 42, was added to as the work expanded and progressed. Below are set out the duties performed by each Section:

I.S.9(W)   Interrogation of escapers, evaders and repatriated service personnel; Preparation of all Reports and Appendices; internal distribution of Reports and correspondence.

I.S.9(X)   Escape and evasion planning; location of P/W Camps; collection of material for M.I.9 Bulletin; Selection, recording and co-ordination of despatch of escape material to P/W Camps; Preparation of escape and evasion maps.

I.S.9(Y)   Preparation of code messages to P/W Camps; liaison with outside secret departments with regard to special cases; correspondence with P/W Camps; liaison with selected relatives of Ps/W; decoding, editing and passing to M.I.9 of information received from all Camps; maintenance of Camp Records, names of attempted escapers, helpers, code users, etc.; dealing with Censorship slips; dealing with Special Questionnaires from Reception Camps; interviewing "Special" Repatriated Ps/W; preparation of Historical Record of each P/W Camp.

I.S.9(Z)   Experimental work; production of escape and evasion equipment; preparation of P/W parcels. Distribution of gadgets and special clothing for I.S.9(D)P.15 agents etc.; weekly and monthly stock sheets. Despatch of supplies to all theatres on M.I.9 indents; records, indents, despatch notes, packing etc.

I.S.9(D)-(P.15) Employment and training (under auspices of S.I.S.) of agents sent to enemy occupied countries of Western Europe to assist escapers and evaders to return to U.K.; preparation of plans for evacuation of escapers and evaders from France, Belgium and Holland; communication with I.S.9 agents in these countries.

I.S.9(AB) Interviewing helpers of British and American escapers and evaders in France, Belgium, Holland, Denmark; investigating and settling financial claims; making recommendations for awards to helpers. (This work was carried out in close conjunction with the Americans and the Intelligence Services of the countries concerned.)

Section "W"

Formation

Like other Sections of I.S.9, I.S.9(W) originated in M.I.9(b), but whilst the other Sections were separated from the War Office branch on the formation of I.S.9 in Jan 42, the work of this Section continued in M.I.9(b) until Mar 43 when, under a new War Establishment, it was brought into the School. The first interrogations of escapers and evaders were carried out, therefore, by M.I.9(b) and, on the changeover to I.S.9(W), no material change in the system of interrogation and of reports was involved.

Location

Although it was essential for the reports to be recorded and distributed from H.Q., it was found to be necessary for actual interrogations to take place in London. We were extremely fortunate in obtaining the sympathy and interest of the London District Assembly Centre, who put rooms at our disposal for interrogation purposes. This purely unofficial arrangement continued to the winter of 1944. Personnel of all three Services were interrogated at the L.D.A.C. and accommodated there for as long as it was convenient, or necessary, to retain them. During the latter months of the war, with Army and Navy personnel being interrogated at Reception Camps outside London and the R.A.F. at a Camp in London, it became an exceedingly difficult task for I.S.9(W) to cope with the work, but the necessary arrangements were made for all returning escapers and evaders to be interviewed, wherever they happened to be sent; this entailed the employment of additional personnel.

Interrogations
The aims of the interrogations carried out by I.S.9(W) were:

   i.   To obtain information for M.I.9 lectures and the M.I.9 Bulletin.

   ii.   To obtain information which might be of use to I.S.9(X) in their planning of escapes.

   iii.   To supply M.I.9 with information whereby they could make recommendations for awards to escapers and helpers, settle claims for expenses incurred and pay compensation etc.

   iv.   To help M.I.9(d)/P.15 to keep in touch with the progress of our organisations on the Continent.

   v.   To obtain and make available to the three services and other Government departments information on conditions in enemy and enemy-occupied countries and on military and specialist subjects.

   vi.   To keep M.I.5 informed of matters of security interest affecting prisoners of war and evaders and to enable them to interrogate personnel whose cases were regarded as doubtful from the security point of view.

How information was obtained:

Information for outside sections was obtained partly at the I.S.9(W) interrogations, interrogators being briefed on subjects for which a watch had to be kept, and partly by arranging for the outside branch concerned to make its own interrogation. This latter system worked satisfactorily once escapers and evaders had become less of a rarity and there was less temptation for outside branches to pass them on to other departments, more in order to hear their stories than to obtain information from them. Such interviews were later held at the L.D.A.C., so as to lessen the strain on the man being interrogated. Close liaison was kept with M.I.5 during the whole of the war so that the security of escapers and evaders could be considered.

Methods:

At first interrogation was done largely by giving the escaper or evader – other then those of obvious importance – a copy of a questionnaire, a sheet of paper and a pencil and asking him to write his answers. This system worked tolerably well in the case of those who escaped from the column of march or evaded capture in Belgium and France immediately after Dunkirk; indeed, considering that the original interrogation officer had no regular trained help, it was probably the only possible system. But as soon as the need was felt for reports which would give a picture of an escape or evasion from which lessons for teaching could be drawn, the limitations of this method were evident. Near illiteracy was found to be by no means confined to Other Ranks and even the officer or man who could express himself with reasonable fluency and accuracy would not necessarily record those things he had done which others might with profit imitate or avoid. It was found from experience that to get a man to write his own "story" produced results of limited usefulness and that to obtain satisfactory results there was no substitute for real interrogation. This method, which had the added advantage of making every officer and man feel that the value of his performance in evasion or escape was fully appreciated, was therefore adopted and strictly adhered to. Where the numbers to be interrogated were large and time was short, it was sometimes found expedient to issue personnel with questionnaires and ask them to fill in their personal details and answer as many of the other questions as they could. This helped the interrogator to the extent of cutting out routine questions and of having the man already thinking along the lines of the subsequent interrogation; but it was never regarded as a substitute for interrogation.

Personnel

Officers:

Interrogation began in M.I.9(b) under one male officer. This continued till January 1943, when a second male officer was employed. An A.T.S. officer had been taken on for secretarial work in 1942 but was not tried out as an interrogator until the Spring of 1943. This A.T.S. officer proved, however, that the right type of woman is as good an interrogator as a man. In 1944, a W.A.A.F. officer was attached to the Section, who besides being responsible for the whole of the office routine, carried out occasional interrogations very efficiently. In the same year an R.A.F. officer – an escaper from Germany – was added to the Section and from September 1944, when the full results of the invasion of France and Belgium became apparent, additional assistance was provided from other I.S.9 Sections and from M.I.9. Canada was represented by the permanent attachment of one Canadian Army Officer and the part time employment of two R.C.A.F. officers, whilst from time-to-time various R.A.F. and Dominion officers were with the Section temporarily. At earlier stages, American officers and officers of I.S.9 (W.E.A.) attended I.S.9(W) interrogations, and their own reports subsequently became adaptations of the I.S.9(W) style.

Other Ranks:
Other Ranks were not used as interrogators. Shortage of clerical staff was a great handicap when the work was under M.I.9(b), but the position improved greatly under I.S.9. In I.S.9 clerks were pooled and a number were trained to take escape and evasion reports to dictation.

Reports
Reports of interrogations of escapers and evaders were produced as M.I.9/S/P.G. (Secret, Prisoners, Germany) reports. Although, as time went on, interrogation of escapers and evaders from other countries besides Germany were carried out, the S/P.G. designation, which meant nothing to anyone outside the organisation, was kept for all reports of this nature. Later, when repatriated Ps/W returned and were interrogated, other designations were given. These were as follows:

I.S.9/W.E.A.	For ex P/W liberated by the Allies.
U.D.F/P.W/INT/U.K.	For South African escapers.
I.S.9/REP.	For escapers from Germany, via Middle East and Balkans.
P.W/EX/SWITZ.	For Italy-Switzerland escapers.
S/P.G./LIB.	For liberated Ps/W from Germany.
C.S.D.I.C/C.M.F/SKP	For escapers from Italy to the Allied lines.
C.S.D.I.C/M.E/SKP	For escapers from Italy to the Allied lines.
S/PG/MIS/INT.	Miscellaneous intelligence information obtained from liberated Ps/W from Germany.

These designations have little significance and are primarily a matter of internal convenience in keeping separate the various types of reports prepared. The reports, where applicable, were divided into:

i. The main report (originally Most and Top Secret and later Secret). This contained information on an escape or evasion up to the point where the escaper or evader came into the hands of an organisation. No names of persons were mentioned, or any descriptions given which might have identified helpers. The main report had a fairly wide distribution.

ii. Appendix A. (Top Secret). This contained names and addresses of helpers, nature of help given, and relevant dates. This information was intended to help I.S.9(D)-(P/15) and, eventually, the Sections charged with the tracing and rewarding of helpers (now I.S.9 (AB)). "Black List" foreigners were also included in this appendix. It had a very limited circulation.

iii. Appendix B. (Top Secret, later Secret). Military Information. Distributed to Service Departments and others interested.

iv. Appendix C. (Top Secret). This continued the narrative from the point where the escaper or evader came under an organisation. Names and addresses of helpers and their descriptions (where necessary) were included. This to a certain extent overlapped with Appendix A. The distinction between the two appendices was so slight that they might have been merged into one.

v. Appendix D. (Top Secret, later Secret). Details as to the use or otherwise of the aids box, purse and other escape aids.

Welfare

If interrogation is to be carried out efficiently, a certain amount of welfare work is necessary, especially for those officers and men who have been out of touch with their homes for a long time. In the early days it was seldom necessary to retain an escaper or evader at L.D.A.C. for more than one night, and no special provision was made for accommodation or welfare. Later, as the number of subsequent interviews became greater, it was necessary to retain them for several days, often for a week or even longer. The accommodation and welfare of officers presented no problem, but after a time an effort was made, prompted by the higher R.A.F. standard of accommodation, to improve the accommodation of other ranks. The Air Ministry furnished a dormitory and provided an R.A.F. orderly, who also kept the interrogating rooms and conducted men to outside interviews. Dormitories were also provided for Army other ranks. Wherever possible, officers and other ranks were allowed to live with relations and friends in London.

Administration

This presented no special problem till the autumn of 1944. Royal Navy personnel and R.A.F. personnel were sent for documentation to the Admiralty and Air Ministry respectively. Army personnel were documented and sent on leave by the Commandant, L.D.A.C., who in 1944, provided an officer specially for this work. In the autumn of 1944, with the arrival of large numbers of escapers and evaders from France, the problem of administering R.A.F. personnel became acute. The Air Ministry finally provided an officer and two orderlies for administration at L.D.A.C.

Training of Interrogators

It was found that a satisfactory method of training interrogators was to have them work for a period on office routine before beginning interrogation. Reserve interrogators for use in rush periods were trained amongst officers of M.I.9 and I.S.9. It is essential to have such reserves.

Suggestions

The following suggestions, based on the working of interrogation in M.I.9(b) and I.S.9(W) are put forward for consideration should a similar Section ever be required:

(a) Interrogators should be selected and trained before they are actually required. Part of their training should be their employment on other "M.I.9" work in order to get the background of what is required from interrogation.

(b) The selected interrogators should study the questionnaires and the scope of their interrogations in advance.

(c) Additional officers should be trained, so as to form a reserve for emergencies. A few trained interrogators are always better than a large number of untrained.

(d) It is preferable that the officer in charge of the Interrogation Section should himself be an experienced interrogator, to whom difficult cases can be referred. Once interrogation work becomes heavy, the officer in charge of the Section should concentrate on the organising of the work, i.e., the allocation of interrogators, the arranging of outside interviews, and the editing of reports.

(e) To obtain maximum results, interrogation of all Services should be centralised and carried out under one roof. Arrangements for accommodation and welfare should be made as complete as possible from the start, in consultation with all the branches concerned in all three Services.

(f) Suitable office accommodation is a pre-requisite to interrogation. A large and comfortable waiting room is essential.

(g) Escapers sometimes think they are under examination to elicit reasons for their capture; in fact, M.I.9 is interested only in their escape and a friendly non-inquisitional approach must be insisted upon. It should be noted that for this reason M.I.9 cannot help OIC Records as this type of pre-capture investigation might necessitate a different approach.

Section "X"

I.S.9(X) was established in January 1942 as the Planning Section of I.S.9, which had just been formed.

Staff

   (a) It was under an Army officer who had been working in M.I.9 almost since it began, with four officers (Navy, Army, R.A.F. and A.T.S.) under him.

   (b) Owing to the smallness of the M.I.9 staff during the first two years of its existence, there had been little or no time or thought devoted to the planning of escapes from P/W Camps or of collecting information likely to be useful to allied personnel trying to evade capture in enemy occupied territory. I.S.9(X), therefore, started practically from scratch.

Work

The Section began by collecting information of value to escapers and passing it on to I.S.9(Y) (Codes and Communications) or I.S.9(Z) (Technical), for transmission to Camps, and by selecting escape material for I.S.9(Z) to send out. As regards evasion, the work consisted in collecting information and passing it on to M.I.9(d) for inclusion in the M.I.9 Bulletin for issue to operational units. The first part of 1942 was mainly spent in preparatory work.

Collection of Material

Information of possible value to escapers soon started to come in. The most reliable source was from successful escapers themselves who were carefully interrogated in detail on their arrival in this country by M.I.9(b) ad later by I.S.9(W). Valuable information about the Swiss frontier was obtained in this way early in 1942. Maps of the frontier crossed were made on a scale of 1:100,000. They included many landmarks which subsequently proved useful to other escapers. These maps and further detailed information in code were sent out to the Camps. In June 1942, information was received from a successful escaper of a route to Sweden, via Danzig. Maps were again made, and detailed information put into code. These were forwarded to our contacts in the Camps by I.S.9(Y) and (Z).

Combined Operations

(a) During the summer and autumn of 1942 one of the duties of I.S.9(X) was special briefing for Combined Operations. These operations concerned France and Norway. With regard to the latter country, it was soon evident that S.O.E., having a number of Norwegians and British officers who knew Norway well to draw upon, were in the best position to advise on evasion. It was, therefore, decided that it was much simpler for C.O. H.Q., to consult S.O.E. direct on all questions of topography and conditions in Norway, while I.S.9(X) gave advice about wearing civilian clothes and the position of evaders arriving in a neutral country. The Section also supplied cover stories.

(b) The Section had a notable success at the end of the year. Plans were required for the evasion of a party detailed for an operation near Bordeaux. I.S.9(X) briefed the party before their departure with the result that some of them made contact with one of our organisations in the area and were immediately convoyed by them over the Pyrenees to Spain and thence to Gibraltar.

New Developments

(a) In the autumn of 1942 the Section started on new developments. It had become evident that, in two important respects, improvements could be made. The maps being issued in purses to aircrew for evasion purposes were on too small a scale and the periodical M.I.9 Bulletins were becoming unwieldy with numerous references back to previous issues.

(b) Unfortunately, a very large sum of money had been expended on maps during the course of the year and there was need for retrenchment at this time, but the need for new and better maps was persisted in and gradually a series, which gained the approval of all those who used them, was produced.

(c) The Section was responsible for the supply of a great deal of the data for the M.I.9 Bulletin. Practically all the country chapters with the exception of the Far East, were supplied by I.S.9(X). These chapters were brought up to date by amendments issued by M.I.9 about once a month.

(d) With the assistance of S.O.E. a great variety of papers, such as identity cards and travel permits, were forged and sent out to

P/W Camps through I.S.9(Z) channels. These were despatched in the Autumn of 1942. Experience proved that papers of a temporary nature were of more use than the permanent type of pass with which all enemy officials would be familiar, and which were apt to get out of date.

(e) During the course of 1942 the very large development in secret communications with Camps through I.S.9(Y) enabled escape messages to be distributed more widely and escape equipment to be sent to an increasingly large number of Camps.

(f) At Christmas 1942, the first bulk parcel containing nothing but unconcealed escape material was successfully received in a P/W Camp (Oflag 1VC). We had been notified by a successful escaper from the camp that, if we sent a parcel with a specially marked label, described in advance in a code letter, our contacts would be able to break into the storeroom and abstract it. Everything worked according to plan, and we immediately suggested to other Camps that they should adopt a similar method. Eventually 70% of the Camps were receiving escape material by this means.

Changes in Policy
In August 1943, it was decided that there should be a big speed up, especially in the amount of material despatched to Camps. By the end of the year very large quantities began to arrive, including a few cameras, typewriters, wireless sets, civilian clothes, and German uniforms.

Lancashire Penny Fund
An impudent scheme, by which money and maps, hidden in Christmas crackers and sent by an imaginary "Lancashire Penny Fund" direct to the German Camp Commandants, was successful in a large number of camps. A letter with the crackers requested the Camp Commandant in each case to pass them to the S.B.O. or Camp Leader to help brighten their Christmas Party. 50% of these got through.

Hogmanay Scheme
In the month of October 1943 sticks of shaving soap were sent in toilet parcels to eight P/W Camps, mostly working camps, with which we had previously no contact. The soap contained maps, a compass, money and a message giving an address to which to write for further aids. This Scheme achieved success in four of the eight camps.

Further Changes

    (a) At the beginning of 1944, owing to the formation of I.S.9(W.E.A.) under S.H.A.E.F. there was a re-shuffle of personnel.

    (b) The policy of sending large quantities of escape aids was now beginning to bear fruit; also, through the development by I.S.9(Y) of W/T Communications with Camps, it was possible to supply them with up-to-date information about escape routes, etc.

Mass Escape from Stalag Luft III

A mass escape from Stalag Luft III in March 1944, was a tragic climax to the history of escaping in Germany. There had been mass escapes before, but since the Spring of 1943, when the Germans adopted special measures for dealing with such outbreaks, most of the escapers concerned had been recaptured. The Escape Committee at Stalag Luft III knew, therefore, that a mass breakout had less chance of success, but, on the other hand, the tunnel had taken a year to build, which seemed a disproportionate effort if only seven or eight were to profit by it. The result of this mass escape is well known.

Of the 74 who actually got out of the tunnel, only three reached England. The rest were caught by the Gestapo and S.S. Troops and 50 of them murdered. The rest were sent back to Stalag Luft III and reported to the Escape Committee exactly what had occurred. They stated that everyone had strictly complied with the Geneva Convention and had given themselves up immediately they had been challenged, thereby carrying out the instructions laid down for all escapers.

After this example of German ruthlessness P/W were discouraged from escaping in view of their ultimate certain liberation in the near future.

Escape Routes

    (a) But in spite of this tragedy there were several successful escapes during the Summer of 1944, mostly via Baltic ports and with the help of French workers.

    (b) The main escape route during 1944 was via one of the Baltic ports. Stettin was the best, owing to the existence of a brothel, frequented by Swedish seamen, and of two or three camps of French dockers. On the whole the Swedes helped in spite of German threats, although there was one case in which a Swedish captain turned his ship round in order to hand over two R.A.F. stowaways to the Germans.

In the autumn of 1944, it was decided by J.I.C. that, in view of the approaching end of the war and the adoption of severe measures by the enemy, such as at Stalag Luft III, escaping should cease. Instructions to this effect were, therefore, sent to all Camps by code letters and wireless.

The Last Phase

During the last few months of the war in Europe our main attention was turned to the safeguarding of our prisoners of war when the collapse came. We kept in the closest touch with D.P.W. and S.H.A.E.F. with the result that the protection and rescue of our prisoners of war were given a high priority in the operations. On the orders of D.P.W. all Camps were instructed by us to "Stay put", organise themselves and await orders.

When the allied armies began their final sweep, the Germans began to move some of our prisoners of war away from the advancing armies, but in many cases, they had managed to take their wireless sets with them and were able, therefore, to know where the Allies were. In one case our prisoners of war actually transmitted a message giving their exact location.

The Final Liberation

Owing to the rapidity of the advance of the Allied armies and the complete disorganisation of the German military machine, our prisoners of war were rescued far more easily than had been anticipated. We were greatly relieved that the revenge which we feared might be taken on them did not materialise.

Analysis of Escape Routes

Route	Percentage of total successful escapers.
Sweden	29.79
Western Europe	24.49
Switzerland	18.50
Russia	14.29
Balkans	12.93

Conclusions

(a) Although I.S.9(X) was not altogether unsuccessful, it took a long time to find its feet. This was mainly due to the lack of staff in the early days of M.I.9. As a consequence, contacts with other secret departments, such as S.O.E., which latterly proved so useful, were not made early enough.

(b) Owing to the time lag in the transmission of messages by P/W mail it was clear that plans for escapes had to be made in the Camps themselves and the only useful contribution from I.S.9(X) was confined to the provision of maps, escape equipment and information concerning conditions in Germany, frontiers and ports. The information sent out was obtained from returning escapers and evaders and, in a lesser degree, from other secret departments.

(c) With the developments of W/T communications with Camps it might have been possible to plan rescues by aircraft. Several schemes were, in fact, prepared by Escape Committees in Camps and referred by us to the Air Ministry, but they were all turned down on the grounds of undue risk to aircraft.

(d) It was unfortunate that lack of staff prevented the Section from interviewing more Allied evaders and escapers who passed through the Royal Victoria Patriotic School. Only about 50 were seen between the inauguration of I.S.9 in January 1942 and V.E. Day. Reports of possible interest were sent to us, but this was not the same as seeing the individuals personally. Under similar future circumstances it would be beneficial to have an M.I.9 interrogator permanently on the spot.

(e) The policy adopted in the summer of 1943, of sending out escape material in large quantities paid handsome dividends. Although some was discovered and confiscated by the Germans a great amount got through undetected. It must, however, be stressed that such a policy should not be attempted until there is a 99% chance of success.

(f) It was never possible to obtain from S.I.S., contacts or addresses in Germany for the use of escapers. We obtained one or two useful addresses from other sources but in general did not favour sending out the actual names of possible helpers as it might endanger the safety of escapers. We did, however, send out the address of the brothel at Stettin, which was particularly useful. This, incidentally, came from one of the few Allied escapers interviewed by us at the Royal Victoria Patriotic School. It was used by quite a large number of escapers before it was literally blown up by the R.A.F. in the summer of 1944. It was a particularly favourable rendezvous because it was reserved for foreigners, Germans not being permitted to use it.

Italy

This memorandum has been primarily confined to Germany because there was very little escaping in Italy. All possible was done to get in touch with Camps, and some success obtained, but never to the same extent as in the case of Germany. This was due to three main causes:

(a) The inefficiency of the Italian administration handicapped our communications to such an extent that code messages and escape equipment often took more than a year to reach the P/W Camps. In addition, much of the mail was lost or destroyed by the Italian censors, probably through laziness on their part.

(b) Prisoners of war were guarded with much greater care than those in Germany.

(c) The Italian collapse came just as I.S.9 was getting into full stride.

The best escape was made by British Senior Officers from their Camp at Florence. They dug a tunnel under the direction of the S.B.O., Lt.-Gen. Neame, and six officers, Lt.-Gen. O'Connor, Air Vice-Marshal Boyd, Maj-Gen. Carton de Wiart, Brig. Combe, Brig. Hargest and Brig. Miles, made their escape. The two last named reached Switzerland safely, and we were subsequently informed that the escape material, particularly the maps we had sent out to them, had been of great use.

Recommendations

(a) That an adequate staff for planning escapes and obtaining information likely to help evaders and escapers is allowed at the outset.

(b) That immediate and close contact and co-operation be sought with other secret departments, so that information from such sources can be applied to the best advantage of evaders and escapers.

(c) That it does not pay to be too timid. So long as lives of prisoners of war or evaders are not jeopardised, a bold policy in conception and execution should be encouraged and adopted. It is essential, however, that before adopting such a policy a 99% chance of success should exist and that those at the other end (the P/W) should know what to expect and play their part.

(d) That the control of all planning should be centralised.

(e) That escapers should not be considered as the only sound authority on plans for evasion and escape. Experience proved that their ideas on the subject were mostly based on their own methods.

Section "Y"

I.S.9(Y) was established in January 1942 as the Codes and Communications Section of I.S.9 which had just been formed. It was previously part of M.I.9(b) and had been responsible for the collection and dissemination of military and economic information received by secret means from our prisoners of war and for supplying them with information likely to be of help in making escape plans. It had been firmly established as part of M.I.9(b) before being transferred to the School as I.S.9(Y).

(a) The collection of information from P/W Camps through secret communications was the main "Raison d'etre" of the original M.I.9(b). If this could not be accomplished nothing could be achieved. With the agreement of the Admiralty and Air Ministry it was decided that the scheme should run on Inter-Service lines under the direction and control of the War Office.

(b) The services of escapers and prisoners of war of the last war were enlisted and, from them general ideas were obtained as to how to set about the job.

(c) Foreign Office code experts were consulted and gave M.I.9(b) a plain language code to teach to selected personnel in operational units. During the early stages of the war the bulk of those taken prisoner were members of the R.A.F. and, to a lesser extent the R.N. The first code given us was, therefore, taught to them. It was an excellent code in every respect, but could only be operated by means of a dictionary. Later, we were given a second, less complicated code, which was called No. II.

Situation when France Collapsed

An officer had been sent out to the British Expeditionary Force in France to contact I.O.s and explain what M.I.9 was trying to do, but the "phoney war" ended before very much could be done in this direction and, when France collapsed in June 1940, there were no Army Official code users in the B.E.F. registered with us. Actually, at this time, there were only three official code users who were prisoners of war – two R.A.F. and one R.N. – and no communication had been received from them. The British Army prisoners, taken by the Germans after France succumbed, numbered more than 50,000 and we were in the unenviable position of having no secret means of communication arranged with any of them. Added to this was the fact that no prisoner of war mail started to come through, except in very small quantities, for nearly six months.

First Contact
In December 1940 we received our first official code letter from an R.A.F. prisoner of war which established secret means of communication with Stalag Luft III.

Getting in Touch
After the collapse of France about 95% of our prisoners of war in German hands were Army personnel. It was essential, therefore, for us to get in touch with them somehow. The means adopted to make contact were as follows:

(a) Censorship were asked to send us for examination any letters received from prisoners of war suspected of secondary meaning or of containing a private means of communication. They were asked also to send us other types of letters – those giving information about conditions in camps, about morale, treatment, location, etc., so that we could obtain a general picture. We examined these letters carefully and got in touch with the addressees in likely cases. By this method we discovered a few workable private codes, arranged by the prisoners of war before capture. We, therefore, wrote to the prisoners concerned, using the means they had employed and sending the letters from fictitious people and addresses.

Whenever a prisoner of war's mail was utilised in this way, we instructed Censorship to place his name on our Watch List, which was supplied to their sorters, whose duty it was to pick out all letters coming from those on the List and to send them to us for examination. We kept these letters for 24 hours only and then returned them to Censorship for forwarding to the addressees. In the case of our letters to prisoners of war, by arrangement with the G.P.O. we had the correct place and date stamp franked on each envelope. The letters were then sent to Censorship who slit the envelopes in the same way as they slit all letters going to prisoners of war, stuck on the "passed by censor" labels and mixed them with the thousands of other letters being despatched. It was essential that these details should be strictly carried out, so that the letters, when reaching the German censors, were no different from the thousands of genuine ones. In this way we managed to obtain contact with three Oflags in the early months of 1941.

(b) In February 1941 we were notified, through one of the private codes, that an officer had arrived in the Camp with one of our official codes. Although we had no registration of the officer, we obtained his back letters from his wife and extracted the messages. Under Gen. Fortune's orders this officer had taught other officers the code, the names of whom we obtained from his back letters. They covered all the Oflags and, when we had been through the back letters of the officers taught, we discovered that they in their turn had taught others as well. The snowball was now assuming large proportions, and we set about getting our contacts to organise Code and Escape Committees in the Camps, which they did with alacrity and enthusiasm.

(c) The case of the Stalags was different. We had failed to discover a single private code amongst the hundreds of letters from O.R. prisoners of war passed to us by Censorship to examine. We suggested, therefore, to the Oflags that they should approach suitable padres and doctors and teach them an official code with the idea that they should volunteer for service in the Stalags. This suggestion was carried out and both padres and doctors did excellent work in picking out the most reliable O.Rs in the Stalags, teaching them an official code, notifying us their names, etc., and getting Code and Escape Committees organised.

A New Establishment

During the Summer of 1941 our code work grew to such an extent that it was obvious a special Section had to be formed to deal with the volume of work. I.S.9 was, therefore, formed in January 1942, with I.S.9(Y) (Codes and Communications) as one of its Sections. An adequate staff was provided with a Major I.O., in command. Most of the personnel were female officers.

Progress

(a) The work during 1942 steadily increased. We got in touch with all the main Oflags and Stalags and, in some cases, with working detachments separated from their base camps. Many camps were splendidly organised with Code and Escape Committees operating smoothly and efficiently. We were greatly encouraged by messages of appreciation of our efforts which we received from many of the camps, also by what successful escapers told us of the value of our work to those interned. Morale was kept on a very high level as a result.

(b) In the Spring of 1942 we suffered a shock. Code messages were being received from two of the Camps stating that they were receiving messages and parcels from Sweden which were so blatant that the whole of our Secret means of communication was being compromised. The previous year we had had a visit from M.A. Stockholm and had discussed with him the possibility of getting escape material sent out from Sweden, since parcels seemed to arrive much more quickly from that country than from England.

The M.A. in his enthusiasm, had, unknown to us, endeavoured to get in touch with certain of his friends who were prisoners of war and had tried to conceal, in fruit sent out in parcels, the method by which he proposed to communicate with them. Most unfortunately, he had adopted a code system similar to one of our official codes in use in the camps. The messages were discovered by the Germans, and, in consequence, the Official Code concerned was in grave danger of being compromised. We were compelled to discontinue this particular code for a period of five months until we and our contacts were satisfied that the Germans had not discovered it.

New Codes

Our experience in code work enabled us to invent new ones ourselves. When we considered that sufficient personnel had been taught Nos. I and II, M.I.9(d) issued No. III to I.O.s of operational units in this country for teaching. Subsequently, No. VI took the place of No. III and, eventually, the following official codes were in general use in British Camps in Germany:

No. I
No. II (with four variations).
No. III
No. VI

All codes with a number, as above, were submitted to the Foreign Office Code experts for approval before being passed as official.

A few months after the entry of the U.S.A. into the War, American Liaison Officers arrived in order to learn our ways and means of secret communication with prisoners of war. The few American personnel captured in 1942 were sent to British Camps, and we instructed our contacts, therefore, to put them wise about code communication, escape organisation, etc., in anticipation of the time when they would be segregated in an all American Camp. We gave these American Liaison Officers our No. VI code for their exclusive use.

In January 1943 the OIC I.S.9(Y) went to Washington and helped the War Department to institute code communication with their prisoners of war on exactly the same lines as was being done here. Shortly after all arrangements had been made, the American prisoners of war were placed all together in an all-American camp, so that, benefitting from our experience, they were able to get going immediately.

The Section scored a triumph in the middle of 1942. We had been anxious to improve the code communication with Oflag IVC, a camp where persistent escapers were sent. They only had our Code No. II in the Camp. We set out, therefore, to teach them a new code (No. V) by a series of messages in Code II. In due course these messages were acknowledged with an intimation that the new code was understood. We received the first message in the No. V Code in October 1942. It had been encoded correctly in every detail and, from that time, both codes were in use right up to the liberation of the Camp.

No. VII Code was sent to the Middle East for teaching agents going on special operations behind the enemy lines.

No. VIII was given to S.O.E. for their exclusive use.

We also had five codes in reserve, including one for a communication limited to a total of 25 words for the use of British prisoners of war in Japanese hands. Happily, the war came to an end before it was necessary to use them.

The Writing of Code Letters

Our first code letters bore the names of fictitious people. The names and addresses were somewhat unusual so as to draw the attention of the prisoners of war to them. These were limited by the numbers of people available to write them. Furthermore, a change in personnel meant the loss of a code writer. The letters written in long hand were mixed with those typed. It was easy for anyone to copy a fictitious signature at the bottom of a typed letter, but again, we were somewhat limited by the number of typewriters available. Notepaper of various sizes and shapes, with all sorts of addresses embossed or printed on it, was obtained and utilised. Later when the G.P.O. produced a special letter card for the Prisoner of War mail, our notepaper became less important, but it served its purpose, particularly in the early days.

With the increase of our code correspondents we took certain carefully selected relatives of prisoners of war into our confidence and asked them to help us. The response was magnificent and, although it meant a great deal of trouble for them, we never received a complaint of any description. Our method was to receive from the selected relative the letter he (or she) intended to send. We would then paraphrase it, so as to include our code message, using the same wording as far as possible, and return the amended letter for copying. The amended letter was then returned to us for checking and despatch. This system and our own methods of sending code letters from fictitious people enabled us to cover all our correspondents satisfactorily.

We assumed that the German Censors had adopted the case system for censoring, as was done by our own Censors in England, and we were very careful, therefore, to have continuity in the text of our fictitious letters, so that the German Censor responsible for examining the mail of an individual prisoner of war would see that the style and contents were constant and unvaried. Everything possible was done by us to avoid suspicion being cast on the genuineness of one of our letters. This made every code letter a most exacting and painstaking job, but it was essential for the sake of security. We do not know of a single case where any fictitious code letter emanating from I.S.9(Y) was ever suspected by the Germans and our ex-prisoners of war correspondents, whom we have interviewed on their return, are unanimous in their opinion that the enemy had never suspected code messages in any of our letters. They suspected that information was being received from England, but they did not know by what means.

News Letters

We started writing news letters to prisoners of war at the end of 1940, before we were in touch with Camps by secret means. These letters were written in an endeavour to counteract German propaganda which had, at that time, reduced morale to a very low level. They were written sometimes in secondary meaning, sometimes in clear, from fictitious people, in the hope that some would slip through the German Censors and be read in the Camps. We mentioned such things as the result of the Battle of Britain, the wonderful morale at home and our belief in ultimate victory. We felt that no letter was wasted, even those condemned had first to be read by a German. Many of these letters got through successfully and, in consequence, we continued them for a very long time.

Our news letters were also made use of by other secret departments (e.g. Political Intelligence Department of Foreign Officer) who gave us rumours and stories to include in them in order to deceive the enemy. We were able to get these letters to the authorities in Berlin when required by instructing our censors here to delete a few words or sentences before despatching them. We had been informed by code that any letters showing a deletion by our censors were not dealt with at the camp but were immediately forwarded to the authorities in Berlin.

In 1941 we discovered that the morale of Indian prisoners of war was extremely low, mainly because the mails from India were not reaching Germany and the prisoners of war felt that they were forgotten by the Mother Country. We contacted a lady keenly interested in the welfare of Indian prisoners of war who undertook to get a number of people to write regularly to these prisoners, provided we organised the work and made ourselves responsible for the letters written. We consulted the India Office and from time to time received from them directives as to the line to be taken by these correspondents when writing about political matters concerning India. These directives were circulated by us to the 150 correspondents who had undertaken this work.

Most of the letters (about 1,000 a month), seemed to have been received safely. We have no means of knowing how much these letters affected morale, but we do know that it improved enormously soon after these letters were started as a regular service and the Germans themselves remarked upon the change that had taken place. Many replies were received by our outside correspondents which showed only too clearly how greatly these letters were appreciated. Every Indian prisoner of war was adopted in this way and the service continued until the latter months of 1944.

W/T Communication

The most important means of secret communication and the one which had the greatest effect on the morale of prisoners of war was radio. The section had foreseen the possibilities of this method very early on, but, like many other innovations, it took a long time to develop and perfect.

Our first attempt was made by means of the Radio Padre, who spoke on the Forces Programme of the B.B.C. every Wednesday immediately after the 9 p.m. news. We approached him in October 1942 and having obtained his co-operation, adapted one of our codes so that a message could be read by those in possession of the key. The instructions for decoding took some time to arrange with our contacts but, in January 1943, the first message, hidden in one of his talks, was delivered over the radio. The decoding of the message depended so much on circumstances beyond our control – atmospherics, wave lengths, reception, the ability of those listening in, etc. – that this method did not prove to be a great success, although one or two messages were heard and interpreted correctly. It was, however, a beginning.

Our next attempts, this time by morse, were much more successful, particularly as the original morse system was initiated by one of the camps. Eventually, with the co-operation of the Admiralty and S.O.E. we were transmitting messages regularly, all of which were picked up and decoded correctly.

Although several camps had transmitters as well as receivers, on grounds of security they were not allowed to send us messages until final liberation was in sight. Prisoners of war on their return confirmed that this policy was correct.

Types of Information sent and received through Code Messages

Our channels of secret communication between England and Germany were used not only by the three Services but also by other Government departments, such as the Foreign Office, Ministry of Economic Warfare, etc., as well as by other secret sections. Our code organisations were employed to send us information of military and economic value, factory targets, conditions in Germany, morale of the people, details of how our aircraft were shot down (supplied by survivors), and to give us answers whenever possible to questionnaires prepared by various departments who desired periodical information on certain matters affecting their long-term policy. They were also used to send us details of the requirements of the Escape Committees and we, in our turn, notified them of what was being forwarded.

In replying to Loyal Greetings from British and Dutch officers in Oflag IVC, H.M. The King and H.M. The Queen of Holland used our means of communication. Messages were also sent to camps at various times from the Chiefs of Staff, Air Chief Marshal Harris (Bomber Command), and the Prime Minister (The Rt. Hon Winston Churchill). These special messages were tremendously appreciated by the recipients.

Italy

Code communications through the P/W mail operated in Italy on the same lines as in Germany, although on a smaller scale. The inefficiency of the Italian administration, however, made it more difficult and less effective, as the time lag was at times appalling, but we had a fairly regular communication with certain camps, particularly with the General's camp in Florence. Before the first paratroop raid on Italy took place in January 1941, M.I.9(b) had taught certain of the personnel taking part our No. II code. When, therefore, some of them were taken prisoner, we were at once in touch with them by code. They did their work well and taught other P/W. By this means the code spread to other camps. The codes in use in Italy up to the time of the Armistice were Nos. II, III and, to a very limited degree, VI.

Statistics

The following figures give some idea of the volume of work performed by I.S.9(Y) during the war:

Germany & Italy

Year	Messages sent:		Messages received by mail	Total
	By mail	By radio		
1941	581	-	799	1,380
1942	1,115	-	2,228	3,343
1943	944	17	3,527	4,488
1944	546	204	2,630	3,380
1945	41	50	289	380
(4 mths)				
Total	3,227	271	9,473	12,971

It will be noted that the peak year was 1943. The development of radio communications in 1944 reduced the number of messages to be sent by mail very considerably and the defeat of Italy in 1943 reduced the number of messages despatched to us during 1944.

Conclusions

(a) The success of our code work was due to the great care with which every letter was written and to the marvellous security prevailing in all P/W Camps.

(b) Our code work proved that prisoners of war can be utilised with advantage as suppliers of intelligence, even though because of the time lag the information may be of value only on a long-term policy.

(c) Communication by W/T was the most important development of all and should be given priority in any future planning of communications by code between Prisoners of War and the War Office. Its use reduces the time lag by half.

Section "Z"

Like other Sections of I.S.9, I.S.9(Z) came into being in January 1942. It was responsible for the production, distribution and despatch of escape and evasion aids. Prior to the formation of I.S.9 it had been part of M.I.9(b) and had already passed from the experimental to the productive stage when it became a separate Section under a Major, I.O.

The Early Days

There was very little to go on when the work of providing aids to escapers and evaders was embarked upon. In the case of P/W Camps, the methods of getting escape material to Ps/W during the last war had been disclosed in detail in books written by successful escapers and other Ps/W. These books had been carefully studied by the German High Command and, as we early discovered, formed the basis of the instructions issued to all German Camp Commandants as to how to prevent escapes and how to discover escape material sent in parcels to Ps/W. These published details made our work a hundred times more difficult.

The old ways had, in the main to be discarded and new methods of concealing escape gadgets devised. Ways of concealing compasses for personnel going on operations were also invented and, eventually, vast quantities of gadgets were produced, the variety and volume of which will be found enumerated elsewhere in this summary.

Parcels to P/W Camps

It was evident very early on that our Ps/W would have to depend largely on the British Red Cross Society for food. It was decided, therefore, that so far as our clandestine work was concerned no attempt should ever be made to get contraband articles into the Camps under the protection of Red Cross labels. Next-of-kin parcels (one every quarter to each P/W) were also banned, since they were sent under the auspices of the Red Cross. We never broke this rule in any way.

The means adopted for getting escape material into Camps was mainly through certain fictitious firms, clubs and organisations which we invented. In order to gain the confidence of the Germans we first sent a letter to each Camp Commandant stating that money had been collected to supply our Ps/W with games, books and comforts, in an endeavour to lighten the burden of their captivity and that a consignment of parcels would shortly arrive which we hoped he would allow the S.B.O. or Camp Leader to distribute. The first, and one of the most successful, of our "phoney" organisations was given the name "The Prisoners Leisure Hours Fund". A list of the organisations, firms, etc., used at various times is given below.

In order to conceal the contraband material as well as possible, a few well known and reliable firms were taken into our confidence who entrusted the work of making cavities in the articles to be despatched, and of loading them with escape material to a few of their most trusted workmen. It speaks well for the integrity of these craftsmen that, so far as we know, never once was the game given away in this country. In 1943 through the skill and ingenuity of the Ps/W themselves, it was possible to send out all contraband parcels to many Camps without any concealment of the articles inside the parcels whatsoever, the Ps/W themselves being able to steal them before they were handled or examined by the German censors.

The method of despatch of parcels entailed detailed arrangements with the Post Office Censorship Dept. The parcels were sent in sealed mail bags to their P/W Section at Aintree. On receipt each parcel was stamped as having been examined, although no examination was actually made by the Censorship officials. The parcels were then mixed with genuine parcels despatched from various stores and other licence holders and sent to their destinations.

The following statistics show the volume of work involved in the despatch of parcels to our prisoners of war:

Parcels Despatched:

Type	1941	1942	1943	1944	1945 (3 months)	Total
Straight	329	4844	2556	1410	144	9283
Special	618	1024	929	854	100	3525
Total	947	5868	3485	2264	244	12808

Straight parcels included several hundred packages of tobacco and cigarettes which were used for bribing the guards and also for exchanging into German currency.

The despatch of parcels to P/W Camps ceased at the end of March 1945, as the end of the war was by then within sight.

Phoney Funds

The names of 'phoney' Funds, Firms, Societies and Organisations used for the purpose of sending escape material to Ps/W were as follows:

Authors' Society.
British Local Ladies Comforts Society.
Brown's Sports Shop, St. Albans.
C & H Sports, Exeter.
Counties Club.
Crown and Anchor Mission.
East Street Sports Shop, Brighton.
Edwards Sports House, Watford.
Empire Service League.
Fussell's Sports Depot, Luton.
Gamley's, Dorking.
Harper's, Athletic Outfitters, Colchester.
Harris's Sports Depot, Bristol.
Jigsaw Puzzle Club, London.
Lancashire Penny Fund.
League of Helpers.
Licensed Victuallers Sports Association.
Liverpool Service Men's Club.
Mayflower Fellowship Society (London Chapter).
Nu-Sports Co., Grantham.
Prisoners Leisure Hours Fund.
Public Institutions & Hospitals Association.
Service Men's Club, Chatham.
Sports Craft (MFRS), Newport.
The Peabody Fund.
The Travellers' Association.
The Wilberforce Foundation.
Vincitas Disinfectants Ltd.
Welsh Provident Society.
Welsh Sports Ltd, Cardiff.
West End Sports, Glasgow.
Women's United Services Association.

Labels were also used for 'Phoney' parcels as from:

P.W. Smith and Co. Ltd.
Gem Tobacco Co. Ltd., London.
Chris James, High Street, Bromley.
Richmond Smoking Mixture.

Aids sent to P/W Camps
Below is given lists of the types and quantities of escape aids and articles despatched to P/W Camps in Germany and Italy during the war.

Money

Currency	1941	1942	1943	1944	1945	Total (3 mths)
Sterling	-	-	-	£300	£60	£360
Marks	27,200	33,040	147,200	460,890	39,400	707,730
Lire	141,900	117,950	78,700	-	-	338,550
French Frs.	4,850	65,400	22,800	38,300	-	131,350
Belg. Frs.	-	2,000	56,500	-	-	58,500
Dutch Gldrs.	-	1,305	5,400	-	1,600	8,305

Escape Aids

Description	1941	1942	1943	1944	1945	Total (3 mths)
Maps	1296	860	2833	3836	422	9247
Compasses	213	656	760	1489	20	3138
Hacksaws	-	270	668	180	1	1119
Wirecutters	-	-	36	37	5	78
Files	-	-	156	95	-	251
Screwdrivers	-	-	58	43	-	101
Passes	-	6	482	1444	10	1942
Passport Photos	-	-	21	40	-	61

	1941	1942	1943	1944	1945	Total
Identity cards	-	-	7	-	-	7
Chisels	-	-	-	14	-	14
Knives	-	-	-	16	-	16
Special blankets (for tailoring)	-	204	67	26	-	297
Convertible Uniforms	-	24	12	6	-	42
Sets of Dyes	-	100	101	215	11	427
Civilian Suits (with accessories)	-	-	3	23	4	30
German Uniforms (with emblems)	-	-	-	4	-	4
Celluloid Cylinders (for concealing maps)	-	-	150	-	-	150

Other items included railway maps of Germany, ties, hats, socks, shirts, suit-cases, German uniform badges, needles and thread, overalls, jodhpurs, Benzedrine tablets, brief cases, buttons, make-up boxes, composite tools, rain coats, purses, razors and blades, Tommy cookers, special rope and rope shoes.

W/T Material

Description	1941	1942	1943	1944	1945	Total (3 mths)
Receiving sets	-	-	14	8	3	25
Crystals	-	-	5	14	-	19
Valves (sets)	-	-	5	14	3	22
Insulating tape (rolls)	-	-	-	12	-	12
Copper wire (lbs)	-	-	-	14	-	14
Condensors	-	-	-	14	-	14

Other items included silver paper, flex, transformers, earphones, resistance meters and glue crystals.

Miscellaneous

Description	1941	1942	1943	1944	1945	Total (3 mths)
Sets of keys	-	-	35	22	-	57
Rubber stamps	-	-	24	89	7	120
Sets of drawing						
material	-	-	13	46	-	59
Cameras	-	-	15	12	-	27
Instructions re						
German A/C etc.	-	19	39	23	5	86
Special messages						
on handkerchiefs	-	-	58	-	-	58
Special messages						
on shirts	-	-	30	-	-	30
Sets of photo-						
graphic material	-	-	1	32	2	35
Magnifying glass	-	-	-	17	1	18
Typewriters	-	-	-	5	2	7
Torch & battery	-	-	-	16	-	16
Sets of letter						
paper	-	-	-	175	-	175
Sets of G.S.G.S.						
maps	-	-	-	6	-	6

Other items included plastic wood, carbon paper, tracing paper, printer's ink, marking ink and electric soldering irons.

Evasion Material
As the war developed it became more imperative than ever that aids to avoid capture, particularly in cases where operational units were likely

to land in enemy occupied countries, should be produced. I.S.9(Z) worked on the production of an aids box which eventually contained the following articles:

Water bottle, sweets, peanut bars, compass, razor and soap, Halazone tablets (for purifying water), Benzedrine tablets (for counteracting fatigue), fishing line. It was a standard pattern and was issued to all Fleet Air Arm, R.A.F. and American Air Corps operational units, not only to those based in this country but to those in other theatres of war as well. It was also issued in large quantities to special assault troops, raiding parties, etc.

In the Far East, a special form of packing was devised for this Far East box which preserved the contents under tropical conditions.

Purses, containing maps, a compass, a hacksaw and currency of the country over which they were operating to the value of £12 were also issued to units.

Other items issued included special flying boots (the tops of which could be cut off, converting them into shoes), blood-chits, phrase cards, posters for placing in briefing rooms, etc. etc.

The following list will give some idea of the magnitude of the work carried out by I.S.9(Z) who were responsible not only for the issue and despatch of the articles but also for arranging for their manufacture:

Description	1942	1943	1944	1945	Total (4 mths)
Compasses:					
Round Brass	231,568	314,522	692,862	62,985	1,301,937
Medium	750	70,369	59,230	0,212	140,561
Midget	-	8,338	6,056	-	14,394
Tunic	2,033	28,301	19,888	14,874	65,096
Pin Point	-	3,212	19,347	200	22,759
Pencil	-	5,470	7,772	-	13,242
Pen	-	600	735	41	1,376
Comb	-	3,741	11,367	3,211	18,319
Pencil Clip	10,165	32,461	45,339	12,389	100,354
Fly Button	40,060	99,447	160,774	58,947	359,228
Pipe	8,525	990	-	4	9,519

Stud	34,483	30,585	26,523	-	91,591
Marching	-	-	1,100	-	1,100
Swinger	47,706	52,746	86,543	10,072	197,067
Cigarette Lighter	-	-	5,766	16,544	22,310
Maps:	391,945	404,439	692,862	176,676	1,665,922
In Purses	85,819	128,048	211,332	43,325	468,524
In Pouches	4,938	4,879	2,991	1,679	14,487
Hacksaws	132,706	221,319	241,874	147,651	743,550
Aids Boxes	135,515	139,408	248,168	37,109	560,200
Blood Chits	15,856	11,624	-	35,230	62,710
Posters	1,440	2,036	1,127	-	4,603
Flying Boots	3,314	3,725	-	-	7,039
Escape Books	10,540	20,014	15,700	356	46,610
Special Knives	-	1,362	2,619	2,511	6,492
Phrase Cards	-	15,124	270,827	62,151	348,102
Far East Aids Boxes	-	-	11,334	48,652	59,986
Special Peanut Packs	-	3,500	-	-	3,500
Recognition Aids	-	-	18,945	8,016	56,961
Telescopes	-	100	13,032	7,673	20,805
A/C Instructions	-	-	8,740	340	9,080
N/B Instructions	-	-	1,944	141	2,085
Heliographs	-	-	20,007	80	20,087
Needle Packs	-	-	10,000	-	10,000
Water Bottles	-	-	32,780	15,000	47,780
Special Food Boxes	-	-	50	38,276	38,326
Bexoid Boxes	-	-	1,500	-	1,500
Special Matches (boxes)	-	-	-	504,000	504,000
Iodised Salt Tablets	-	-	-	10,000	10,000
Pocket Containers	-	-	-	4,990	4,990

The following were also despatched in small quantities: Minox Cameras and films, Jungle boots, waterproof watches, medical boxes, milk and tea tablets, Horlicks, Ovaltine, padlocks, torches and batteries, banding machines, R.A.F. battle dresses, braces, belts, prismatic compasses, wire cutters, fishing lines, shrimp netting, rotators, razors and blades, sleeping bags, typewriters, language records and ski-boots.

I.S.9(D)/P.15

During 1943 and 1944 I.S.9(Z) clothed and equipped many agents selected by I.S.9(D)/P.15 for work in connection with our clandestine organisations in Western Europe. The preparation of containers for dropping supplies of all kinds to our agents on the Continent was also a big part of their work. A special clothing store in Regent Street, London, W.1., was instituted where agents could be fitted out.

During 1944 the Section was also used for the purposes of obtaining special boating equipment for Holland in connection with the evasion activities of I.S.9(W.E.A.).

The following items indicate the variety of articles issued on behalf of I.S.9(D)/P.15, and, through them, I.S.9(W.E.A.): Food, special food packs, clothing, aids gadgets, maps, torches, batteries, special knives, suitcases, aids boxes, tyres, binoculars, purses, phrase cards, toothbrushes, wireless equipment, soap, cotton, razor blades, needles, hacksaws, compasses, first aid equipment, special type waders, infra-red equipment, "Q" type dinghies, flasks of rum and whiskey, silent Sten guns.

In addition to the above, special equipment, such as "S" phones, canoes and certain types of explosives were drawn from other departments and included in the items despatched.

Awards Bureaux

On the establishment of our Awards Bureaux in France and Belgium during the autumn of 1944 (and after V.E. Day in Holland), I.S.9(Z) despatched thousands of parcels of food for our helpers, also clothes of all descriptions. Many of our helpers were compensated in kind, in preference to money payments, particularly in Holland where goods were practically unobtainable. The parcels contained such items as tins of meat of all kinds, tea, coffee, sugar, salt, biscuits, jam, suits, shirts, ties, shoes, hats, cloth lengths, overcoats, bicycles, etc. Shipping the goods across the Channel was the biggest problem, but by perseverance and persistence we managed to get space allotted by both air and sea.

Conclusions and Suggestions

(a) It is generally acknowledged by all three Services and the Americans that the work performed by I.S.9(Z) was an important contribution to the war effort as a whole. Many people owed their lives and liberty to the equipment devised and issued by this Section.

(b) The reports received from returning prisoners of war on wireless activities in P/W Camps were most impressive. It is considered that I.S.9(Z) might have been able to do more than it did in this matter if it had possessed more expert knowledge of the subject. In the event of another war, it is reasonable to expect a considerable use of wireless communication with P/W Camps. It is suggested, therefore, that a fully trained wireless expert should be allowed for in a future establishment of this Section.

(c) The Section was handicapped by not having its own workshop and mechanics to experiment in devising and making new evasion and escape equipment. It is strongly recommended that in a future I.S.9(Z), a fully equipped workshop and trained instrument mechanics are supplied.

(d) Once the experimental stage has been passed and a more or less standard pattern of escape equipment agreed, the emphasis is then upon production in bulk, and I.S.9(Z) becomes a producer and distributor on a large scale. Whilst time spent on reconnaissance is seldom wasted, too much effort put into experimenting can jeopardise the output of articles badly needed by the troops.

Section I.S.9(D)/P.15

This Section was formed in the spring of 1941 for the purpose of assisting evaders and escapers in enemy occupied Western Europe to avoid capture by the enemy and to return to this Country. It was controlled in its activities by the over-riding authority of S.I.S., and was, in fact, started as M.I.6(D), with an office in Broadway and a staff of one junior officer and two clerks.

The Build-Up

Clandestine escape work as a specialist form of Intelligence was an entirely new development. It had no tradition or technique derived from the last war. The oft repeated statement that Nurse Edith Cavell, who apparently worked for S.I.S. during the last war, had been discovered through assisting a prisoner of war seemed to dictate the whole attitude of S.I.S. towards the Section. They were determined to prevent evaders and escapers from involving them in any way. This attitude may have been correct from their own security aspect, but it was a terrific handicap to those trying to build up an organisation.

It was only after two years that S.I.S. began to realise the need for more than nominal support of I.S.9(D)/P.15. This was due to their realisation that increased numbers of evaders on the Continent were coming within the orbits of their organisations and endangering their agents. This rather negative form of support continued to the last and had the inevitable effect of restricting the scope of I.S.9(D)/P.15's work in every country with which it was concerned. Nevertheless, as the final results prove, certain considerable successes were achieved.

Agents

The Section had great difficulty in obtaining suitable agents for the work. Most of our contacts with the French, Belgian and Dutch Intelligence Services were originally arranged by S.I.S., whose ignorance of and lack of interest in the rapidly increasing evader problem spread to their opposite numbers in the Allied Services. The French and Belgians were, therefore, inclined to adopt the attitude that the problem was so unimportant that a very low priority should be given to I.S.9(D)/P.15 in recruiting agents. Moreover, it was not until 1943 that they really saw any point in assisting anybody but their own nationals out of enemy-occupied territory.

The Dutch, in the same way, were totally disinterested and openly hostile to risking Dutch lives in this manner. They omitted to realise until too late the quite important political consequences that work done on behalf of British and American subjects in this manner might have. They have now realised the extent of the organisations built up in Holland, particularly during the months after Arnhem, and are more than a little mortified to find that they knew literally nothing about the work done by their compatriots employed by the Section.

This apathy towards the work of I.S.9(D)/P.15, however, was probably the main cause of its considerable success, for, to achieve anything, it had to work on its own. It led to the Section running an organisation which few people in England knew anything about, but which had a marked influence on public opinion on the Continent. The better type of underground worker distrusted his own Intelligence Services and preferred to enrol in an escape movement which had no political bias and a more human aspect than mere espionage. The Section, therefore, was able eventually to obtain a remarkably high standard of agents without the assistance either of S.I.S. or of the Allied Intelligence Services.

Operations

The high quality of agents enrolled led to this small section of three officers being able to achieve considerable success in the operational sphere. This was particularly true of sea operations and air landings. During the months of 1944 when M.T.B.s were crossing to Brittany, I.S.9(D)/P.15 was quite outstanding in its successful handling of boat evacuations. The enthusiastic co-operation and support of the Royal Navy were most important contributing factors to these successes.

Air Ministry

Unfortunately, the Air Ministry took little interest in the work of I.S.9(D)/P.15. In spite of the enormous numbers of rescued Airmen who made strong representations to the Air Ministry, no support was forthcoming. The particular interest that the Section had in Air Ministry support was in obtaining sufficient priority in aircraft from Bomber Command and special squadrons to carry out air evacuations and parachute droppings, but priority was always low. This attitude was quite comprehensible, in view of the dangers involved of loading aircraft and the fact that the time factor, insofar as evaders were concerned was of relative unimportance.

Conclusions

(a) I.S.9(D)/P.15 was hampered all through by lack of staff.
(b) The subservience of one secret Intelligence organisation to another did not pay. The work of S.I.S. and I.S.9(D)/P.15 was quite different, and it was only natural that the young organisation, with no tradition behind it, should be looked upon with suspicion by the parent organisation.
(c) The W/T and training facilities supplied by S.I.S. were much appreciated, but it did not help when operations planned as a result of the facilities given were obstructed on the grounds of policy.

Recommendations

(a) In the event of another war it is strongly recommended that if the necessary War Establishments can be obtained, a separate M.I.9 organisation should be set up with its own communications and agents. By this means the evasion organisation can be studied as a subject separate from other forms of Intelligence. The training as given by S.I.S. is considered the model on which agents should be instructed. The matters which would mainly concern our agents would be:

W/T, codes, parachuting and pick-up training, details of which could be supplied by S.I.S.

PART II

FIRST-HAND ACCOUNTS
OF ESCAPEES

Compiled and retained on the original file for instructional and training purposes

BRIGADIER JAMES HARGEST, D.S.O. AND TWO BARS

New Zealand Army
Captured: Sidi Aziz, 27 November 1941.
Escaped: Campo 12 (Castello di Vincigliata).
Left: Gibraltar, 28 November 1943.
Arrived: Whitchurch, 29 November 1943.

Capture

I was captured by the Afrika Force, which was under the direct command of General Rommel, at Sidi Aziz on 27 November 1941.

I commanded the 5th Brigade of the New Zealand Division, and in the battle which commenced on 18 November, my task was the capture of Fort Capuzzo and Sollum heights, and the blocking of the entrance to the enemy fortress of Bardia.

I successfully accomplished these tasks in the early stages of the battle, and my Brigade lay athwart the enemy's line of communication between Bardia and the German position at Helfaya Pass and blocked both the northern and southern exits from Bardia. On 25 November Rommel broke away from the battle before Tobruk and, passing round the south along the Trig-el-Abd, crashed into the rear of the British positions around Sidi Omar and reached Helfaya.

Here after replenishing his supplies from our supply dumps, he proceeded to Bardia, into which he had no difficulty in entering because of his powerful force. Meanwhile I had been given the additional task of holding the cross-roads and the air-landing ground at Sidi Aziz to enable our reconnaissance planes to operate.

I had at my immediate disposal my Brigade H.Q., three troops of artillery, one platoon M.Gs., and one Company of Infantry, about 500 men in all with 11 guns.

On 27 November at 0700 hours, the German force approached from the south and attacked me with a force of approximately 100 tanks and

71

48 guns, with supporting infantry – the whole of General Rommel's armoured force.

The battle lasted for two and a quarter hours – till 0915 hours, when, after all my guns had been destroyed, the enemy tanks assaulted the camp and forced our surrender by overwhelming us and then driving the men into small groups.

I had been hurt by two shell fragments which, though not serious at the time, subsequently caused me great pain and illness. General Rommel was present and expressed his admiration for the way the troops under my command had fought. His treatment of my force was correct and humane, he himself visiting the dressing station to see the condition of our wounded.

Bardia.

I was taken into Bardia by car with my Brigade Major and Staff Captain and interviewed by General Schmidt, the German Commander of the Fortress. He offered me my liberty inside the position on condition that I gave my parole. On my refusing, he handed me over to the Italian Commander, who thenceforward took charge of me and my men.

3 December, Benghazi.

I was locked up in a compound with about 1,000 British prisoners of war for several days, and was then placed on an Italian submarine, and with 29 other officers and my servant taken to Benghazi, which we reached on 3 December.

6 December, arrived Italy.

On 6 December I was sent to Italy in a torpedo boat, and after being detained at Messina for some days was despatched to Sulmara.

1942. 13 March, Castello di Vincigliata.

After four months – on 13 March 1942 – I was taken in company with Brigadier R. Miles of the New Zealand Forces, and two other Brigadiers to Florence, where we were placed in prison at Campo 12 (Castello di Vincigliata). I remained there until the night of 30-31 March 1943 when, in company with Brigadier Miles, I escaped into Switzerland.

During my detention in Italy, I was reasonably well treated and have no complaints, except in respect of the treatment of my injuries. Notwithstanding my frequent applications for treatment and after at least three X-ray examinations, the Italian medical authorities did nothing whatever towards assisting my condition.

Escape from Campo 12 (Castello do Vincigliata).

For a period extending over twelve months a party of officers in Castello Vincigliata made preparations for escape.

The party comprised Lieutenant General Sir R. O'Connor, Major General Carton de Wiart, V.C., Air Marshal Boyd, Brigadier J. Combe, Brigadier R. Miles and myself. We were loyally assisted by almost all the other officers and men in the camp, and especially by General P. Neame, V.C., Brigadier D. Stirling, and Lieutenant Lord Ranfurly. We spent several months in the preparation of maps, the collection of provisions, the making and dying of clothes, and a careful reconnaissance of the prison camp with a view to finding the best method of escape. Some of our efforts were abortive and were found to be impossible, and one attempt made by General O'Connor was frustrated as he lowered himself from the top of the outer battlement.

1942. August, tunnel plan.

In August 1942, we decided to tunnel out from the Castello Chapel by first sinking a shaft 10 feet deep in the Chapel porch, then tunnelling for about 30 feet under the castle walls, under the driveway and the outer battlements, and to come to the surface immediately under the shelter of the outer wall.

The tools we had were a kitchen knife, some half-inch iron bars sharpened in the kitchen fire – we used these mainly as levers – some gardening buckets, and some rope for hauling the buckets to the surface.

We used the Chapel as a spoilage dump and, by taking a lead from the lights there, were able to have a chain of electric lamps in the tunnel.

1 September. Digging begun.

We commenced work on about 1 September 1942 and completed the tunnel to within five inches of the surface about mid-March.

In the actual escape we chose a very wet night when the sentries would be in their boxes.

0130 hours.

To defeat the very close inspection of our beds which was made nightly by the Italian officer and N.C.O. on duty at 0130 hours, we resorted to the manufacture of dummy figures.

1943. 30 March, escape through tunnel.

We broke the surface on the evening of 30 March 1943 and at 2130 hours, were free of the castle. Generals O'Connor and de Wiart elected to walk to the frontier and left us immediately. I did not see them again. The remaining four of us walked into Florence and took a train for Milan via Bologna, separating but keeping each other in sight and meeting from time to time on the journey. We changed trains at Bologna where we were compelled to wait for several hours owing to the lateness of the trains due to overcrowding.

31 March, Milan.

We reached Milan at 0830 hours, 31 March to find that no trains ran towards the frontier from the main station until noon. We decided to go to the Stazioni de Nord by tram in two parties. Air Marshal Boyd and Brigadier Combe, entering a tram ahead of us, set off. We did not again see them, and subsequently heard that they were recaptured.

Como.

Brigadier Miles and I proceeded by tram to the station and after buying coffee at the buffet took a train at 10.30 hours for Como, where we arrived at noon.

Chiasso.

We at once walked towards Chiasso, and as soon as we could we left the roads and took to the mountains which had some trees, sufficient to give us a little shelter from view.

Crossed frontier.

We encountered the frontier fence after stalking a patrol in the darkness and succeeded in cutting a hole with wire-cutters and so entered Switzerland at 2230 hours – 25 hours out from Vincigliata.

1 April. Surrendered to Police.

The Swiss Police to whom we surrendered early next morning (1 April) were most correct and courteous to us and handed us over to the Army, who conveyed us to Berne. We were freed within three days and handed over to the British Military Attaché.

The attitude of the Swiss people is most cordial towards the Allies and they did everything possible to welcome us. I would say that they are at least 75 to 80 per cent strongly pro-British and they made no secret of their belief in our cause. I believe that this was the case even in the darkest days of 1940, and the feeling is strongest in the German-speaking part of the country.

Journey to Spain

On 11 October 1943 we were informed that the Dutch Military Attaché in Berne (General van Tricht) was prepared to assist Brigadier Miles and me to proceed to England via France and Spain, using the Dutch organisation. He did this as an act of personal friendship towards us and Colonel Cartwright but stated that it could be done for us only and that he could not collaborate with the British P.C.O. at Geneva. Brigadier Miles left Berne that night and succeeded in reaching Spain, where he unfortunately met his death on 21 October.

I was to be ready to leave on 20 October but not to start until the guide had returned to Switzerland to pick me up. No news came until 26 October when the M.A. received a cablegram from London informing him of Brigadier Miles's death.

In the circumstances General van Tricht was disposed to close down the organisation – but later, on hearing that it had not been "burned", agreed to send me. The War Office was cabled, and at once replied consenting to allow me to proceed.

I left Berne on Saturday evening (30 October) in company with Colonel Cartwright who drove me to Lausanne, whence I proceeded to Geneva by train on Sunday morning (31 October). Here I met the head of the Dutch organisation (M. Niftrik), who went with me to the Swiss police to obtain the necessary documents to enable me to proceed through France.

Here also I met my guide, Doctor Georges Prontas, a Frenchman of 23 years of age. He is a doctor in the Toulouse Hospital, working every day and at the same time controlling the whole of the Dutch escape organisation in France. Since last March he has sent between 300 and 400 men out of France into Spain, using the services of a large number of young men in all sorts of positions, all of whom work voluntarily and absolutely refuse to accept any renumeration.

We left Geneva in the afternoon and, after some trouble in finding a suitable spot, crossed over the double barbed-wire fence near the village of St. Julian about 1715 hours in full daylight. I was dressed in ordinary civilian clothes with a dark great coat and carried a despatch case. At St. Julian we were met by a young man who dressed some wounds in my hands caused by my hasty crossing of the wire and then drove us in his car to Annecy, 35 kilometres away.

We took first-class rail tickets and left at 1930 hours for Toulouse. At Chambry we were informed that the railway line ahead had been blown up, and we were sent back to Aix-les-Bains and switched through to Lyons – thence southward to Valence. Here the train was held, but my guide secured seats for us on a German troop leave train which took us beyond our desired junction (Tarascon) to Arles. We arrived at 0700 hours (1 November) and breakfasted at the railway buffet with a large number of German soldiers. At 0800 hours we caught the Marseilles-Bordeaux express for Toulouse and during the journey we lunched in the refreshment car with two German officers at our table.

At Toulouse I was taken to a house in one of the main boulevards where I remained for four nights, staying indoors all the time.

On Tuesday, 5 November, my guide and I set off for Foix, where he had a friend who owned a chateau, and who offered to keep me until the following Tuesday (9 November). At Toulouse station we met this young fellow who told my guide that the Germans had discovered a store of arms he had, and had arrested his cousin. They were both officers of the Patriot Army and he believed they had been betrayed, so he was making for a hiding place in the mountains until the situation cleared up.

We were mysteriously handed fresh tickets for St. Gaudens, about 85 kilometres on the Bayonne line, and, leaving at 1700 hours, we arrived there at 1830 hours. Here I was again quartered in a house with a family and remained indoors until the following Tuesday morning (9 November) when a lady came for me and took me back to Toulouse to the same house as before. I changed out of my clothes into blue working overalls, heavy working boots and a beret and so became a working man. At 1600 hours we left for Foix, travelling 3rd class and taking bicycles on the train.

We arrived at Foix at 2000 hours and bicycled out to a village in the hills some kilometres distant, where we stayed the night with a *chef du train* and his wife. Next morning (10th November) I dressed up in a railwayman's peaked cap and coat and became a *cheminot*. I was given a new passport with a new description and name and also a "safe-conduct" form for use in the forbidden frontier zone, signed by a German official at Toulouse.

We left the cottage at 0530 hours and boarded a frontier bound train at 0600 hours. Here my guide left me and went back to Toulouse.

My disguise was now that of a porter on the train, and at the stations I received parcels, carried German soldiers' kits and loaded their bicycles on and off the train.

At Tarascon we stopped for two hours and I sat with the railwaymen coming off and on duty in their room in the station. They must have been aware that I was a stranger, but they never by word or act disclosed the slightest notice of my presence, and when a German sergeant came into the room and sat down, they turned their backs upon him and froze him out.

From this point onwards the Germans increased their vigilance, a patrol passing through the carriages continually examining the papers of everyone. Although they came to the van at nearly every stopping place and looked in closely, they did not address me. I busied myself with parcels and when this was finished, totted up figures on papers in pigeon holes.

At Porta, three stations short of the frontier, I left the train carrying the mail bag to the station office, the *chef du train* carrying my small pack. Once inside I was hustled upstairs into the living quarters of the stationmaster, while the *chef* hurried the train out of the station. This was at noon.

At 1500 hours the *chef du train* returned with the train, and coming upstairs, told me I would be called for about 1800 hours by a young man who would accompany me over the mountains and the frontier early next day. At 1800 hours the new guide, also a railwayman, arrived with two bicycles which we rode for about 6 kilometres towards the frontier until we reached his cottage at Carol where I spent the night.

At 0500 hours on 11 November, the *cheminot's* wife went out on a reconnaissance of the village and returned with the news that she could see no patrols. We set out up the mountainside. At 0700 hours we crossed the frontier at a lonely spot above the forest line and then, finding a path, turned left along it towards Puigcerda. At 0800 hours my guide left me, and I walked down the mountain into the town without being accosted by anyone.

I found a Guardia Civile and asked to be taken to his Chief and, finding him at his house, gave myself up at 1030 hours. He was extremely kind, as was his wife, who gave me a meal and dressed my hands. After taking my disposition he handed me over to the Secret Police, where my treatment was somewhat different. The Chief was offensive and after beginning an interrogation of me left me sitting in his office for over four hours. About 2100 hours a number of plain clothes men arrived and searched me, and then interrogated me very searchingly with the aid of a crude and completely inefficient interpreter.

They were satisfied, however, and handed me back all my money and effects with the exception of some razor blades.

I was then handed over to the *Comandancia* of the 65th Infantry Regiment, who with his officers and men treated me with the utmost courtesy and kindness until I left Puigcerda under escort on 13 November at 0900 hours for Gerona. I was given my liberty and invited to stay at a hotel, but I declined, owing to the proximity of the town to the frontier which was only one kilometre away.

On the last evening when I was walking, I was sought and found by several agitated officials who told me that the Gestapo knew of my presence and that a Gestapo car had just come up from the frontier. The *Comandancia* was afraid of my being kidnapped and asked that I remain in his office until I could be escorted to his mess, which, of course, I was glad to do.

On Saturday evening, (14 November) I arrived in Gerona to find the Acting British Consul-General there, together with Mr. Ferrer-Smith, and I was at once handed over to them by the Spanish military authorities.

Notes on Dutch Organisation
The success of the Dutch escape organisation is mainly due to one young man – Dr. Gabriel Nahas, who works under the alias of Dr. Georges

Prontas. He is aged 23 and is a practising doctor in Toulouse Hospital but controls all the work in his escape organisation and twice each month goes to Switzerland to personally conduct the more important escapers across France. He leaves Toulouse on Saturday, arrives in Geneva on Sunday and is back in his ward on Tuesday morning.

He is completely reliable and fearless and very religious and controls the work only from a spirit of patriotism. Neither he nor any of his colleagues, many of whom are in very humble circumstances, will accept any renumeration whatever for their work.

Since March last he has sent nearly 400 men into Spain. Now he feels that nearly all the men who have recently passed through his hands are unimportant, and he is anxious to handle British officers and airmen who are more valuable to the Allied cause. He told me that he could bring out young men in groups of fours or fives as often as twice weekly, and when next in Switzerland at the end of November he would like to contact the Military Attaché at Geneva.

I append below my suggestion as to how it could be done. I desire to point out, however, that the Dutch Military Attaché, who agreed to my being taken through only out of friendship, would require to be consulted. I feel sure he would co-operate.

If a telegram could be sent to Colonel Cartwright fairly soon stating that "Georges" will ring him from Geneva about the end of the month it would set the matter going. He could go down and meet the doctor. Dr. Prontas will ring the Legation and ask for "Henry" but will speak to no one else.

It is important that arrangements be made to pass that message through to Cartwright and that he understands its import.

This will require a strict watch to be kept in the Chancery, where the attention to the telephone calls is notoriously bad.

Dr. Prontas has asked a special favour of me which I pass on to the British Consulate with the strongest recommendation.

He was once arrested and detained for a fortnight for writing anti-collaborationist pamphlets and distributing them. Now he feels that there is a possibility of his being suspected and pursued which will necessitate his moving into Spain. He asks that the British Consulate give him whatever assistance they can to obviate the tedious business of going to prison in Spain. Should this happen, he desires to be passed through and assisted into getting an appointment in the British Army as a medical officer. He speaks English very well.

I strongly recommend that he be especially cared for should he become a fugitive and also that when the time is opportune, he be rewarded by the British Government for his courage and devotion.

Additional notes

1. It is imperative to success that instructions sent from France to Switzerland on the subject of clothes and equipment, etc, be strictly carried out. Clothes and boots are plentiful in Switzerland, but difficult to acquire in France.
2. For those travelling over the route I followed two sets of clothing are necessary to start with:
   (a) the dress of a fairly prosperous business man who travels first class on the railways – good but inconspicuous.
   (b) The dress of a working man – blue or black trousers, heavy working boots, blue or black shirt with a shabby tie. A beret can be used for both types of dress. The outer clothes in (a) must be left in France, as there is no way of getting them through the last 20 miles.
3. Food can be obtained, but some should be carried, and in this respect tea and coffee are especially appreciated by the women in whose houses escapers must be put up. Soap is valuable.
4. The first half mile and the last 20 miles are the most critical parts of the journey.

Most important

In addition to the Emergency Certificate, every officer and man should carry a certificate signed by the M.A. in Berne, giving the military rank of the escaper. This entails no additional risk but is of great value on arrival at the Spanish frontier post, where every effort is made to discount one's story.

LIEUTENANT 200507
RICHARD MICHAEL CLINTON
CODNER
457 LIGHT BATTERY, R.A., *AND*
FLIGHT LIEUTENANT 117660
ERNEST WILLIAMS
7 SQUADRON RAF

Left: Stockholm, 28 December 1943.
Arrived: Leuchars, 29 December 1943.

Lieutenant Codner.
Captured: Medjez-el-Bab, 15 December, 1942.
Escaped: Stalag Luft III (Sagan), 29 October 1943.
Date of Birth: 29 September 1920.
Length of Service: Since 17 October 1940.
Peacetime profession: Student.
Private address: Redfern, Burnham-on-Sea, Somerset.

Flight Lieutenant Williams.
Captured: Kluse, 19 September 1942.
Escaped: Stalag Luft III (Sagan), 29 October 1943.
Date of Birth: 13 July 1911.
R.A.F. Service: Since June 1940.

O.T.U.: No. 11 Bassingbourne.
Post in crew: Bomb aimer.
Peacetime profession: Architect.
Private address: 88, The Drive, London, N.W.11.

A. Lieutenant Codner

This officer was captured at Medjez-el-Bab on 14 December, 1942. He was sent first to Rome and then, by mistake, to Dulag Luft (Frankfurt-am-Main). From there he went to Oflag XXI B (Schubin) and then Stalag Luft III (Sagan). Escape from Sagan is exceedingly difficult; no one had got home direct from Sagan or had succeeded in making a break from the East Compound, where Lieutenant Codner was imprisoned, for over a year. Wire schemes are suicidal and orthodox tunnels are always found. The only method for escape from the East Compound was something entirely new. Lieutenant Codner with Flight Lieutenant Williams started such a scheme with Flight Lieutenant Philpot as third participant.

On 8 July, 1943, the three men began digging a tunnel. A hollow vaulting horse was constructed under which the digging went on. The diggers were carried out daily inside the horse, and the dirt similarly removed, whilst a squad of prisoners of war did vaulting exercises under the nose of a nearby sentry. The tunnel was 95 to 100 feet long, and the exit was in the open about 15 feet outside the wire. On 29 October, 1943, the tunnel was complete and the three men escaped. For the rest of the journey Lieutenant Codner and Flight Lieutenant Williams were together. They were dressed in civilian clothing improvised in the camp. They went by train to Frankfurt-an-der-Oder and then to Stettin via Kustrim, arriving there on 30 October. On 1 November they entered the dock area, hoping to board a Swedish ship unaided, but this attempt proved unsuccessful. Contacts were made with Frenchmen, but it was not until 6 November that they were put in touch with a Danish sailor who offered to help them. They were smuggled on board and hidden in the foc'sle of a Swedish ship. On 7 November the ship docked at Copenhagen. Lieutenant Codner and Flight Lieutenant Williams were hidden by the sailor in a flat outside the town. On 10 November, having returned to the ship, they hid in the chain locker for a day and a night. On 11 November they were put ashore at Strömstad (Sweden). The next day they reached Göteborg and finally Stockholm on 12 November 1943.

Capture

1942.

On 23 December 1942 I had orders from the C.R.A., 78 Division, 1st Army, to carry out a reconnaissance of the hill tracks in the high ground north-west of the Medjez-el-Bab – Terbourba road. I was to base myself on the Northants Battalion of the 11th Brigade, 78 Division and to accompany one of their patrols.

I carried out the patrol on horseback, accompanied by a captain from the Battalion, and located the necessary tracks, returning at nightfall.

14 December captured. Medjez-el-Bab.

During the patrol, our position was frequently given away by Arabs using smoke signals. The next morning (14 December) before returning to H.Q.R.A., I was told to pass on my information to an isolated forward company, via a route held to be safe. But the Arabs had guided the Germans to a position from which they could command the road. I was on a motor-cycle, when I heard shots coming from the left and front, and my cycle was hit in several places and the engine failed. I was unhurt and flung myself into a shallow ditch and tried to engage with my revolver. But two Germans with Sten guns got me in enfilade from about 20 yards, and I was forced to surrender. Their shooting was fortunately poor.

Ferryville Tuapani (Sicily).

I was taken back without delay to Ferryville, and within 24 hours had been flown across to Tuapani, Sicily, where I was detained in a cell until 26 December.

Sicily – Germany

26 December, Naples and Rome.

On 26 December I was flown to Naples and thence by train to Rome. I had not been briefed as to the possibility of escaping to the Vatican, but later heard that someone had gone that way.

Dulag Luft.

In Rome I stayed about three days, and was thence sent on by error to Dulag Luft, Frankfurt-am-Main.

Up to this point searches and interrogation had been perfunctory. At Dulag the search was rigorous, but the interrogation futile, as they were only concerned with Air Force matters, of which I knew nothing. They were loath to believe that their Prisoner of War Department had made a mistake in sending me there, and at first thought I came from a mythical Airborne Division.

1943. Schubin. Sagan.
From Dulag Luft I was sent to the following camps:
15 January 1943 – 4 April 1943: Oflag XXI B (Schubin).
4 April 1943 – 29 October 1943: Stalag Luft III (Sagan).

Dulag Luft

On reaching Dulag Luft I was first searched very thoroughly, and then put into a cell, about 9 feet by 6 feet with windows barred on the outside and locked on the inside. The idea seemed to be to leave you for 48 hours and let you become thoroughly bored, so that you are more eager to talk. When I asked to see an officer, I was told that all officers were on leave. The guards also refused to open a window, to allow exercise, reading, writing or smoking. I was told that all these would be allowed when the officer had expressed himself "satisfied with me".

Some sort of Red Cross form was also shown me, but for some reason I was not pressed to fill in any compromising details. I think they were rather non-plussed at being sent an Army man instead of R.A.F. and did not have the necessary filed information for interrogation. They tried, however, the usual trick of over-heating the cell, and refusing to open the windows. I think this was done as a matter of routine, more than anything else, as on the fifth day I was let out into the compound.

Apart from one "Kultur" conversation with a Feldwebel, who seemed painfully eager to avoid military topics, I had only one interrogation from an officer. The officer spoke perfect English and did nearly all the talking himself, chiefly a string of complaints against the organisation which had sent an Army officer to a Luftwaffe interrogation centre.

B. Flight Lieutenant Williams

Dulag Luft.

On arrival at Dulag Luft I was searched by a Feldwebel who was very thorough, making me strip to the skin and going through every article of clothing with care. He then gave me a Polish tunic and breeches, taking my own, as he said, to be X-rayed. I managed to retain the silk maps and compass from the escape kit. After the search I was locked in a cell 3 metres by 2 metres and kept there for nine days. The window was of obscured glass protected by iron bars and throughout the nine days was never open. I protested but with no result. My guard expected me to sweep out my own cell, but I refused. I repeatedly asked to see an officer but was not allowed to do so for two days. When at length an officer appeared to interrogate me, I asked for cigarettes, a book, exercise and a bath, but was refused all these unless I would give my squadron number, bomb load, and target. I refused and the officer walked off, saying that he would come back in a day or two to see if I had changed my mind.

I was interrogated by three people in all, each adopting a different approach. They were as follows:

(a) Bogus Red Cross Representative. This man had a form which he wanted me to fill in. The form started off perfectly innocently with name, date of birth, mother's and father's names, whether dead or alive and such like, personal questions, but gradually led on to date of joining R.A.F., where trained, for how long, where stationed, station commander's name, etc. The whole form was rather cunningly done and might easily lead one on to say more than one should. When I ran my pencil through the form and handed it back, the "Red Cross" man lost his temper. I imagine that he had experienced this reception too often for him to see it as a joke. He informed me that unless I filled in the form my people would not know that I was a prisoner.

(b) Operational Type. This officer told me that he was an operational pilot on rest. He tried to gain my confidence by telling me that he was not an intelligence man and hated doing the job. His attitude was "knights of the air" and he did not carry paper and pencil, but continually tried to lead the conversation round to my target. He told me that one of my crew had already told him all he wanted to know and when I told him that I did not for a minute believe him, he said that I was a stupid man. On his next visit he produced a printed book containing the names of a lot of stations in England and told me that we were from Newmarket. I told him that if that was what he thought I was quite content.

(c) Confidential Type. This man I consider to be the most dangerous. He would talk for a long time on social matters, on art, national characteristics, and of how Germany did not hate the English, but was surprised and hurt when we declared war.

He, also, did not produce paper and pencil or attempt to interrogate me. His line was that the interrogators and interpreters were university professors who had copious forms and reports which they had to fill in. He said, "It's all red tape, you know, just a matter of form. Just tell them what they want to know. They will then lock the form away and be happy. Then you can go. There is too much form-filling in Germany, but these chaps have single track minds and I'm afraid they will not pass you through until all their nice little forms are completely filled."

During the whole time I was in the cell I had no exercise or fresh air and nothing to read or smoke. My diet consisted of two thin slices of bread, one dry and one thinly smeared with some sort of spread, and Ersatz coffee for breakfast; a plate of thin soup for lunch; and the "breakfast" again for supper. The cell was intolerably hot, the heating being controlled from outside the cell. When I complained the guard turned the heat on still more.

After being released from the cell I was taken across to the transit camp, where I waited for about 12 days before being taken to Schubin in Poland.

15 December 1942-April 1943. Schubin.

We arrived at Schubin on 15 December 1942 where I remained until April 1943, when I was moved to Sagan, whence I made my escape.

C. Lieutenant Codner and Flight Lieutenant Williams

Tunnel scheme
1943, 8 July. Tunnel begun.

On 8 July 1943 we began the tunnel described in the report of Flight Lieutenant O.L.S. Philpot. Philpot eventually joined us in the scheme.

29 October. Escape through tunnel.

On 29 October the tunnel was ready for breaking. Codner went down at 1300 hours with the luggage and was sealed in at 1400 hours. Philpot came later. The tunnel was broken at 1800 hours. All the events leading up to our emergence from the tunnel are described in Philpot's report.

Equipment and documents
We had the following equipment and documents:

(a) Lieutenant Codner:
i.   Clothes. Converted naval tunic, converted naval battledress trousers, standard brown shoes, civilian shirt and collar and tie, R.A.F. mackintosh, home-made beret and woollen gloves, light under-clothes. I was also carrying a home-made canvas valise containing washing, shaving, and boot-cleaning tackle, food, a polo-collar woollen dicky and spare socks. I am sure that for this type of escape it is necessary at all costs to look respectable and clean and to be carrying reasonable luggage. I think it would also be an advantage to be able superficially to change

one's appearance – i.e., sometimes to wear a hat, sometimes a collar and tie, and to change by removing the hat and wearing a choker or high-necked sweater, as this work entails a great deal of hanging about in rather suspicious areas.

ii.   Documents. I was in possession of:

Vorlaufiger Ausweis.

Arbeitskarte.

Police permission to travel.

Reason for travelling supplied by the firm on Reichsbauamt.

A Swedish seaman's pass (highly questionable).

50 Reichsmarks.

At no time did I ever have to show any papers other than the *Ausweis*. The Swedish pass would have been dangerous rather than otherwise, but it had been designed solely to baffle a simple official in case we were stopped. I think it advisable to be in possession of the other papers in case an official proves more persistent.

iii. Food. I was carrying five tins of concentrated foodstuffs prepared in the camp, also a little chocolate. It would have been better to have taken more food, particularly biscuits, as the Germans frequently order beer and coffee at a restaurant and eat food with it produced from their pockets in paper bags. This is done even in the best hotels, often by Army officers.

(b) Flight Lieutenant Williams.

i.   Clothes. I was dressed in a beret made from a German blanket, an Imperial Airways raincoat, a Marine's black converted uniform, and black shoes. I carried a small leather attaché case in which I had my escape food, shaving kit, and a black roll-collar sweater for my role as a Swedish sailor. For the actual break I wore woollen combinations dyed black, with a black hood over my head. My jacket and raincoat were in a long sausage-shaped bag, also black. I was clad in long woollen underwear but found this insufficient when sleeping out at night.

ii.   Documents. My papers consisted of:

Vorlaufiger Ausweis.

Arbeitskarte.

Police permission to travel.

Reason for travelling supplied by the firm on Reichsbauamt.

A Swedish sailor's pass (doubtful).

150 Reichsmarks.

A photograph of a stunning girl inscribed 'A mon cher Marcel – Jeanne'.

Two letters written in French to myself, Marcel Levasseur.

Break and journey
Left tunnel

We had arranged to break the tunnel at 1800 hours on Friday, 29 October, in order to catch the Frankfurt train, which departs at 1900 hours. We all worked without ceasing until 1805 hours when we emerged.

We managed to reach the woods without being seen by the guard and, once there, we took off our black camouflage suits and hoods and cleaned one another down. We then walked to the station, where Codner bought two tickets to Frankfurt. In the booking hall of the station, Williams came face to face with the German doctor who had been treating him in the hospital only two days before. Fortunately, he had cut off his rather heavy moustache, and was not recognised. The train journey was uneventful. The train was extremely crowded and perfectly dark. We stood in the corridor.

Frankfurt-an-der-Oder.

We arrived at Frankfurt-an-der-Oder at 2050 hours and tried to get a room at four hotels. These were all full, so we walked out of the town and spent the night in a drain. It was dry and sheltered, but extremely cold. We had intended to spend all our nights under cover and had not taken enough warm clothing. We came out before dawn (Saturday, 30 October).

30 October

We walked about the streets until dawn. There were a number of people about, the Germans being very early risers. We then had coffee in the station waiting room and booked tickets to Küstrin. Codner again bought the tickets, his own *Ausweis* being sufficient for the two tickets. The train was a *Personenzug* (local stopping train) as, once clear of Sagan we wished to avoid fast trains and travel with local workers if possible. The train was very crowded, and once again we had to stand. The first carriage we entered was full of Russian prisoners of war. We were turned out by the German guard. Fortunately, the Germans are very used to incompetent foreigners, and one has only to say, "*Ich bin Ausländer*" and look helpless.

Küstrin

We left at 0850 hours and arrived at Küstrin about 1000 hours. There were no train checks. At Küstrin we walked into the park, where we cleaned up and ate some food. At 1200 hours we had a *Stammgericht*, or coupon-less meal, at a café and sat in a cinema until 1630 hours.

Stettin

At 1708 hours we caught another *Personenzug* for Stettin. By this means we managed to travel with workers on local trains for the whole journey.

We arrived at Stettin at 2000 hours and, although we had been warned to expect a check, we managed to leave the station without being asked for our papers. We again tried about four hotels, but they were all full for the weekend, so we walked out into the suburbs looking for a place to sleep. After some time, we came to a path which led to the back gardens of a row of houses. Each house had an air raid shelter dug in the garden and, choosing the most comfortable, we spent a cold but secure night.

We again moved off before dawn on Sunday, 31 October, and cleaned up in a lavatory in the town. We had not been able to shave since leaving the camp, but we looked respectable enough to book a room at the Hotel Schobel at about 0930 hours. We had to produce our *Ausweis* and fill in a form stating that we were French draughtsmen on our way to Anklam to work at the Arado Flugzeugwerke. We managed to book for two nights, explaining that we were visiting a director of the firm in Stettin and that he would not see us on Sunday. We then shaved and went out to look at the docks.

Visit to docks

We located the Freihaven and then walked about 4 kilometres to Reiherwerder coaling station, where we expected to find a Swedish ship. We could not see any Swedish flags and could not go very near the docks, as there was a policeman on guard on the bridge. We then spoke to a French worker but received no help. We returned to the hotel to eat some of our food. At 1900 hours we went out into the town and drank beer at several cafés. We did not meet any Frenchmen and, as we were not sure about a curfew, we returned to the hotel at about 2200 hours.

1.   November

About 0730 hours on Monday, 1 November, Codner made contact with a Frenchman, who confirmed that there were Swedish ships in the Freihaven but appeared to scared to assist us. Later we walked carefully all round the dock and located a Swedish ship. We could not read her name, but fixed her position by a large German vessel called the *Walter*. We decided that if we had not contacted a Swedish sailor by that evening, we would climb into the dock and stow away.

Returned to Freihaven

We spent the afternoon in the cinema, and in the evening, we put all our food in our pockets, leaving our bags at the hotel. We tried a number of cafés and, meeting with no success, we walked to a spot we had marked during the morning and climbed over the wire into the dock. There were high lamp standards at intervals round the wire, but our spot was fairly dark and we entered unseen.

We reached the quays without being stopped but found that the Swedish ship had sailed and there was a German vessel in her place. We explored several ships, but they were all German and we decided to move to another part of the dock. We had been compelled to use a torch to read the names of the ships, as it was very dark. Just then a light began to move up the quayside towards us, forcing us to retreat to a siding, where we saw another man with a torch coming towards us. We were caught between the two and could not get away. We rolled under the platform of the siding and after about 10 minutes they both moved off. We had a short conference and decided that it was useless trying to find a Swedish ship in the dark and to return the next day.

Stopped by guard

We had to cover about 100 yards lit by arc lights before we could regain cover, so we walked boldly across as if we had a right to be there. An armed guard intercepted us and demanded our papers. We produced our *Ausweis*, which appeared to satisfy him. After a casual enquiry about the time, we walked to the dark spot in the wire and climbed out again. We then decided that climbing into the docks involved too great a risk of capture, and that the only certain method of escape was to contact the sailors outside the dock. We returned to the hotel and planned an intensive campaign among the French workers.

2 November – Meeting with Frenchmen

We left the hotel next morning, Tuesday, 2 November, and went down to the docks, where we found a sympathetic Frenchman. Up to now we had not divulged our true identity, but we decided that for the French to trust us we must trust them. This proved to be the case. This man arranged to meet us at his camp that evening. We were to climb in over the wire and go to his hut, where he said there was a man who spoke English. We had a coupon-free meal at midday, and spent the afternoon at the cinema. In the evening we went along to the French camp and met the English speaker who could offer us no practical assistance. We told him to spread the news among the French that two English prisoners wished to make contact with Swedish sailors, and arranged to meet him two days later to hear his news.

As we had no room for the night, we hurried back into the town and managed to book a room for two nights at Hotel Gust. We did not book for more than two nights at a time, as we expected the police would have to be notified of a long stay.

3 November

On Wednesday, 3 November, we had breakfast with a Colonel and two Captains of the German Army, all three producing bread from their pockets to eat with their coffee. We produced American ration biscuits, feeling quite in order. During the morning we walked round the docks, making a note of the likely-looking cafés to visit that evening. We had a "*Stamm*" lunch at midday, and went to the pictures again in the afternoon, as we thought the cinema one of the safest places. There are not many cinemas in Stettin and only one comfortable one. We saw the same film four times and did not understand a word of it.

At about 1900 hours we once more started our rounds of the cafés. During this we consumed large quantities of German beer, which is very inferior in quality and seems to contain absolutely no alcohol. At one café we met a Frenchman who was very anxious to help us, but was so furtive in his manner and so obviously a conspirator that he was rather a liability than an asset. He took us to another café where he sat us down at a table and told the waitress in a loud voice that we were Swedes and that if any more Swedes came in, they were to be shown to our table. He then walked out, and a German woman came across to us and started to talk in Swedish. Williams immediately mumbled something and walked out, while Codner tried to explain that Williams was Swedish and he was French. It was a nasty moment.

4 November – Meeting with Daix

In the morning of Thursday, 4 November, we again walked out to Reiherwerder, but could not see any Swedish ships. We took a tram back to the Free Dock and sat in a café which a Frenchman recommended. The only customers were Germans. We returned to the hotel for our bags, and booked a room for one night at the Hotel Sack.

We kept our rendezvous with both the English-speaking Frenchman and the Furtive Type, but neither had any help for us.

We then contacted two more Frenchmen who were themselves trying to escape and thought at first that we were Gestapo agents. We made an appointment with them and moved on to the Café de l'Accordion which, they said, was a haunt of Swedish sailors. Here we met another Frenchman who said that he could help us. Codner returned with him to his Commando, where he met Andre Henri Daix, a former Sergeant in the French Army, who told him that he was leaving for Denmark the next night. He did not think there would be room for us.

5 November
On Friday, 5 November, things began to look rather grim, as we were running short of food and had stayed at all the available hotels we could find. We had been warned about the Hotel Timm, where the proprietor speaks fluent French. We decided to return to our air-raid shelter. We felt that the word was getting round the French that we were there and that we should be successful in the end. That night we again kept our appointments, but with no luck.

Shelter at French Commando
About 2230 hours at the Café de l'Accordion, we made a contact who, on hearing that we had no bed, insisted on taking us back to his Commando. We hesitated, as the punishment for the French would be severe if we were discovered. The Frenchman insisted, however, and we returned with him to his camp several miles outside Stettin.

6 November – Boarded Swedish ship
At 0730 hours on Saturday, 6 November, next morning, one of our other contacts, a Frenchman, arrived, having walked several miles from his own camp, to tell us that he had found a Danish sailor who would take us. We hurried down to the docks where we met a sailor who said he would take us on board. It appears that this was the same ship in which Daix was going to Denmark. We walked onto the dock, using Daix's pass, and found him already on board. He had told the crew "boss" that we were in Stettin. Once on board, we were hidden in a tiny compartment in the foc'sle until the ship had been searched. Once the search, carried out with the help of dogs, was over we were put into the sail locker where we remained until clear of Swinemünde. We were then given food in the foc'sle and slept there that night.

The ship, whose route was Stettin – Copenhagen – Oslo – Göteborg, docked at Copenhagen at about 1200 hours on Sunday, 7 November.

7 November – Copenhagen
We were taken by the sailor we had met in Stettin and hidden in a flat some distance from the town.

8 November
On Monday, 8 November, we lay up all day in the flat.

9 November
On Tuesday, 9 November, the sailor who was extremely careful, took us to meet the crew "boss" who arrived late and very drunk. He insisted on talking English at the top of his voice, both in the street and in a café. The sailor then took us for a meal at the other's expense. The other man did not go with us. We then returned to the ship, where we were told that we had been seen by the first mate who wished to see us. We were taken to his house, where he told us that he would look after us. We then returned to the ship.

10 November – Oslo
On Wednesday, 10 November, we sailed for Oslo about midday. We were put in the chain locker, where we remained for the rest of the day and night. We were very ill.

11 November – Strömstad (Sweden)
We remained below until just after midday on Thursday, 11 November, when we were brought up to see the first mate, who had arranged for us to go ashore with the Swedish pilot, whom they were dropping at Strömstad. This was considered safer than taking us to Göteborg. We were put ashore at 1700 hours and were taken to the police station, where we had a bath and a meal and spent the night in the cells.

12 November – Stockholm
On Friday, 12 November, we were taken to Göteborg, where the British Consul met us and after giving us a meal sent us to Stockholm.

LIEUTENANT DAVID PELHAM JAMES, R.N.V.R.

Commanding M.G.B. 79

Captured:	28 February, 1943, off Dutch coast.
Escaped:	10 February, 1944, Marlag-Milag Nord.
Left:	Stockholm, 15 March, 1944.
Arrived:	U.K., 16 March, 1944.

Date of Birth:	25 December, 1919.
Peacetime Profession:	Student.
Navy Service:	Since 7 December, 1919.
Private address:	Brackley Grange, Brackley, Northants.

1943

Capture

On 27 February 1943, M.G.B. 79, under my command, was one of a unit commanded by Lieutenant-Commander Hichens.

Our orders were to escort a unit of M.L.s on a mine laying operation off the Dutch coast, and thereafter we were given freedom of action until dawn.

At about 0300 hours, on 28 February, an enemy unit was encountered off the Dutch coast, and in the course of the ensuing action M.G.B. 79 received multiple hits aft, severing the steering gear abaft the emergency position, and severing all electrics, telegraphs and hydraulics.

While I was in the engine room attempting to manoeuvre clear, further hits were received in the petrol compartment, setting the ship on fire. Having got out a distress signal and destroyed C.B.s we abandoned ship.

Some of the crew were picked up by other ships of the unit, but, owing to the proximity of the enemy, they were unable to remain to rescue us all.

At about 0400 hours, the Germans picked up myself, together with:
A.B. Barker.
A.B. Levitt.
A.B. Edwards.
A.B. Westwood.

28 February 1943

The enemy ship was a modern built trawler (1939). We were well treated, and given food, drink and medical attention. No interrogation was pressed, but our names and ranks were taken.

Rotterdam

At about 1000 hours (28 February), the ship docked in Rotterdam and at about 1600 hours we were taken under escort to the station, and then by train to Wilhelmshaven.

Wilhelmshaven. 28 February-12 March.

For the next twelve days myself and my crew were confined in a sort of converted hotel. I was in a room by myself in comparative discomfort, was given nothing to read, three cigarettes a day, and simple O.R.s rations.

I was interrogated four times by an elderly Kapitan zur See. The interrogations were carried out in comfort. I was placed in an armchair by a fire, but on refusing to answer questions the interrogation was not pressed.

12 March, 1943 – Marlag-Milan Nord

On 12 March we were moved by train to Marlag-Milan Nord (Westertimke), where I last saw the four members of my crew, as they were taken to the ratings' compound.

April 1943. Wire-cutting scheme.

Early in April two others, Lieutenant W.E. Rodwell, R.N.V.R. and Lieutenant R. Eggleston and myself, having obtained some wire-cutters, set out on a wire-cutting expedition, originally conceived by Rodwell, but we were forced to give up the attempt, since it was too late in the season and the nights were too light. (Incidentally this method was employed later by Lieutenant Rodwell successfully, but he and his co-escapers were apprehended on the Dutch frontier.)

June 1943. Tunnelling scheme.

First escape attempt
About June, several others and myself started a tunnel scheme, with the tunnel opening under the dining room. The Germans used to inspect the ground underneath the floors of huts weekly for signs of tunnelling. There was a brick wall supporting the partition between the galley and dining room, and to overcome this difficulty a dummy wall was built by us, four feet nearer the inspection hole, and the shaft sunk in the intervening space. This scheme was conceived and the work organised by Lieutenant-Commander Cheyne, R.N.

September – Tunnel discovered by Germans
By early September, when about 120 feet of the necessary 140 feet had been dug, the Germans, who were suspicious that something was afoot but could find no clue, suddenly exchanged the officers and ratings quarters. They then started to dig a trench six metres deep round the officers' camp and after a fortnight exposed the tunnel. They filled it in, and we were moved back to our old quarters in about three weeks' time. We at least had the satisfaction of knowing that the Germans had to expend six months' labour in digging. They were still digging when I left the camp in February of this year.

Second escape attempt
In September I thought out the following scheme. There was a certain standard form of letter, instructing the Germans to move officers from place to place, and I had ascertained that action was usually taken on these letters immediately on receipt. Lieutenant-Commander Linton, R.N.V.R., the Camp Paymaster, who knew the German writer-staff, was going to obtain one of these letters and, with it as a guide, we were going to forge instructions that I was to be repatriated via Spain forthwith. Lieutenant Orchard, R.N.V.R., who was repatriated in October, brought details of this scheme to this country, and my father, who was in a position to use influence with the British authorities in Spain, set the ball rolling. Unfortunately, at that moment the Germans changed their writer-staff and it was no longer possible to obtain the original form.

Method employed in escapes 1 and 2
My next scheme was the following:

Bath house.

Every Thursday the Germans would escort us in parties of 40, for a hot bath, to a bath house which was outside the camp. The bath house consisted of a central shower room, with changing rooms on either side. In bad weather the German guard used to come and sit in the changing room while we took our shower, instead of patrolling outside the building. From one of the changing rooms there led a lavatory which was divided by a partition only, from a lavatory which led into the open, and which was used by the staff. My scheme was to climb over this partition and pick the lock of the outside lavatory.

The weakness of the scheme lay in the fact that we were carefully counted, both before leaving the camp, and at the bath house before our return. As against this, however, I relied on the fact that:

1. The German guards stood to get a prison sentence of three weeks for letting a prisoner go, so that it was reasonable to hope that they might themselves cover up their lapse in the hope that it would never be traced to them, and
2. In the event of the guards reporting my absence, the Germans would hold a 'Tally *appel*', when every officer would have to pass with his official number disc. I had secured a second tally disc and another officer, rather similar to me in build, was going to show himself twice, first using my disc, and then his own.

    (Referring to the above, I heard later from Messrs. Campbell (S/P.G.(G)1832) and Kelleher (S/P.G.(G)1843) who left my camp twelve days after me, that the guard of the bath party did, in fact, report that they were one short on return from my second attempt. The Germans then held a 'Tally *appel*' and Warrant Officer James, R.A.F. answered for me as well as himself, passing the Germans first in a naval greatcoat, with my tally, and then in an R.A.F. coat with his own.)

    It was further arranged that in order to give me a clear start from the area I should be covered for the routine afternoon and evening *appel*s. This was facilitated by the fact that the Germans used to count those sick in their barracks. It was comparatively easy to arrange for one man to be counted sick twice in two separate rooms, thereby falsifying the total.

    The main difficulty, once outside the camp, would be getting out of the area, as, being near the coast, it was littered with troops, and as a British bomber-lane the German Home Guard were out every night looking for airmen who might bale out. Rail communication consisted of a small gauge railway, which took one and a half hours to cover the 29 kilometres from Tarmstedt (3 kilometres from the camp) to Bremen. It has always been considered that to use this train would be too risky. It therefore occurred to me that its very improbability might render it the safest as well as the quickest method.

'Lieutenant Bugger-off'.

Owing to the large number of uniforms to be seen in Germany I resolved to attempt to escape in full British naval uniform, carrying a card purporting to be a Bulgarian naval identity card, which was forged by a Lieutenant R.N.V.R., and a letter written by a Sub-Lieutenant R.N.V.R., as from the First Secretary of the Bulgarian Legation, to the effect that I was a Lieutenant Ivan Bagerof (pronounced bugger-off) and "employed on liaison duties of a technical nature involving me in much travel. Since my knowledge of German was limited, it was hoped that all authorities would afford me their usual benevolent assistance".

First escape

On Thursday, 9 December, I joined the bath party. There happened to be a thick fog, and I managed to climb through a window, thus saving me the trouble of picking the lock of the outside lavatory, and successfully got clear of the bath house.

I was wearing grey flannel trousers over my naval uniform, and had my naval buttons covered with black silk covers, as our uniform was well known on the local train.

Christoph Lindholm, a Dane

I was carrying a small suitcase, containing some food, change of clothes, etc., and for this part of the journey had a forged "*vorläufiger Ausweis*" to the effect that I was Christoph Lindholm, a Dane employed by the A.E.G., Bremen. My story was that I had been injured in a recent raid on Bremen and had been sent to the country for a week to rest my nerves. On the way to Tarmstedt I bandaged my head, further to substantiate my wound story.

Just outside the village I was stopped by the local policeman, who asked for my papers, and searched my bag, but I succeeded in satisfying him as to my identity.

I had obtained about 150 German reichsmark, so was able to buy a ticket to Bremen at Tarmstedt station, catching the 1150 train, which was filled with local shoppers.

9 December, 1943 – Bremen

On reaching Bremen at 1320 hours, I went into the lavatory at the Park Bahnhof, took off my button covers and grey flannel trousers, blacked my moustache (which I had grown) and eyebrows and emerged as

Lieutenant Bagerov. I walked to the Hauptbahnhof and went to the "Wehrmachtseingang". On production of my papers the military policeman on duty sent an assistant, who bought me a ticket for Lübeck, told me time and platform of my train and finally, having ordered me a beer, left me in the waiting room. I caught the train to Hamburg and had dinner in the station restaurant. I was eyed with curiosity by a gentleman in the Afrika Korps, but he made no approach. I then caught the 2000 hours train to Lübeck.

Bad Kleinen

In my compartment there was a Hauptgefreiter and a civilian, who, in the course of conversation, asked me where I was going. I replied that I was a foreigner going to Lübeck, and asked them where I could spend the night. They advised me not to stay in Lübeck because of the raids, but on my saying that my next place of call was Stettin, advised me to spend the night in a waiting room at Bad Kleinen. They purchased my ticket and left me in the waiting room there.

10 December, 1943 – Stettin

Next morning (10 December), I caught a train at 0500 hours, arriving at Stettin at 1420.

Neubrandenburg.

A search of the docks revealed no Swedish ships, so after a "pub crawl" in Stettin, I caught the train towards Lübeck, spending the night at Neubrandenburg. When about to enter the civilian waiting room here, I was stopped by the military policeman on duty, who said "Not in there, here, in the Wehrmachtsunterkunft please", where I was given free soup and coffee by a Red Cross sister. I did not sleep very well, owing to the proximity of a German naval officer, and about twelve ratings, who, however, failed to recognise my British naval uniform.

11 December, 1943. Lübeck.

Next morning, I caught the first train to Lübeck, arriving there at about 1100 hours. I went to a good hotel, where I had a shave, followed by an excellent lunch. I then went down to the dock, where I located two Swedish ships lying alongside the Halbinsel.

Boarded Swedish ship.

I succeeded in walking straight past the sentry, without being challenged, and boarded the nearer of these ships, which was a small coaster of about 300 tons. I knocked at the first cabin door I saw, and made my identity known to the steward who emerged. He seemed anxious to help, and consulted the engineer, with a view to hiding me in the coal bunker. We learnt, however, that this was impossible as the ship was coaling that day. He then suggested that I should try the ship astern, which was a sister ship of the same company, and due to sail that evening. After a few minutes discussion I went to board her, but she sailed as I arrived alongside.

11 December, 1943 – Recapture

I went back to the first ship, and after further discussion the steward said he would give me a passage if I returned on Monday. There was nothing for it but to leave, and on going out, I was challenged and apprehended by the sentry at the dock gates.

After interrogation by the duty officer, and then at headquarters, I was taken to the "Wasserschutzpolizei" who saw at once that my papers had been forged. There was nothing for it but to admit my identity, and after they informed my camp, I was handed over to the military authorities.

13 December, 1943 – Return to camp

On 13 December two guards arrived to take me back. We reached Hamburg at 1800 hours, where I was lodged for the night, as my guards preferred to stay there, thinking it was safer to remain in a town which had already been badly bombed. Next morning, we entrained for Bremen, our journey being complicated by the fact that the line had been damaged by an air raid the day before. We arrived in the camp that evening and I was given a sentence of ten days' cells.

Preparations for next escape

As soon as I got out of the cells I started to prepare for my next attempt. This time I decided, since I speak some Swedish, to go as a Swedish merchant service officer, who had been wounded in a raid on Bremen, and was returning to his ship. I took with me a "temporary Swedish passport" and a "letter from the Swedish Consul in Bremen" to the effect that "Since this national of a neutral power has suffered so much, both physically and mentally, during his stay in Germany, it is hoped that everything will be done to make his journey home a pleasant one". The letter was drafted, as previously, by the same Sub-Lieutenant R.N.V.R., whilst the forgeries were made by a Lieutenant-Commander.

I again planned to go in my uniform and greatcoat, this time with merchant service buttons and cap badge. I also took a set of civilian buttons with rings sewn to the back, so that with the aid of split pins I could completely change my appearance within a few minutes. Since I was likely to be recognised in the early part of my journey I had a most realistic make-up, consisting of scabs made of cardboard and stuck to my face with a gluey concoction of violin resin in a solution of surgical spirit.

Escape

10 February, 1944. Escape from bath house. After waiting for three weeks for suitable weather conditions, I left the bath house as previously, under cover of a snowstorm, on Thursday, 10 February. I lay up all day in a wood near the camp and caught the evening train into Bremen.

Bremen. Inspection of papers.

I had to spend the night in the station waiting room, where a very efficient railway policeman inspected my papers, and expressed himself completely satisfied.

With the intention of directing any hue and cry on to Lübeck, I purposely tendered the wrong change at the booking office, and mispronounced the word Lübeck when purchasing my ticket.

11 February, 1944 – Rostock. I caught the 0405 express to Hamburg, continued to Lübeck and immediately bought a supplementary ticket to Rostock, which I reached at 1100 hours (11 February).

12 February, 1944. Stettin.

A search of the docks revealed no ships, so I continued to Stettin, spending the night at Neubrandenburg en route. I arrived at Stettin at 0900 hours on 12 February, but again drew a blank with regard to Swedish ships.

Nearly recaptured

In Stettin an incident occurred which very nearly terminated my attempt. I went into a restaurant for lunch, and, when washing, had apparently washed a small scab, caused by my cap, off my forehead. While sitting at the table a man at the table next to me drew my attention to the fact that blood was pouring down my forehead. I went to the lavatory to staunch the bleeding and he courteously accompanied me. Out of pure politeness he asked me who I was, and on hearing that I was a Swede, he told me in fluent Swedish that he had been in Sweden for ten years. As my Swedish was hardly up to this standard, I must have thoroughly aroused his suspicions, and those of the proprietor, who was hovering in the background. I was able to get clear, abandoning my beer.

Feeling certain that they would inform the police, I went straight to the nearest public lavatory, changed my merchant service buttons to civilian ones, removed my cap badge, and, thus altered in appearance, took the first train out of town in the direction of Danzig.

Koslin

I got out at Belgard, and had dinner, and then continued to Koslin, where I spent the night in the waiting room.

13 February, 1944 – Stolp and Danzig Next day being Sunday (13 February), I was not anxious to continue to Danzig looking for ships, so I spent the day at Stolp. I went to church, went for a walk in the park, and then caught the afternoon train to Danzig, arriving there at 1830 hours. Again, I spent the night in the waiting room, being asked for my papers, which passed muster.

14 February

My position on the morning of 14 February was such that I only had six reichsmark left, and was reaching the end of my tether with regard to keeping up a respectable appearance. I therefore felt that I had either to board a ship that night or obtain assistance from some of the numerous French workers in Danzig. Inspection of the free harbour showed only two Danish ships. I approached three separate groups of French workers, but, although they were sympathetic, they had no offer of food or accommodation. I therefore resolved to board one of the Danish ships; these were lying on the westward side of the spit dividing the two arms of the free harbour. There was a sentry patrolling between the gangways of the two ships, but no sentry on the eastward bank of the arm.

Boards Danish ship

I had by now used up my last six reichsmark, so, going down the unguarded side of the spit, I lay up between the warehouses till dark, and managed to avoid the sentry and board one of the ships.

I went straight down to the engine room, and within a quarter of an hour made contact with a stoker, who told me that the ship was going first to Lübeck with grain, and then on to Denmark. This was not ideal for my purpose, but I felt that "where there's life there's hope", and decided to remain on board.

16 February
For the customs search, when the ship left harbour on 16 February, the stoker covered me with coal. He only divulged my presence to one other stoker.

Lübeck again
They brought me food, and I was on board amongst the coal until 19 February, having reached Lübeck on the 18 February.

19 February
On the evening of 19 February, the stoker informed me that the ship was doing a trip to Königsberg before proceeding to Denmark. As I did not fancy the idea of spending the next 21 days in the coal in pitch darkness, with no guarantee of safety at the end of it, I decided to leave the ship as soon as possible, since I knew Lübeck sufficiently well to stand the chance of boarding another ship under cover of darkness.

Having been buried in coal for five days, I was such a sight that it was essential that I should find a ship before daylight. I spent the night boarding various ships in the Burgtor Hafen, having discarded my shoes, which I had in my pocket. I boarded a big ship with a Scandinavian name, in the timber yards. I crept up to the saloon, where a party was in progress, but was disappointed to hear only Finnish voices, which I recognised, having myself spent a year in a Finnish four-masted barque. I left the ship, and having inspected them turned down a timber schooner of unknown nationality, and an 'M' class sweeper. Crossing the bridge to search the other side of the harbour, the air raid sirens sounded, and I spent about an hour underneath a lorry, as I could not risk being seen moving about or being challenged.

At the Svea wharf, where the Klug Hafen joins the Hansa Hafen, lay a large merchant ship. I managed to board her without being seen by the sentry, who appeared to be absent at that moment. I saw him ten minutes later, when I was already on board. The ship appeared to have steam up, but I could find no clue as to her nationality, or any signs of life. Finally, I heard snores issuing from the galley, where I found the night-watchman asleep. By his side was a peculiar type of Finnish knife, which I immediately recognised.

Finnish ship
As it was now too late to board another ship, I waited outside in the shadow till the night-watchman came out a few minutes later. I addressed him first in German, to make certain that he did not speak it,

and then asked him in Swedish the ship's nationality, name, destination and time of sailing. He replied that she was a Finnish ship and was due to sail in under two hours for Stockholm with a cargo of oranges. He then asked me who I was and I said "German customs", which seemed to satisfy him.

Stowed away

I found my way down to the engine room, where I met a stoker, stressing the fact of having been a year in the Finnish merchant service, I disclosed my identity to him and asked him to stow me away to Stockholm. He said that although he personally liked the British, he was doubtful about taking me, since our countries were at war. I offered him the sum of £200 if he would take the risk. He agreed, and hid me under the boilers.

20 February, 1944 – Ship sails

A few minutes later the ship's inspection party arrived. They actually tapped the boiler-casing where I was, but did not discover me. The ship sailed at about 0700 hours on 20 February.

I stayed under the boilers until the ship reached Stockholm on 22 February. For two watches out of three, I was able to keep a manhole into the stoke hole open, through which I received plates of soup and porridge, but for the third watch, which was not reliable, I had to be sealed in. I could then only find sufficient ventilation by keeping my nose low down in the bilge.

The second engineer discovered my presence, but was the only officer to do so. He agreed to pretend to know nothing about it.

22 February, 1944 – Stockholm

We reached Stockholm at 1500 hours, but at the crew's request I agreed not to leave the ship until after dark.

At 1800 hours I went ashore, and having made contact with the British Consul and gone through the usual police formalities, was freed next morning.

Unlike most successful escapers, I have since had the pleasure of hearing from Lieutenant Campbell (SS/P.G.(G)1832) and Lieutenant Kelleher (S/P.G.(G)1843) of how the Germans learned of my absence. A fortnight before my second attempt Sub-Lieutenant Jackson, R.N.V.R., had made a most ingenious escape, and when I left the Germans were most apprehensive lest he should have got away with it, thereby spoiling their then clear record. On the morning after my departure the

Camp Commandant came to *appel*, with face beaming, and said to our man-of-confidence, in full hearing of the entire camp, "I'm delighted to be able to tell you, Kapitän Lambert, that Lieutenant Jackson has reported back from leave". Commander Lambert, R.N., replied "And I'm delighted to be able to tell you, Captain Bachanson, that Lieutenant James has just gone off on leave again".

Lieutenant Hussey, R.N.V.R., forged the identity card, stating that I was a Bulgarian Naval Officer, that I used on the first occasion that I got out of Marlag-Milag Nord (Westertimke). I also carried a letter written by Sub-Lieutenant Jackson, R.N.V.R., purporting to have come from the First Secretary of the Bulgarian Legation and stating that I was employed on liaison duties. Jackson drafted the letter from the Swedish Consul that I carried on my final escape and Lieutenant Commander O'Sullivan completed the forgeries. On this occasion the camp M.O., Major Knight, prepared a most realistic set of scabs and wounds for me which he stuck to my face.

The ship I sailed in from Lübeck to Stockholm was the Finnish ship *Canopus*.

FUSILIER 4270748
JOSEPH PURVIS

7th Battalion, Royal
Northumberland Fusiliers

Captured: St. Valery-en-Caux, 12 June, 1940.
Escaped: Merkers, 29 April, 1943.
Left: Marseilles, 5 October, 1944.
Arrived: U.K., 4 November, 1944.

Date of Birth: 22 September, 1912.
Peacetime Profession: Miner.
Army service: Territorial Army since July, 1934.
Private address: 51 Maple Street, Ashington, Northumberland.

Following his capture at St. Valery-en-Caux on 12 June, 1940, Purvis was transferred to Germany, where he was imprisoned at Stalag XXC, Stalag IXC and subsidiary working camps. When employed in salt mines at Volkerode during September, 1941, he made his first attempt to escape; with one companion he emerged from a mine shaft, collected their hidden store of food from the baths, climbed through a window and over the fence. Although after three days' freedom his companion was compelled through illness to give himself up, Purvis continued alone towards Switzerland. On the tenth day of his solitary journey, he was discovered by a hunting party and handed over to the authorities.

Transferred to Merkers in December 1942, he participated in a mass break-out but was recaptured within forty-eight hours. At the beginning of February 1943, Purvis planned an escape with another prisoner employed nearby. On 29 April, 1943, the details were complete, and, whilst two other prisoners attracted the guard's attention, Purvis climbed the 12′ wire fence. In anticipation of being joined by his companion, he remained in the locality for three days, but on 2 May, he hid in a wagon and covered himself with salt. Half an hour later the truck was sealed. After travelling thus no less than five days Purvis heard both French and German spoken, and getting out he discovered that he had reached Switzerland.

For fourteen months he remained there before he was evacuated to France. When the arrangements for the remainder of the journey broke down, he was compelled to join the Maquis. Before reporting to a British officer at Decize on 30 September, 1944, he took part in four battles against the Germans in the area south west of Toulouse.

This solo escape into Switzerland by a private soldier was a first-class performance.

Capture
12 June, 1940. Captured at St. Valery-en-Caux.

I was captured with the whole of my section at St. Valery-en-Caux on 12 June, 1940.

Camps in which imprisoned

Fort XVII (Stalag XX A): July-September, 1940.
Stalag IX C (Bad Sulza): One night.
Camps attached to Stalag IX C.
Volkerode (Germany, 1:100,000, Sheet 85, 7581). September 1940-August, 1942.
Molsdorf (Sheet 98, 2741). August 1942.
Romhild (Sheet 111, 9685). September-December, 1942.
Merkers (Sheet 97, 7832). December 1942-April, 1943.

Attempted escapes

(a) From working camp at Volkerode.
I made my first attempt to escape in September 1941, from Volkerode where I was working in a salt mine together with a private from a London Regiment (name not remembered).

We left the mine at 2100 hours and went straight to the baths where we had hidden the food which we had been collecting for some weeks. We climbed through the window and over a fence without any difficulty and walked for about two miles to some woods close by where we removed the blue working overalls we had been wearing. We stayed in the woods till 0400 hours the next morning. We then took our bearings with the compass we had brought with us which had been made in the camp and travelled south with the intention of making for Switzerland. We continued walking south for three days keeping to the woods and fields. At the end of the third day my companion fell ill and was forced to go to the nearest farm and give himself up.

Re-captured on tenth day and sent back to Stalag IX C.

I continued my journey alone for ten days avoiding all towns and sleeping in the woods. On the tenth day I was discovered while I was sleeping in a wood, by a stag hunt party. I was put into the military prison of the small town nearby (name not remembered) for three days. After that I was sent to Stalag IX C where I was interrogated and remained here for eight days. I was then sent back to the camp at Molsdorf. I was interrogated again here and after three weeks I was sent to the camp at Romhild.

(b) Second attempt

In December, 1942, I was sent to the working camp at Merkers. The conditions here were appalling, and the mattresses and bed clothing were full of bugs and lice. There were 47 men in the camp and at the end of two days we all decided to escape. We had discovered a part of the wiring which was weak and worked at it with pick axes whenever we had the chance. On the night of the third day after I had arrived at the camp all but 12 men got out. I went with Private Dukes (Regiment unknown) and two other men. We were making our way to Fulda but were captured two days later in a snowstorm. We had reached a railway siding and climbed up into an empty goods wagon which shortly afterwards was moved into a nearby station where we were caught.

Four guards and an officer came for us and marched us three kilometres to the town (name unknown) with our arms above our heads. If we lowered our arms, we were hit on our finger ends with rifle butts while the two guards behind kept prodding us with their bayonets. When we arrived at our destination, we were made to stand with our faces to the wall for another hour with our hands still above our heads. Then we were marched to a house where we were made to strip while our clothing was examined. We were put into a civilian prison for three days and then sent back to Merkers.

The 12 men who had been unable to get out of the camp at the time of our escape were severely beaten up. All the escapers were eventually rounded up.

As a punishment for escaping, we were made to work an extra two hours a day digging trenches. This was in addition to the eight hours we were already doing in the mine. Our food was very bad during this time. We received two meals a day consisting of dry bread and coffee for breakfast and sauerkraut or potatoes for our evening meal.

Escape

About February, 1943 Gunner Martin, R.A., and I planned to escape again. We collected food for the next six weeks by taking a sandwich to work with us each day. I hid mine in the salt factory in which I worked.

Martin was working on the railway a quarter of a mile away from the salt mine. We decided to wait for a misty morning when we could escape and hide independently in the woods close by for the day. We intended meeting at midnight that night at the power station. We were then to hide ourselves in a salt wagon bound for Switzerland.

29 April, 1944. Escaped from working camp at Merkers.

On 29 April, we decided to put our plan into effect. That morning I went to the latrines with two other men while the guard waited outside. My two companions covered me while I eluded the guard by going round the back of the latrines. I had intended to hide under the salt tanks but seeing several German civilians there I changed my mind and ran straight for the 12 foot wire fence. I seized the top of the fence and heaved myself over. As I reached the top, I was seen by an engine driver who shouted at me. I dropped down on the other side and ran hard for the woods where I remained in hiding for the rest of the day in spite of search parties with dogs.

At midnight I returned to the power station and waited till 0130 hours for Martin but he did not turn up. I returned to the factory unobserved, collected my food, stole a bottle of coffee from the civilians' canteen which was unlocked and returned to the woods. I stayed in the woods for the whole of the next day (30 April) and once again returned to the power station at midnight. I waited till 0200 hours and then went back to the woods for the whole of the next day (1 May). That night I came back past the power station in case Martin should show up. I climbed over the fence into the salt factory which was not guarded and hid under a weighing machine.

2 May, 1944. Hid in salt wagon bound for Switzerland.

I remained under the weighing machine until 0930 hours the next morning (2 May) when the Germans went to the canteen for breakfast. I then left my hiding place and made my way towards the salt wagons. I chose one marked 'Ausland, Italien' and got into it, covering myself with salt. Half an hour later the guard came along and sealed the wagon.

Shortly afterwards the wagon was hitched to an engine and we started to move. We reached Fulda where we remained till nightfall. For the next few days we travelled between 2000 and 2300 hours, and 0200 and 0630 hours. We went through Vacha (Sheet 97, 7233), Meiningen (Sheet 111, 0004), Mannheim (Sheet 131, 6183), Rastatt (Sheet 137, 4113) and Freiberg (Sheet 151A, 1417).

6 May,1944. Reached Basle.

We arrived at Basle on 6 May. Here the trucks were inspected and resealed.

Arrived in Switzerland.

Six hours later we crossed into Switzerland though I did not know this at the time. I was desperately thirsty by this time and had almost decided to risk getting out of the wagon when we started to move again. After two hours we stopped again. I listened to the people talking and heard only German spoken, so I remained where I was. We continued our journey for another hour and stopped once more. This time I heard both German and French being spoken and left the wagon through a small window. I approached a railway worker and asked first in English and then in German for something to drink. He took me to a hut where he gave me some wine. While I was drinking the wine the Swiss Military Police entered.

I was given some food and then taken to Barasone (not marked on map) where I spent the night in the local prison. The next day I was sent to Berne where I contacted the British Legation.

I remained in Switzerland till July, 1944. I worked at the press department of the British Legation for a few months and then went to stay at Le Basset on Lake Geneva.

Left Switzerland
24 July, 1944. Crossed Franco-Swiss border.On 24 July, 1944, I left Switzerland accompanied by two Belgians.

Toulouse
We arrived in Toulouse on 29 July. Here we stayed in a boarding house for two days. A woman then called for me and took me back for the night to her house. The next day a man came and took me to a house two miles outside Toulouse where I remained for two days. I was then told that it was impossible to send me back to the U.K. and that the only alternative was to join the Maquis. I was taken to the station where I met an officer of the Maquis who took me to a small town which was at that time held by the Maquis. From here I was taken to a small town which I think was La Bastide du Salat south west of Toulouse. I remained fighting with the Maquis till 30 September, and took part in four battles with them.

On 30 September, I contacted a British officer at Decize. On 1 October, I left the Maquis and made my way to Marseilles by American transport. Here I met up with the first contingent of repatriates from Switzerland and reported to a British officer.

I remained at Le Bassett on Lake Geneva till the summer of 1944 when I was sent for by an official of the British Legation and told that I was being sent out of the country accompanied by two Belgians.

I posed as a French traveller and was given passes to that effect. My only instructions were to make for Toulouse where I was given an address to go to.

We left from a point near Reney, accompanied by a Swiss official who took us to the border which we crossed without difficulty. We reached Annecy via St. Julien en Genevois on 26 July. From here we went to Chambery and Lyon and reached Toulouse on 29 July. A Dutch official in Switzerland had given the two Belgians an address in Toulouse where we could contact an organisation. We went to this address but were told that the organisation had ceased to exist. We tried to contact another organisation without success and were forced to spend the next two days staying in a boarding house.

I had been given an address in the Rue des Temps and a password which I gave to the Belgian. He tried to make contact with this organisation, but again was unsuccessful. He was told that we would either have to return to Switzerland or join the Maquis.

Two days later a lady came to the boarding house and asked for me. She took me back to stay at her house for the night and the next day I was taken by a man to a point two miles out of the town. Here I remained two days and was then told that I would have to join the Maquis.

I was taken to the station where I was met by an officer of the Maquis who eventually took me to a town in the mountains about 160 kilometres south of Toulouse.

While I was with the Maquis, I took part in four battles against the Germans and was given a certificate to the effect that I fought in the Battle of Lioran, Mur de Barrez, Lyon and Decize, signed by Captain Goaille, who was commanding our battalion. I was also given two other certificates, one describing the action I took part in on 9 and 10 August, when 18,000 Germans surrendered to the battalion and the other commending my general behaviour during the whole of the time I was with the Maquis. I handed over these three certificates to I.S.9(W) when I was interrogated on my return to the U.K.

On 30 September I contacted a British officer at Decize and the next day I left by American transport for Marseilles.

I left Marseilles about 5 October, for the U.K. via Naples.

INTERIM ACCOUNT OF ESCAPE OF LIEUTENANT AIREY NEAVE

1 Searchlight Regiment, R.A.

Captured: 26 May, 1940.
Escaped: 6 January, 1942.
Arrived: Switzerland, 9 January, 1942.

Capture

I was Troop Commander in 2 Battalion, 1 Searchlight Regiment, R.A. we retired from Arras and took up position 2 kilometres south of Calais on 19 May, 1940. On 24 May I was wounded while defending a forward position and was taken to a French hospital, which was shelled and bombed during the next two days. On 26 May I contacted the last line of defence of the British forces, but it was impossible to evacuate the wounded. I was captured on a stretcher on the shore at about 1730 hours on 26 May.

Being wounded, I did not reach Germany till August and from then I was in three camps altogether.

Oflag IX A, Spangenberg, near Kassel, Hesse.

August 1940-March 1941.

This was a well-guarded Schloss, considerably over-crowded by 250 Prisoners of War. Medical stores were scanty, and health was bad as a result. No Red Cross parcels had as yet arrived and food was poor. There were several cases of brutality.

Stalag XX A, Thorn, Poland.

March-May 1941.

This was the reprisal camp for Fort Kingston, Canada. The following conditions obtained:

Underground rooms with no daylight. (Windows were boarded up if necessary);

Guards with rubber truncheons;

Three *appel*s a day;

Revolting sanitary conditions;

Officers were locked in their rooms at 2000 hours till 0700 hours.

The effect on morale was negligible, and the Germans seemed rather ashamed of the whole affair. After a month most of the restrictions were withdrawn. The food was the same as elsewhere.

1st escape

On 16 April I attempted to escape to Russia, but was captured near Warsaw and handed over to the Gestapo. During my escape I observed:

i.   All crucifixes and any religious monuments have been deliberately destroyed in occupied Poland.

ii. In Leslau I saw a young member of the Hitler-Jugend beat an old Pole about the head and stamp on his hat in the street amid roars of applause.

iii. I was told that the Ghetto in Warsaw is in a bombed quarter of the city and that leaving the boundaries of it was punishable by death.

iv. I was in the Strafgefängnis in the town of Płock. It is run by the Gestapo and political prisoners of both sexes were mixed with thieves and other criminals. I saw people being kicked and heard sounds of beating.

v.   Members of the Gestapo admitted to me that hundreds of Germans were being murdered by the Poles.

vi. The morale of the Poles is remarkable and they are always ready to help escaped prisoners.

Oflag IV C. Colditz.

May 1941-January 1942.

This is a camp for "Ausbrecher", or escapers. There were also Jews and political prisoners there. The total number was over 550 and it is very strongly guarded by a complete battalion. General morale was very high and everything was done by escapes, demonstrations, etc., to keep guards occupied. The result was a series of minor incidents and reprisals. There is overcrowding and little opportunity for exercise. Medical attention is poor, but parcels come in well. Censorship of letters and books is very inefficient.

Account of escape

6 January, 1942. Escape

On 6 January, 1942, I made my escape with a Dutchman, both of us dressed as German officers. By a complicated scheme involving breaking through a ceiling, we emerged from the guard house and passed two sentries without arousing suspicion.

Leipzig

At 0545 hours we took a train from Leisnig to Leipzig. There we learnt that the best train left at 2052 hours. We therefore spent the day in the town, visiting the cinema twice. From Leipzig to Regensburg (where we changed) and then to Ulm we travelled without difficulty. At 1030 hours on 7 January, we attempted to take a ticket to Engen near Singen in the frontier district. We attracted some suspicion here and were handed over to the Reichsarbeitspolizei, to whom we presented our Dutch papers. They seemed satisfied with these, but said they were not valid for travel beyond Ulm. A policeman accompanied us to the Reichsarbeitsdienst where we were supposed to report. Fortunately, he said that as we spoke such good German, he would wait for us below. We went upstairs and managed to make our exit through a door at the other end of the building.

8 January, 1942. Singen

As it was now impossible to travel by express to the frontier, we walked and travelled by local trains until we were 3 kilometres from Singen about 0400 hours on 8 January. There we were questioned by workmen on bicycles who seemed suspicious, and we heard them say they would inform the police. We had hoped to get over the frontier during darkness, but we were obliged to hide up for a whole day. We hid in a small hut and slept there. Weather conditions were terrible and the temperature very low. At 1800 hours we left the hut carrying large spades and a couple of long white coats found in the hut.

A Hitler-Jugend patrol stopped us and we satisfied them that we were Westphalian workmen. They told us they were looking for two prisoners of war who were reported in the district. We entered Singen and from the station we walked west as far as a signpost to Gottmadingen 4 kilometres. There we travelled north and then round a large wood that fringed the Gottmadingen-Singen road, eventually travelling south over the railway line that runs north of this road to a point where road and frontier meet for about 50 yards. There we threw away the spades and put on the white coats. An open space lay before us with woods all round. Seventy metres away we saw a sentry at a barrier and cars being stopped. This was to our left.

9 January, 1942. Ramsen

At about 0030 hours, walking and crawling, we crossed the road and this open space which was about 200 yards across and thus passed over the frontier. We saw no Swiss guards and no lights. After accidentally crossing back into Germany (which we discovered by observing a sentry to our left – i.e., to the east) we followed compass line to Ramsen and were there interned at 0100 hours.

Notes

1. As far as our observations went, no one but the military were asked for passes in trains.
2. It would attract undesirable attention to eat chocolate in public or smoke too much.
3. Station waiting rooms may be dangerous, as I have noticed that railway police ask civilians for passes, particularly on large stations at night. Coffee and beer can be bought without difficulty.
4. Cinemas are good places to rest in.
5. It seems probable that the local civilian population in the frontier areas are instructed to question strangers who may be prisoners of war.
6. Since the black-out in Switzerland at 2200 hours there will be no lights visible as a guide after that hour.
7. Trains are very stringently controlled in occupied countries, especially Poland, and it was generally thought too dangerous to travel in them.
8. Advantages can be taken from the presence of two sorts of foreigners in Germany:
    (a) Volksdeutsche (German nationals) who may speak very little German and who have been repatriated from places like Bessarabia, Volhynia, and Lithuania. This is particularly useful for those escaping in Poland where large transplantations of the population have taken place.
    (b) Workers from occupied countries and Italy, especially Dutch, Walloons, and Flemish. There are many of these in industrial areas of Germany adjoining Holland. All of these speak only a certain amount of German.

MAJOR RONALD BOLTON LITTLEDALE, D.S.O.

2nd Battalion, K.R.R.C., 30th Infantry Brigade

Captured: Calais, 26 May, 1940.
Escaped: Oflag IV C (Colditz) 15 October, 1942.
Left: Lisbon, 24 May, 1943.
Arrived: Whitchurch (Bristol) 24 May, 1943.

Date of Birth: 14 June, 1902.
Peacetime Profession: Regular Army.
Army Service: 20 years Regular Army.
Private address: Bunbury, Cheshire.

Capture

On 25 May, 1940, I was Brigade Transport Officer of the 30th Infantry Brigade at Calais. I was with the Staff Captain and Brigade H.Q. details in the railway station, Brigade H.Q. being in the Citadel. At about 1300 hours we received a W/T message instructing us to collect petrol and to deliver it to tanks in the area of 2/K.R.R.C. At the same time a message came instructing details of Brigade H.Q. to reinforce a Rifle Brigade Company outside the station. The Staff Captain told me to see to the delivery of the petrol, which I collected and handed over to Brigade H.Q. 2/K.R.R.C., there being no tanks to be found in that area.

When I returned, I could find no trace of Brigade H.Q. details, either at their former location or with the Rifle Brigade Company referred to above. I moved over to the Fort at the harbour mouth and next morning, while trying to make contact with British troops, I was taken prisoner by a German patrol.

Mid-June. Oflag VII C at Laufen.

With other officers taken in Calais I was marched across France for about 10 days. From a small station north west of Luxembourg we went by train to Trier, thence to Mainz, where we stayed three days, and finally to Oflag VII C at Laufen.

1941. Fort 8, Stalag XXI D, Posen.

Early in March 1941, I was included in a party of about 400 officers sent to Fort 8, Stalag XXI D, at Posen.

First escape. 28 May

In September, 1940, a tunnel was begun by a party of six officers. Those whom I remember were Captain P.R. Reid, R.A.S.C., Captain Barry, Oxfordshire and Buckinghamshire Light Infantry, Captain Elliot, Irish Guards, and Lieutenant P. Allan, Argyll and Sutherland Highlanders. Allan speaks German very well. I believe that all these officers successfully got clear of the camp. Some of them were captured two days later south of Salzburg, and the remainder four days later, west of Bischofshofen.

In October, Captain Lewthwaite (regiment unknown), concealed himself in a garbage cart. On this occasion the cart was driven to a different destination from the usual one. He therefore jumped out, and was soon caught.

In October, 1940, with the approval of the escape committee, a party of twelve officers began work on a tunnel from the music room, which opened from the recreation room. These officers included Lieutenant A.M. Sinclair, K.R.R.C., 2nd Lieutenant E.G.B. Davies-Scourfield, K.R.R.C., Lieutenant A.A. Rolt, Rifle Brigade, Lieutenant Forbes, Welsh Guards, and myself. Our intention was to dig a tunnel about 20 yards long under a road and into the cellar of an empty house on the other side of it, and clear of the camp.

About the end of January, 1941, we knew that some stranger was tampering with our work, but we did not know whether he was a German or an inquisitive prisoner of war. We stopped work for a fortnight but eventually resumed it.

One afternoon towards the end of February, 1941, Sinclair and I were working on the tunnel while Davies-Scourfield and some others were keeping watch above. A party of Germans suddenly rushed into the music room, arrested Davies-Scourfield, opened the entrance to the tunnel and pulled Sinclair out. Sinclair told them there was no one in the hole. They then tried to induce an Alsatian dog to enter the tunnel, which it refused to do. While they were searching above me with the dog, I managed to get out of the hole undetected and to slip through a door, normally locked, and apparently opened that afternoon by the German search party. I then joined a crowd of prisoners of war walking in the yard outside.

Sinclair and Davies-Scourfield received 28 days cells, and the floor of the room in which we had been working was ripped up by the Germans.

Prior to our escape from Stalag XXI D on 28 May, 1941, Captain Hancock, R.A.S.C., who spoke German very well, had made contact with the young Pole Klowski, who had previously helped another officer escaper from this camp.

Sinclair, Davies-Scourfield and I were wearing clothes altered and dyed in the camp. Officers from Fort 8 were allowed to visit a dentist in the Stalag itself. During these visits we obtained some Reichsmarks from British N.C.O.s there who had changed their "Lagergeld" for Reichsmarks with some French prisoners of war. From the same source we obtained a compass each. We had brought with us from Oflag VII C a tracing of a railway map.

The N.C.O.s in the Stalag had contrived to secure a wireless set from an old car and to smuggle it into their camp. By this means the officers sometimes received the B.B.C. news.

The Commandant Müller at this time allowed us to receive tins unopened. By this means we were able to save some useful food for our journey. We also hoarded some chocolate and bully beef. When we left the camp in the rubbish barrow, we took this food with us in small bags.

On 28 May, 1941, Lieutenant A.M. Sinclair, K.R.R.C., 2nd Lieutenant E.G.B.D. Davies-Scourfield, K.R.R.C., and I escaped from the Fort.

We had noticed that each day two orderlies carried rubbish in a hand barrow from the Fort into a rubbish pit about 50 yards outside the entrance. The barrow they normally used was too small to hold a man, but as there was a lot of spare wood available, we had a larger one made. Captain Laurie (Regiment unknown) was in charge of the orderlies thus engaged, and gave us a good deal of assistance. Sinclair speaks German fluently, and I can speak a little, but Davies-Scourfield could hardly speak German at all. We had managed to make contact with a young Pole in Posen, and our plan was to be carried out of the camp separately in the hand barrow, and to hide in the rubbish pit, later making our way to our Polish helper's house.

In the morning of 28 May Sinclair was carried out to the pit without incident. He was wearing an old French army coat which had been altered and dyed black, a pair of black trousers, and a civilian shirt. In the afternoon Davies-Scourfield and I were similarly taken to the pit. Davies-Scourfield was wearing a Dutch overcoat and a pair of trousers, both dyed black, while I was wearing an old mackintosh, and a pair of flannel trousers, also dyed black. We both had civilian caps.

We had collected a small sum of money (about 180 Reichsmark between us) and had managed to obtain a compass each.

Davies-Scourfield and I had arranged that Sinclair should proceed to the Polish helper's address and arranged for him to meet us at a tram terminus about three quarters of a mile from Fort 8, at 1630 hours. We proceeded to this rendezvous, where our helper, Klowsk, met us and took us to his house, where we found Sinclair.

Here there was in hiding a young Polish girl who claimed to have been a wireless operator for a secret organisation. Her father had been already taken by the Germans. Later that evening we proceeded to the house of Frau Markiewicz where we stayed till about 8 June. In the meantime, we were planning to try to reach Russia. Frau Markiewicz told a Polish doctor that she was sheltering us. He had a double-barrelled name and had lost an eye in this war. I believe that he had formerly been acting Hungarian Vice-Consul in Posen.

That evening we were taken to different houses, and next morning were taken to another address. For the next ten days we all hid in a very small room about the size of a railway carriage, which we left for no purpose whatsoever.

Łódź

Our helpers gave us each a better suit of clothes and some kind of green identity cards in German and Polish. These had no photographs attached. As they considered Klowski to be rather indiscreet they told him we had already left Posen.

One morning we were taken by a car, accompanied by a Pole, and driven by a Volksdeutsche who was unaware of our identity, to Łódź. We arrived at Łódź that afternoon and were taken to a house, where we spent a week. There were two Polish evaders also hiding here.

On 20 June, 1941, we left in two parties to cross the Demarcation Line between the Warthegau and the territory of the General Government of Poland. I went with Roma and a Polish woman. I went by tram to the eastern edge of Łódź and spent the night in a house by the tram terminus. Early next morning we went in a horse-drawn cart to a point near Borowa, whence we walked to Gałkow. About midday I met Davies-Scourfield here. A village girl then joined us and while the German frontier guards were having their mid-day meal we slipped out of the village and walked to a house on the railway, about two kilometres south of Kaluski.

We stayed here till the evening of 22 June, when Sinclair, Nicodem and Maria joined us. We then walked to Lubochnia Gorki. Maria had gone on ahead and met us here and took us to her sister's house. She then returned to Łódź. We stayed in this house while Nicodem and

Roma went to Tomaszów Maz to reconnoitre our route. When they came back, they told us that the Germans had invaded the U.S.S.R. It was therefore decided that we could not continue our original plan and Roma left us.

Nicodem agreed to go to Warsaw by train and to warn some friends of his there to expect us. We were to follow by ourselves on foot.

21 June. Borowa
Next morning my companion and I travelled in a horse-drawn cart to a point north of Borowa and walked to Gałkowo, where we breakfasted at a farmhouse. There were German frontier guards in the village, but in the course of the morning I was moved by stages from house to house till I reached the eastern end. In a house here I met Davies-Scourfield.

Kaluski
While the German guards were enjoying their midday meal, Davies-Scourfield and I were taken to a house on the railway, about two kilometres south of Kaluski. Our helpers told us that the German control on the Demarcation Line in this district is considered very dangerous.

22 June. Lubochnia-Gorki
On 22 June, we met Sinclair who was accompanied by a Polish ex-soldier and a woman. We walked to Lubochnia-Gorki. We stayed in a house here until 23 June, while two of our helpers went to Tomaszów Maz to reconnoitre our route. When they came back, they told us again that the Germans had just invaded the U.S.S.R. Our helper said it would be impossible for us now to enter Russia, but one of them agreed to go to Warsaw and to warn some friends of his there to expect us. He told us that we must make our way to them by ourselves, and by road.

23 June-26 August. In hiding in Warsaw
We were now informed that the Germans had heard of our hiding place. At 0300 hours on 23 June, 1941, we set off on foot along the main road to Warsaw. We carried razors and shaved when necessary. We arrived in Warsaw on 25 June and went to the address we had been given, a sweet shop at Chmielna 28 or 26, which was occupied by cousins of Nicodem. That evening Dolniak's son met us here and took us to his flat. We stayed here for two days when Mme. Makoska took Sinclair and Davies-Scourfield to 11 Piusa. I was taken to M. Oszewski's flat. From this time till 26 August, I was in several different houses

for short periods. For the last six weeks I stayed with M. Romanski at Spitalina 8, in the Wedel building. Here I met Mr. Charles Whitehead, an Englishman whose mother was a Wedel. Whitehead was working in a chocolate factory belonging to his mother's family. He has two brothers in England.

Mme. Makoska and Oszewski made arrangements to send us to Hungary. We were given identification papers. As far as I can remember mine described me as a farmer, and had my photograph upon it, but Sinclair's had no photograph. It was not found possible to include all three of us in this party and Davies-Scourfield therefore remained in Warsaw. He was recaptured by the Germans in March, 1942, and is now in Oflag IV C.

26 August. Kraków
On the evening of 26 August, Sinclair and I with the three Poles caught the night train to Kraków. We spent the night here and at about 1500 hours on 27 August, caught a train to Zakopane near the border of Slovakia.

27 August. Zakopane
About 2100 hours we got out at the station before Zakopane, where we met another Pole. After a meal we then walked all night to a small village north west of Zakopane, which I cannot identify. There were 25 German frontier guards in this village.

29 August. Entered Slovakia. Crossed present Hungarian frontier to Rožňava
After dark, on 29 August we were guided across the frontier into Slovakia, where we were met by a car and driven to Rožňava, now in Hungary. We then walked some distance to another car in which we drove to the first railway station south of Rožňava. At 0900 hours on 31 August, we caught a train for Budapest.

The Poles bought our tickets and paid for the cars. Throughout our journey we carried shaving kit and boot cleaning materials and took great pains to maintain a respectable appearance. The Poles carried a change of lower garments.

31 August. Budapest
We arrived at Budapest about 1600 hours on 31 August, and were taken to a house. Later, we were moved to a pension where we had all our meals in our bedroom.

We stayed here for a month. We were given passes representing us to be Polish internees on leave in Budapest from a Hungarian internment camp. After a time, the Hungarian Police began to make enquiries about these passes. We therefore were moved to another address and were given new passes made out in different names. Later Sinclair and I were separated for a time.

9 November. Szeged. Crossed Yugoslav frontier

About 9 November, Sinclair and I with six other people were sent by train into Yugoslavia. Our identity cards showed us to be *Volksdeutsche*. We went by train to Szeged, where we arrived at about 2200 hours. We then walked across the Hungarian-Yugoslavia frontier and boarded a train at a small station in Yugoslavia.

10 November. Pancevo, Belgrade

From here we travelled to Pancevo, outside Belgrade, where we arrived about 1300 hours on 10 November.

From here it was necessary to take a ferry across the Danube to Belgrade. This ferry was most carefully controlled by German troops. One of our party could speak Serb. There were many travellers trying to board the ferry boat, and in consequence I was not asked to show my pass, though Sinclair and the Poles were required to produce theirs. Luggage was also examined here by a German official in uniform. The ferry crossing took three quarters of an hour. On landing at Belgrade there was another control but not quite so rigorous. Here we all had our identity cards scrutinised.

One of our party then took us to a house where we had a meal and went to sleep.

11 November. Jagodina

Next morning, 11 November, 1941, we caught a train to Jagodina, where we arrived about 1600 hours. Our guides left us here and returned to Budapest. Jagodina was garrisoned by about two companies of German soldiers, who were said to have come from Russia, and who appeared to be of all arms.

16 November. Bela Palanka

On 16 November, Sinclair and I with two Polish women left by train for Sofia. After about four hours we reached Bela Palanka. Here one of the Polish women left us. The other was a young woman of about 22, far advanced in pregnancy, who could speak Serb. She was trying to join her husband in Turkey.

17 November. Crossed present Yugoslav-Bulgarian frontier
About 0600 hours on 17 November, with this woman, Sinclair and I were taken in a horse-drawn cart across the Yugoslav-Bulgarian frontier. We went by side roads and drove straight past some Yugoslav frontier guards (presumably Quislings?). We went to a farm, owned by a Serb, between the Yugoslav and Bulgarian frontier posts. This farmer took us round a Bulgarian frontier post to a village on the Bulgarian side of the frontier. Sinclair and I were wearing the civilian clothes we had procured in Warsaw, and were each carrying a small suitcase.

It had been arranged that another cart was to meet us at this village and to take us to Pirot (now in Bulgaria). The owner of this cart was not at home, and the farmer who was guiding us got hold of a friend, and I presume must have told him to find another cart for us.

Arrested by Bulgarian Customs guards.

While following this man along a country road, about midday on 17 November, we met a Bulgarian Customs official. He asked for our passes and demanded to see our baggage. As we possessed only Yugoslav passes, he ordered us to follow him. The Polish girl told us it would be wiser to obey him, and that we should be able to bluff him without much difficulty.

Taken to Pirot (now in Bulgaria)
We were then all taken in a cart, with an escort of Customs officials, to Pirot. Here the Commander of the Customs Guards interviewed us. The Polish girl and Sinclair spoke German to this officer, and told him that we were Germans. He replied civilly that in that case he would at once get in touch with Germans nearby who might be able to help us. We then told him that we were really Poles. On learning this, all but one of the officials present appeared very sympathetic.

Handed over to Bulgarian police
We were then taken to the Police H.Q. at Pirot, and handed over to the Bulgarian police. The Polish girl and Sinclair were questioned here in German. I was not questioned, possibly owing to lack of time. We were searched, and kept in separate cells in Pirot gaol for two days. The girl was quite reasonably treated.

19 November
Taken to Sofia. 19-27 November, imprisoned and interrogated by Bulgarian police.

Early in the morning of 19 November, we were all taken by train with a police escort to Sofia, where we arrived at about 0800 hours that day. After breakfast we were taken to the Sofia C.I.D. Here they took our fingerprints and asked us to write out statements in French. This did not work very well, and later they produced a Bulgarian woman who spoke French to act as an interpreter.

About 1100 hours we were taken to another prison in Sofia, where Sinclair and I were put into a smallish cell with six other men, all Bulgarians. The place was filthy, and alive with vermin. The Polish girl was kept under similar conditions in the women's part of the prison. We received no food other than bread and water. On 20 November, we were removed to another prison at the Police H.Q., which was clean, and where conditions were much better. We were kept in separate cells. I had as companion a Bulgarian lorry driver who managed to make me understand that he was accused by the Germans of being a "Communist". From him I also managed to gather that it was virtually impossible to cross the Bulgarian-Turkish frontier on foot.

On 24 November, 1941, we were questioned separately by the Bulgarian police with the aid of a male interpreter who spoke French. The Polish girl was interviewed first, then Sinclair, and lastly myself.

Sinclair and I decided that we should still pose as Poles. He could speak a certain amount of Polish and maintained that he was a Polish student attempting to leave Poland. I, who can speak only a few Polish phrases, said that I was a Pole who had been living in America and had visited some of my relations in Poland just before the war and had then gone to Hungary.

Our interrogator told us that our stories were false, and that unless we told him the truth, he would have to hand all three of us over to the Germans. Sinclair told me later that he then declared himself as a British officer and a prisoner of war, escaped from German hands. His interrogator said that if he gave a full account of his route, with the names of any persons who had helped him, we would all be sent to Turkey, possibly in a couple of days.

When my turn for interrogation came, the interrogator already knew that I was a British officer and an escaped prisoner of war. He told me that if I gave a detailed statement of my routes and helpers, he would send me to Turkey. I thought this attitude most suspicious, and I began to write out a statement in English giving imaginary routes and helpers. This plan Sinclair and I had previously agreed to adopt should we fall into German hands. While I was writing out this statement Sinclair was brought in. He said to me in French, "We must tell the truth", and was then taken out again. I therefore thought that he must have had some experience during his interrogation that I had not.

Accordingly, I wrote out a true statement of our routes and helpers. On 27 November while visiting the prison barber, I met Sinclair, who signalled to me that things had gone wrong. Later we were taken to collect our baggage. While thus engaged Sinclair told me that the Chief of Police had again seen him and had told him that he regretted he was unable to send us to Turkey and would have to hand us all over to the Germans. He gave as his reasons: (1) that Bulgaria had just signed the Anti-Comintern Pact and (2) that the Germans already knew of our whereabouts.

Sinclair also told me that when the Chief of Police saw him there was a German N.C.O. in the room. Sinclair added that he had refused to say anything while this German was present, and had demanded to speak to the police official who had originally seen us. This request was eventually granted. Sinclair protested vigorously to this man that our statements had only been made because we had been definitely promised that none of us should be handed over to the Germans. Eventually, the original statements made by Sinclair and myself were handed to him and he was allowed to burn them. He asked if there were any copies and was assured that there were none. Later we found an opportunity to have a short conversation with the Polish girl and she told us that subsequent to the burning of our original statements, she had noticed on the desk of our first interrogator a typed copy of one of them.

27 November. Handed over to German authorities in Sofia
Sinclair and I were then handed over to a German N.C.O. who took us by car to the city gaol in Sofia. Here we were lodged in a special wing under German control. On the way to the gaol, I asked a Bulgarian police official who came with us, and who spoke English well, whether he would inform the United States Consul of our fate. He said that he doubted whether he could.

On 30 November I was taken before two Bulgarian police in plain clothes. One of them spoke English well. He told me that I could write a short letter to my father, but that I must not say where I was.

I protested most empathically at our treatment by the Bulgarians, and demanded to see the Chief of Police myself. I also said that we were particularly anxious to prevent the Polish girl from falling into German hands. He immediately said, "She is not agent, is she? She has not done anything against the Germans?" I replied that all she had done was to use the knowledge of Balkan languages to help Sinclair and myself to reach Bulgaria.

2 December. Taken to Vienna Military Prison

On 2 December the Polish girl, Sinclair and I were taken by train with an escort to Belgrade. Here the girl was handed over to a German soldier. Sinclair and I were then taken to the Military Prison in Vienna. We remained here from early December 1941, until 17 January, 1942.

In the Military Prison at Vienna our treatment was good. There were a number of Austrian military prisoners and also Austrian guards. Some of both categories were sympathetic to us, and expressed their dislike of the Germans.

1942 second escape. Escaped from train at Roudnice (Czechoslovakia)

About 0900 hours on 17 January, 1942, Sinclair and I, escorted by a Feldwebel (an Austrian) and one soldier, were taken by train from the Franz Josef Bahnhof. When the soldier was out of our compartment the Feldwebel told us that he disliked Germans, and complained of the manner in which they ill-treated Russian prisoners of war. Later he told us that he was taking us to a place near Dresden.

Sinclair and I agreed to escape from the train if possible. We reconnoitred the window of a lavatory and without detection contrived to break the supports which held it in place. We were still in plain clothes, and had our shaving kit with us, and soft hats in our pockets. We had no money, and no food beyond portions saved from our lunch ration that day. Between Prague and Roudnice the train began to slow down. Sinclair, on the plea of visiting the lavatory, left the compartment with the Feldwebel, who remained in the corridor.

I followed a few moments afterwards, having asked permission of the private soldier to stand in the corridor beside the Feldwebel "to get some air". I had arranged that if Sinclair left through the window of the lavatory, he should leave the latch of the lavatory door in a certain position. When I got into the corridor, I saw that the latch was in this position. I walked past the Feldwebel, entered the lavatory, locked the door and got out of the window, feet first. In the meantime, the train began to gain speed. While I was hanging on the near side of the train, I felt a touch on my leg and saw Sinclair below me on the step of the train. We then made our way to the buffers between two coaches.

As the train approached Roudnice Station it slackened speed, and Sinclair dropped off. As he did so a door in the carriage opened and the Feldwebel looked out and saw him. I was crouching out of his sight and was not noticed. Almost immediately afterwards the train stopped. The Feldwebel leaped out and chased Sinclair, while I remained hiding on the buffers. Apparently, Sinclair had hurt his head in falling, and was slightly dazed, for he was soon caught. Two black-uniformed railway police came and stood just below me and flashed their torches about. I heard them discussing Sinclair's escape. A timely escape of steam from a pipe fortunately obscured me from their view.

When Sinclair had been caught the hue and cry in the immediate vicinity of the train died down. I slipped off the buffers and walked down the line southwards. It was bitterly cold and I had no greatcoat. I felt, therefore, that my only hope was to find a helper very soon.

I walked into Roudnice. As I knew I was in Czechoslovakia I decided to speak in German to any potential helpers whom I met, and to ask them the time. If they replied in Czech or in bad German, I would then declare myself to them. If, on the other hand, they replied in good German I would approach some other person.

This plan worked well. The first man to whom I declared myself as an English escaper said that he would have to report me to the police, but took no further action. The second man said that he lived some distance away and could not help. The third person I approached was a boy of about 17. He took me to his house, and fetched a relative who had lived in America and spoke English. I stayed in this relative's house for two nights. He gave me a big jacket to wear in lieu of an overcoat, and a pair of boots. He also collected some money (I think about 30 crowns) from some of his friends and gave it to me. I wanted to obtain the address of a possible helper in Prague but was unsuccessful in this. Later I was given an address in Krabcice.

19 January. Krabcice

On 19 January, I visited this address, and obtained an address in Prague. My informant gave me a little more money and told me not to attempt to travel by rail, but to walk. He added that it might be safe for me to ask for a lift upon a coal lorry. I walked by side roads and at one place stopped at an inn and had a hot drink.

Zdiby

Eventually I arrived at Zdiby. Here I declared myself to a man who directed me to a farm, where I met two farm workers. One of them was very inquisitive about my identity, but I felt that I was safe in telling him the truth. He immediately replied by saying "I am a German". He seemed so stupid as to be almost an idiot, and contented himself by telling me to go away. I immediately walked away quickly towards

Prague and caught a train which took me to the middle of the city, where I arrived about 1900 hours.

1900 hours arrived Prague. 19 January-18 May in hiding in Prague.

The person whom I hoped to see at the address I had been given was away. I was very tired and lame, and it was bitterly cold. I tried to obtain shelter at various places, but unsuccessfully. I then sat in a railway station until 0100 hours on 20 January. Then I noticed that the police were checking passes, so I went into the street. After a time, I accosted a man and told him who I was. He took me to a restaurant which was open all night. Next morning, 20 January, I again visited the address I had been given. This time I met the person I wished to see. He made me give him a sample of my handwriting on a bit of paper, and told me to call again that afternoon. When I did so I told him that my plan was to try to reach Switzerland, when the snow on the mountains had melted, which would be in about two months. He told me he would try to help me and took me to a flat. Later I moved to various other addresses in Prague, where I stayed till 18 May.

18 May. Husinec
On 18 May a helper took me by train to Husinec.

20 May. Linz
On 20 May another helper took me to Linz by train. I stayed that night in a house and next morning travelled alone to Innsbruck. I travelled by slow trains and third class and bought my tickets in stages. At Salzburg I had to change trains. I arrived at Innsbruck at 0800 hours on 22 May and went to a certain address there. A potential helper here was ill in bed and could neither help nor advise me. At 1000 hours I took a slow train to Bludenz.

Bludenz
I arrived here about 1400 hours and walked about the town. I found an old man working in the garden, told him my story, and asked him whether it would be possible for me to cross into Switzerland. He replied that the snow was impassable, and that the frontier was very strongly guarded. I then went to the Lion Hotel, where I had a drink, and that night I slept in a barn.

23 May. Schruns
About 0730 hours on 23 May, I went by train to Schruns. Here I met an old priest who had been in India and spoke English. I asked his

advice and he told me it would be quite impossible for me to cross into Switzerland. Another man to whom I spoke confirmed this view.

At this time, I imagined Liechtenstein to be occupied by Germans, I therefore decided to retrace my steps and to make another attempt in June when the snow had melted.

23-25 May. Linz, Prachatice, Husinec

I returned via Linz and Prachatice to Husinec, where I spent two days in bed with fever.

On the evening of 27 May my helpers told me that Heydrich had been murdered that day, that police activities were widespread, and that my position and theirs were very precarious. I therefore decided to try to reach Prague and hide there. While trying to board a train to reach Prague at 0800 hours on 29 May a Czech gendarme asked me for my pass.

29 May. Arrested at Husinec

I possessed none but I spoke to him in German and told him I had lost it. He then arrested me. Knowing him to be a Czech (not a Sudetenlander) I told him my true identity and asked him to help me. He replied "On no account", and thereafter took the greatest care to see that I did not give him the slip.

Taken to Budweis

A few hours later I was handed over to the German Criminal Police in Budweis. My fingerprints and photograph were taken and I was interrogated as to my previous camps, routes and helpers. I was shown a list of missing persons wanted by the police which contained my name. I do not remember any other names upon this list. I told my interrogator the camps I had been in but I invented false routes and helpers. I spent the night in prison in Budweis.

30 May. Taken to Prague

Next day, 30 May, I was handcuffed, and taken to Prague, to the Gestapo H.Q. On the following day, 31 May, I was questioned by the Gestapo.

Interrogation by the Gestapo at Prague

My first interrogation lasted for three days (31 May-2 June). At first two interpreters were present, a Czech woman who could speak English, and a Czech man who translated my replies into German. My interrogation lasted from about 0900 hours to 1600 hours each day, with a break for lunch which was brought to me from a canteen.

My interrogator was very correct in his manner, and I got the impression that he disliked his job. He began by asking me some personal questions. He told me that as it was known that Heydrich had been murdered with the aid of English weapons, he regretted that he could not treat me as an officer and an escaped prisoner of war and that I was suspected of criminal activities, if not of actual complicity in the murder. He then asked me to tell him my precise route since my escape, and the names of my helpers. He added that if my replies were unsatisfactory I should have to be brought before a military court, which would almost inevitably order my execution.

I told him that possibly the people at the Lion Hotel at Bludenz might remember that I had called there with a suitcase on the night of 22 May. I also said that I had been in Linz during the period of Heydrich's murder, and until 28 May, and that I did not know the names and addresses of people who had helped me.

Another German in the same room as my interrogator was almost apologetic in his attitude, but a third man later came into the room and attempted to shout at me. My reaction to this was immediate, and I refused to speak while he was present. In consequence the other two men apparently told him to go out of the room, which he did. The Czech woman interpreter was not present on the second and third days of my interrogation.

My interrogators told me that they had captured a Squadron Leader Bushell in a house in Prague a few days previously. They assured me that though helpers had been arrested, their son and daughter had not been penalised in any way.

I asked if I could write a letter to my father. My interrogators replied that they could give me no guarantee that it could be sent until after the war.

The Czech woman's place as interpreter was filled by a barrister named Tschober. This man had been in England a good deal and spoke English very well. He said that he had had "many good times" in England, and that he disliked extremely having to treat me as a criminal. He then spoke at great length in order to justify the attitude of my interrogators, and to impress me with the gravity of my legal position.

I was again repeatedly asked to give the names and addresses of my helpers. On the third day of my interrogation, the chief interrogator, aged about 40, slim, height about 5 feet 11 inches, with hair getting somewhat thin, gave me his word of honour that if it was proved that my helpers were involved in no other activities beyond helping me as an escaped prisoner of war, they would suffer no worse fate than imprisonment. I asked him if the chief of his department would agree to this also.

In due course a man calling himself the chief of the department came in, and assured me that normally the penalty imposed on people who had merely helped escaped prisoners of war was two years' imprisonment, and nothing worse. Tschober from his experience as a lawyer also assured me that this was the case.

Eventually I inclined to believe these statements and repeated assurances. Since I also believed that, to the best of my knowledge, the character and activities of Frau Skskova, the schoolmistress in Prague, were irreproachable and that she could not therefore suffer any worse punishment than a term of imprisonment, I gave my interrogators her name, and her name only.

My interrogators then told me that I would have to remain for six weeks solitary confinement in the Gestapo's hands while my case was investigated.

While undergoing this punishment I was kept on a starvation diet. I was twice again called out for questioning during my confinement. On both occasions I was asked to give details of my other helpers. This I refused to do. While awaiting interrogation I was kept waiting in a large room – on the second occasion for about six hours. there must have been about 40 men and women mostly Czechs seated on benches in this room. The guards in the room wore a badge with the letters "S.D." Some of these men seemed almost insane, and were very brutal, especially to young men.

We had to sit with our hands upon our knees and our eyes fixed upon a point on the wall. We were not allowed to move in any way. If people moved, they were immediately made to stand up with their faces to the wall, and were abused and sometimes struck by the guards. I saw two young men in handcuffs brought in and made to do "knees bend" until they were completely exhausted. They then had to stand with their faces to the wall, and a guard kicked one of them several times. Messengers were sent from time to time to take those waiting into another room, presumably for interrogation.

Somewhere about the middle of July, my original interrogator sent for me and told me that he had obtained certain details about the people who had helped me in Prague. At Bergauer's house I had left a number, 17/1/14/6/02. This number was composed of the date of my escape at Roudnice (17 January), and of the date of my birth (14 June, 1902). I had left this with my helpers in order to enable my identity to be checked later if I was successful in reaching Switzerland and wished to get in touch with them for any purpose.

My interrogators were obviously of the opinion that this number had a sinister significance. They told me that they knew that Frau Skskova had taken me to Husinec. They asked me who had taken me to Linz, and whether the clergyman at Husinec had helped me. I replied that I had first met Frau Skskova at the clergyman's house, because I thought that this might make things easier for the clergyman himself.

On 15 July, 1942, I was removed from the Gestapo prison to a military prison in Prague. From here I was sent to Oflag IV C (Colditz), where I arrived that evening. During the journey I was not allowed to make use of the lavatory.

Third escape – Oflag IV C (Colditz)
This escape was arranged with the approval of the escape committee. Lieutenant-Commander W.L. Stephens, R.N.V.R. and I broached the idea to the Committee of passing across a sentry's beat, even though in bright reflector light, while his back was turned. We asked for two other volunteers to form a second pair, one of whom should have some skill in lock picking. The inclusion of the lock-picker would enable the whole party to pass out of the camp through a part of the Kommandantur building after passing a sentry. Captain P.R. Reid (R.A.S.C.) and Flight Lieutenant Wardle were chosen for this second pair.

Site of the escape
The camp is an old Schloss, consisting of an inner and outer courtyard completely enclosed by high buildings, with exits through archways and gates, all guarded. The prisoners of war were in the buildings surrounding the inner courtyard. The kitchen gave on to some flat roofs over a boiler-house in the outer courtyard, by means of a window barred on the outer courtyard side. This window was in full view of the windows of the outer courtyard buildings, in bright reflector light, and in view of the sentry for part of his beat. The main Kommandantur entrance was by steps to a dimly lit terrace. The plan of escape necessitated passing this to the door of a carpenter's store in the buildings opposite the boiler-house. It was hoped to unlock this door, pass through the store, and find an exit on the outer side of the outer courtyard. Thence, by descending three terraces of an old moat also in reflector light and near the dog kennels, it was possible to reach a road leading out of the camp. This road ran past the married quarters blocks and had at the end iron gates in a high wall, with a small amount of barbed wire on top.

The action

The kitchen was entered at night through a window. The attention of the sentries in the inner courtyard was distracted on the four previous nights, which enabled the rivet head of the transverse bar of this window to be cut. The rivet was found to be hot sweated, and the loosening of the bars only accomplished by means of a screw press manufactured in the camp. This was designed by Captain Reid and made by E.R.A. Hammond, R.N. and E.R.A. Lister R.N.

It was constructed from a fire bar, a square thread screw, and soft iron bed slats. The other tools used were a hacksaw and file. The screw pins applied very heavy pressure, forcing the rivet out of the bar. This work had to be done very silently, and without trace, through a window which normally was kept locked by the Germans, and which had to be opened to enable the work to be carried out. Squadron Leader McColm removed all traces of our work upon this window after we had left.

On 14 October at 2100 hours Reid and Wardle proceeded on to the flat roof, thence dropped to the ground (10 feet), and waited two hours in a convenient door entrance in shadows owing to the failure of a signalling system by accordion music. Finally, they went ahead and crossed the sentry's beat when his back was turned, and thence along the foot of the Kommandantur terrace. At one point a German soldier passed within a yard of Reid who was lying flat on a grass border in the open, but was not noticed.

At the end of the terrace, near the carpenter's store, Reid and Wardle found a cellar, in which they rested; in the meantime, Stephens and I followed their route and joined them. The door of the carpenter's store could not be unlocked, but an exit was found through an extremely narrow flue running at ground level from the cellar, to the outer, or moat, side of the outer courtyard buildings. This flue was barred, but one bar was successfully loosened. The process of getting through this flue took an hour, during which time no concealment against a patrol was possible. Three stages of terraces each about four metres high (a moat in former times) were then descended by aid of a sheet.

The top terrace was within a few yards of sleeping Germans, and the bottom some ten yards from the dog kennels. Twice during the descent an Alsatian dog was roused and barked furiously, but no action was taken.

Each of the four members of our party carried attaché cases which were muffled with shirts and sheets during the process of exit. Though a great hindrance at the time, their contents of civilian clothes etc., were invaluable later. Arriving at the bottom of the terraces, we proceeded along the road between the married quarters, and then scaled the gate in the wall surmounted by barbed wire. At this point, as arranged previously, our party split, Reid and Wardle, forming one pair and Stephens and I the other. We parted at 0400 hours, on Thursday 15 October.

15 October – Rochlitz

0400 hours	Separated from Reid and Wardle, and walked to Rochlitz.
0730 hours	Arrived Rochlitz
Chemnitz.	
0805 hours	Departed by train for Chemnitz.
0920 hours	Arrived Chemnitz. Booked through to Stuttgart. Questioned by railway police – papers satisfactory.
0940 hours	Departed Chemnitz.
Hof	
1500 hours	Arrived Hof, and changed. Walked round the town and drank beer in station restaurant until:
1930 hours	Departed by "D ZUG" to Nurnberg.
Nurnberg	
2300 hours	Arrived Nurnberg.

16 October

Drank beer and slept in restaurant until:

0530 hours	Departed by Schnellzug for Stuttgart.
Stuttgart	
1015 hours	Arrived Stuttgart. Went by train to the suburb Esslingen. Took electric train to Plockingen, Reutlingen and Tubingen.
Tubingen	
1500 hours	Arrived Tubingen. (The object of this round journey was to avoid booking towards the frontier from Stuttgart main station, which we had been told by a Polish officer in the camp was strictly controlled.):
1839 hours	Departed Tubingen for Tuttlingen.
2230 hours	Arrived Tuttlingen. Owing to a mistake we took the wrong road out of Tuttlingen, and were compelled to spend the night six kilometres south east of the town in a wood.

17 October

Immendigen	In the light we made out our position by aid of a small-scale map and a home-made compass, and went on foot across country to the railway just south of Immendigen, and rested till dark.

Engen.

1915 hours	Moved on down valley, in which the railway ran, to a wood above Engen.

18 October

Singen	We lay up in the wood until dark, about 1915 hours. The day was uneventful except that a man was shooting rooks in the wood with a rifle, and later a terrier came to look at us, but made no sign. We walked in the fields parallel to the railway and came into sight of Singen shunting yard about midnight. We retraced our steps and in crossing over the main line by a bridge were stopped by a sentry. We showed him our papers and satisfied him that we had lost our way to Singen Station. After crossing the railway further north, we found the point where the main Helsingen-Singen road meets the wood, shown to us as leading to the frontier.

19 October

Swiss Frontier	We followed the wood, but it eventually became clear that we were wrong. We therefore lay up until dawn and then reconnoitred to fix our position. Having done this, we lay up till dark, and then, following a more easterly branch of the wood, arrived on the frontier road at 2100 hours. We were challenged by a frontier sentry, but owing to his credulity we were able to move away. We remained hidden until the moon went down, and crossed the wood north of Ramsen.

20 October

Ramsen (Switzerland)

0300 hours	Ramsen, where we arrived about 0300 hours on 20 October. We remained hidden until dawn and then reported to the Swiss police in Ramsen.
Schaffhausen	Later that day the Swiss police took us to Schaffhausen, where we stayed for the night in a hotel. Here a self-styled "journalist" asked us (I think in English) for details of our crossing of the frontier. The patronne of the hotel called me out into the passage and warned me to be very careful how I answered this individual's questions, adding that his reputation with the police was not good.

21 October
On 21 October we were taken to a Military Barracks in Berne. Here a member of the Swiss General Staff asked us some questions on military activities in Germany. We were then taken to the British Legation.

25 January 1943
Left Switzerland for Spain. I stayed for about 10 days with the Military Attaché and later went to a hotel. On 25 January, 1943, with Flight Lieutenant Fowler I left Switzerland for Spain, as described in his report.

30 January
Crossed Franco-Spanish frontier. Arrested La Junquera. After our arrest at La Junquera on 30 January, 1943, we were not confined in cells, but in a room which appeared to be part of the police office. Our Spanish guide was bullied by the police and had his face slapped, but I do not think he was otherwise maltreated while we were there.

30 January-22 February
Imprisoned Figueras. Released. 22 February-1 May. Barcelona. 1 May-12 May. Jaraba. On 22 February, 1943, after my release from prison in Figueras, I went to Barcelona, where I stayed in a hotel. On 1 May, 1943, two Civil Guard officers took me by train to an officers' internment camp at Jaraba.

Madrid
On 12 May, I left by car for Madrid, where I reported to the British Embassy. I stayed with a member of the M.A.'s staff till 15 May, when I left by train for Gibraltar, where I arrived at 1400 hours next day.

16 May
Gibraltar. On the morning of 23 May, I left by air for Lisbon.

23 May
Lisbon.

CAPTAIN 77940 G.F. COLLIE

H.Q., 51st (Higland) Division R.A.S.C.

Captured:	St. Valery-en-Caux, 12 June, 1940.
Escaped:	Paris, 8 April, 1942.
Left:	Gibraltar, 12 August, 1942.
Arrived:	Bristol, 13 August, 1942.

Army service:	T.A. since 1938.
Peacetime profession:	Solicitor.
Private address:	Morken, Cults, Aberdeenshire.

Capture

I was wounded at St. Valery-en-Caux on 12 June, 1940, and taken to a Field Dressing Station which was captured by the Germans the same day. Twelve hours later I was operated on at a German field surgery in a wood near Rouen (about 20 miles from St. Valery). I was then moved by ambulance to various German casualty clearing stations, eventually being kept at one at Forges-les-Eaux. At this time, I was ten days without food, being unable to take anything but special diet, which was not available.

1 July, Rouen; 12 August, Amiens;15 September, Neuilly-sur-Seine

On 1 July, I was moved to a hospital in Rouen which was being run by the R.A.M.C. I was then transferred to a French hospital in Amiens (12 July), where I remained till 15 September, when I was sent to a special facial centre, the only one of its kind in Occupied France, at the French Military Hospital at Neuilly-sur-Seine, Paris. In January 1942, this hospital was damaged by the R.A.F. raid on the Renault works, about 2 miles away, the upper floors being completely destroyed. These were occupied by the Centre Maxillo Facial, where I was being treated. The centre was then transferred to the Hôpital Foche, in Paris, where conditions were much less comfortable.

January, 1942. Hôpital Foche, Paris
At this time, myself, Sergeant Aston, W.H., No. 1 Base Sub-Depot, R.E. and Driver Flack E., 51 (H) Division, R.A.S.C. Ammunition Company, were the only British military wounded left in Occupied France. Technically we were prisoners of war in German hands, but the German medical service in Paris, which was run by Czechs and Austrians, had not allowed us to be sent to Germany, where we would not have been able to obtain the special medical treatment we required. The medical service also refrained from telling the Kommandantur in Paris of our presence. In the spring of 1942, the three of us decided to escape, as we were certain that, though the French authorities at the hospital were willing to keep us, we were likely to be sent to Germany at an early date.

We spent a month laying our plans. A French woman who had visited us in hospital and whose husband had business connections with Unoccupied France, made arrangements for us to be taken across the Line of Demarcation and for our journey to Unoccupied France. We also sent parcels of food to addresses in Angoulême, Limoges, Grenoble, Lyons and Annemasse, which we thought might lie on our route, and to two addresses in Paris, in case the start of our journey should be held up. We considered these caches of food would make it possible for us to do without ration cards. We had no difficulty in collecting the food, for, in addition to receiving Red Cross parcels regularly, we were kept supplied with food by French people.

We were allowed unlimited visitors in hospital in Paris, and about 500 different people must have visited us – over 100 of them regularly. I had fresh grapefruit for breakfast every morning and always had fresh butter; these were only two of the gifts we received. In addition to the food dumps, we also took the precaution of getting one of the special food cards issued to French wounded going on leave from the hospital. This card was obtained from a Frenchman whom we supplied with food from our private store so that he did not require to use his card. These cards were never dated and are valid in both Occupied and Unoccupied France.

As we had no identity cards, we typed on a borrowed typewriter copies of the form of "permission" granted to the French wounded in the hospital. This form is accepted by the police in both Zones in lieu of the *carte d'identité*, the French wounded soldiers in hospital in France having no proper card till they are discharged from the army. When we had typed the forms, a French lady filled in our own names (we had given ourselves French ranks). Sergeant Aston completed the forms with a fictitious French signature. As the "permission" is available in one place only, we made out copies for Angoulême, Limoges, Lyons, Annemasse, and Marseilles in case we required to go to those towns. To finance our journey, we raised the equivalent of £35 by selling our surplus Red Cross stores to people connected with the Black Market. We sold chiefly cigarettes and tea – the tea fetching £6 per lb. We also raised another £75 by loan against a sterling obligation to be repaid to people now in Britain.

Before leaving the hospital, we distributed our possessions among friends in Paris, through an Algerian patient who took stuff out every morning for a fortnight. We also typed a circular to about 80 of our French friends telling them we were leaving for the Unoccupied Zone of our own accord, thanking them for their kindness, and warning them against visiting the hospital. The circulars were posted the day we left by a friend who came to the station and saw us go off. Several times our departure had to be postponed because one or other of us was undergoing treatment. We had to take an assistant surgeon into our confidence because he was to have performed an operation to remove shrapnel from Sergeant Aston's foot about the time we had fixed for our departure.

There was only one door to the hospital, on which there was a caretaker day and night. To get rid of the caretaker we arranged for a friend to telephone and ask for the resident doctor, who was normally on the third floor. Our friend telephoned at the appointed time, but the doctor, who was on the ground floor then, came unexpectedly quickly and almost upset our plan. Another patient, however, stood between the caretaker's box and the door and covered our exit. We left the hospital at 2030 hours on 8 April, 1942. We wore civilian clothes which we had had in hospital for over a year, having got them once we made up our minds to get away if the Germans came for us.

We walked from the hospital with two French patients, who were the only people there, besides the assistant surgeon, in whom we had confided. The Frenchmen walked well ahead carrying our suitcases, and we followed them on the Metro to the Gare d'Austerlitz. Tickets and seat reservations had already been obtained for us on the train leaving at 2200 hours for Angoulême. A French lady acted as our guide, but avoided us at the station and on the journey, she travelling first class and we third. At the station we saw two other French patients from the hospital, but though they travelled on the same train, they did not spot us, either then or on the platform at Angoulême.

9 April. Angoulême
At Angoulême, which we reached at 0400 hours on 9 April, there was a hitch in the arrangements. The Frenchman who was to have met us did not find us, though he had photographs of ourselves and our guide. The station was packed with German soldiers and sailors. Our rendezvous was in the waiting room, but we could not enter, as there was a German guard on the door asking for papers. After consultation with our guide, we left for an address in the town, a German officer carrying our luggage part of the way. The Frenchwoman left us at the house, where we were later picked up by the man who should have met us at the station.

La Rochefoucauld
At 0700 hours this man took us by car to a quarry in the woods near La Rochefoucauld and left us to be collected in ten minutes by another man. We followed the new guide for a quarter of a mile to another wood, where two farmers were waiting with a cart, to which a false bottom had been fitted. The three of us squeezed into this narrow space with great difficulty, and the cart was loaded with sacks and manure.

Line of Demarcation, between La Rochefoucauld and St. Sornin
The cart was then driven over the Line of Demarcation between La Rochefoucauld and St. Sornin, which was well guarded. We were in Unoccupied France within 12 hours of leaving hospital. I paid the farmers 5000 francs for taking us across the Line. The cart took us on about three kilometres and we then walked along the road to Montbron till we were picked up by the Frenchman with the car.

Marthon
He drove us to Marthon, which is the terminus in Unoccupied France for the railway between Thiviers and Angoulême, and left us.

Marthon was, in fact, a bad choice. Being the railway terminus, with only one train a day, it is well watched by the police. As we were entering the village we were stopped by a man in civilian clothes, who probably belonged to the French Secret Police. We admitted having just crossed the Line of Demarcation, adding, "it's no offence". We denied that anyone had helped us, and said we had just been given a chance lift in the car. When the man asked for papers, we produced the hospital passes for Limoges and said we did not know where we were to stay there, as we were to be met in Limoges Station by another wounded man. He asked our nationality and we said we were French

Canadians who had been volunteers in the French Army. After an hour's delay he returned our papers. Marthon is a place to be avoided. The next station on the line would probably be less difficult.

Limoges

We went by train from Marthon to Limoges, where after some difficulty we got shelter at an office, the address of which we had been given in Paris. The difficulty was chiefly due to our arriving at 2300 hours (9 April), the journey having taken 10 hours. To find the caretaker I had to tell a passer-by who we were and, though he helped us, someone must have given us away, as the police arrived at the office to arrest us two hours after we had left. In my opinion, Limoges is one of the less pro-British towns. The caretaker was expecting us, and we stayed in the office till midday. We then left for Lyons accompanied by a Frenchman.

Lyons, 10 April

We reached Lyons at 2330 hours (10 April) and were refused admission at the house to which we had sent our food parcel. The owner of the house (a brothel) did, however, escort us to a house of a man who had been a patient with us in Paris. It was fortunate he came with us, as it was well after curfew, and when we were challenged by the police, he passed us off as boxers in whom he was interested.

11 April

We arrived at the ex-soldier's house at 0130 hours on 11 April, and were immediately taken in. They were working-class people. They kept us for two months. Fortunately, we were able to pay them amply for our stay.

In Lyons I was able to get in touch with French people who arranged our subsequent journey.

The journey of myself, Sergeant Aston and Driver Flack was arranged by Mme. Tiberghien, Paris, who had done tremendous work for the British wounded. Her husband, Alphonse Tiberghien is controller for the whole of France of all textile, wool, and allied industries. Although he is supposed to be a collaborationist, I do not think he is now. Mme. Tiberghien has (April, 1942) a courier service between Occupied and Unoccupied France, using her husband's office in Limoges. She made arrangements with M. Briggs (a Frenchman), Montbron, Angoulême, to meet us at Angoulême Station. After the delay described in my report Briggs picked us up in Angoulême on 9 April, and saw us over the Line of Demarcation. We sheltered in M. Tiberghien's office during our stay in Limoges, and one of his secretaries accompanied us to Lyons.

The address in Lyons – 3 rue Confort – proved to be a brothel. The man (M. Blazy) would perhaps have taken us in, but the woman refused to have us. They also said they had refused to accept delivery of our food parcel, though they may, in fact, have sold it on the Black Market. This rendezvous had been arranged through a man called Baldwin. M. Blazy did help to the extent of accompanying us to the house of M. Boudrand, 25 rue St. Jerome, Lyons, who had been in hospital with us in Paris. We were two months there.

On 11 April, the day of our arrival in Lyons, I visited Mr. Whittinghill. Our intention had been to get to Switzerland, whence we imagined we could easily travel home on British passports. Mr. Whittinghill explained that Switzerland would be no better than France and advised us either to go to the internment camp at Nice or to remain in Lyons and apply for repatriation at the next meeting of the Mixed Medical Commission at Marseilles on 10 May. He gave us British papers and told us to apply for food tickets as British subjects, although Lyons is an area in which British subjects are not allowed to live.

Through Mme. Santu, Paris, a friend of Mme. Lus, who had acted as our guide from Paris to Angoulême, we got in touch with Mr. Smallwood, a British subject who had lived in France for 20 years and is now a refugee (from Paris) in Lyons. He told us British subjects may not live in Lyons without a special permit and said we ran the risk of arrest if we remained under British nationality. After considering various schemes, we obtained Belgian papers through a friend of Mr. Smallwood who works in the passport department of the Rhône Préfecture.

The Préfecture supplied us with the certified extracts of certificates of birth in Belgium and arranged for the police to get us Belgian passports from the U.S. Consulate, which looks after Belgian interests. We also got a letter of identification as Belgian subjects and a copy of a letter of application for a *permis de séjour* in Lyons with an acknowledgement by the Sûreté that our papers were in order. Once we got our Belgian passports we applied to the Ministry of the Interior in Vichy for exit permits, which were granted, and our passports endorsed. We all assumed Belgian names, mine being Gaston Martens, born in Courtrai, and our ages were changed. We then applied for Spanish and Portuguese visas. The Spanish visas were granted in 24 hours, but the Portuguese visas had not arrived when we left France on 27 July.

At the end of June our friend from the Préfecture warned us to leave immediately, as Vichy had received orders from the Germans to question all persons recently granted Belgian papers with exit visas because German deserters had used this means of escape from Occupied France.

We left immediately and spent three or four days at the house of Mr. Davis, a British dentist, who practices at 59 Cours Gambetta, Lyons. During this time, we visited Mr. Whittinghill who could not help. We then telephoned a very wealthy friend of M. Tiberghien – M. Ricalens, who lives at Laroque d'Olmes. He agreed to receive us. Through the Préfecture we got *sauf-conduits* from Lyons to Laroque. We travelled to Bram by train and then by bus to Laroque (about 27 June). M. Ricalens called in a friend M. Pycke, formerly of the Deuxième Bureau. M. Pycke comes from Roubaix and was condemned to death by the Germans in the last war. He now lives at Bélesta, near Laroque. M. Pycke went to Toulouse and saw the Deuxième Bureau, who said they could get a Portuguese visa to our Belgian passport in four days. This they failed to do during a whole month, during which we stayed at a château at Fanjeaux owned by M. Ricalens.

Eventually we wrote M. Ricalens asking if we could not go. M. Pycke then made arrangements for our journey via Andorra. He accompanied us bringing with him a representative of the Deuxième Bureau who gave us *sauf-conduits* to L'Hospitalet which was on the road running at that point parallel and close to the Andorran frontier. We all travelled in M. Pycke's car to Foix, where we were joined by the Secretary-General of the Préfecture of the Department.

I got into the Secretary-General's car, which preceded M. Pycke's car to L'Hospitalet, where we picked up a guide. We drove past the point where a path to Andorra leaves the road, there being a strong guard on that part of the frontier. We then left the road and scrambled across country into Andorra and joined the path beyond the control. A horse came up for Aston, who has had a foot amputated. We made our way to Soldeu, the crossing taking three hours.

We stayed a week (27 July-2 August) in Soldeu in the only hotel, the owner of which is very pro-British. As a result of our asking Mr. Whittinghill to inform the Consulate in Barcelona of our intention of getting to Spain, Mr. Dorchy (of the Consulate) had got in touch with three Andorrans, who are the non-active heads of the chief smuggling gang (called possibly Casalis). They took us by car to Escaldes on 3 August and handed us over to smugglers. We went on horseback about 10 miles, climbing to 7500 feet. The horses returned and we lay under some rocks all day. In the evening we crossed into Spain, arriving about 2000 hours on 4 August. We then had to walk along the spur of a mountain till 1500 hours next day (5 August), when we got down to a road, where Mr. Dorchy picked us up by car. We were driven at once to Barcelona. I stayed three days with the Consul-General, leaving on 8 August by car for Madrid, where I spent one night. I arrived in

Gibraltar on 10 August and left by air on 12 August, reaching Bristol on 13 August.

Conditions at Madrid

Captain Collie made the following statement on the conditions in which escapers and evaders were living at H.M. Embassy, Madrid:

> In the grounds of the Embassy there is a building which I understood was built expressly for escaped prisoners of war. In this building there are four bedrooms which are used principally for the Embassy guard. It also contains a sitting room and a dining room used by escapers. Food is cooked in this building by Spanish women. The floor is of good quality. There is no lavatory or washing accommodation in this building. The sleeping accommodation for escapers and evaders is in another building in the grounds, known as the annex. It consists of a ground floor room with about 20 beds. The lavatory is in a cellar in another part of the annex. It is also used by Spanish women and is filthy. There are no facilities for having a bath in private. The washing facilities consist of two wash tubs (fitted in), which were dirty, and a bath alongside. I never saw anyone use the bath. I did not know whether or not I was intended to sleep in the same room as the men, and after repeated enquiries I was given a room in the Embassy with a window which did not open.
>
> I arrived at the Embassy at 1050 hours on 9 August, after travelling for over 10 hours by car. Sergeant Aston and Driver Flack, who escaped from Paris with me, accompanied me. We had been brought from Barcelona by Mr. Whitfield. He handed in our papers, and we did not see him again. When we arrived, a clerk was sent down with security certificates for signature. There was no one to receive us and to tell us where to go, and no one came to see us all day. We were left on the steps leading to the hut. Only by chumming up with R.A.F. sergeants did we know where to go. Sergeant Aston and Driver Flack had to find their own beds and bedding and put them up. There is a Frenchman in charge of the hut who does not speak English or Spanish. We got no breakfast – nothing till lunch. The food was good, but the service was indifferent. The Spanish servants speak no English.
>
> I saw no Embassy officials till next morning when I was called to a meeting for which I was late because no one told me earlier to be present. At this meeting I got movement instructions for my journey to Gibraltar. I left Aston and Flack in Madrid. When I left that evening, they had still not been interviewed.
>
> When I was there the other British evaders and escapers consisted of four R.A.F. Sergeants and a boy from 51 (H) Division (Seaforth Highlanders) who had escaped from Germany. They have a library which contains only three books published since 1940. All the other stuff is pre-war "throw-outs". There are no British newspapers. There

is a wireless set in the billet, but it does not get London. The Embassy circulates a duplicated transcript of B.B.C. news and a copy is available. The people passing through are supposed to keep the rooms clean.

(Note: Captain Collie was severely wounded in the face at St. Valery-en-Caux in June, 1940, and has an artificial jaw. Sergeant Aston had a foot amputated in Paris. Driver Flack was also wounded in the jaw and Captain Collie believes he will require a major operation on arrival in the U.K.)

LEADING SEAMAN JX 125054 ALBERT EDWARD PENNY, R.N.

H.M. Submarine *Oswald*

Escaped from Vetralla Camp.
Repatriated from Vatican City.

Captured:	Mediterranean, 2 August, 1940.
Escaped:	Vetralla (Italy), 5 October, 1942.
Left:	Lisbon, 21 January, 1943.
Arrived:	Bristol, 22 January, 1943.

Service:	From 8 October, 1925.
Peacetime profession:	Royal Navy.
Private address:	Whitedale, Hambledon, Hampshire.

I was a member of the crew of H.M. Submarine *Oswald* operating from Alexandria. On the night of 1/2 August, 1940, the submarine was on the surface charging the main batteries. We were rammed by the Italian destroyer *Ugolini Vivaldi* and afterwards depth-charged and subjected to shell fire for half an hour. After the ship was abandoned, we were in the water for two and a quarter hours before being picked up by the destroyer. Only three of the crew were missing. We were taken to Taranto, where we were kept in the naval hospital for about nine days.

Interrogation at Taranto
In the hospital at Taranto officers and ratings were separated, the ratings being put together in a large ward. Two days after arrival we were interrogated. The interrogation struck me as being very poor and without any proper method. It was conducted by a civilian who spoke perfect English. In my case the interrogation lasted about a

145

minute. I was asked my name, place of birth, time in the Service, base of operations, date of departure, and number of torpedoes. While we were still on the destroyer our captain had warned us of the probability of interrogation and on his advice, we all gave different answers, all of them incorrect, to the operational questions.

We were interrogated separately, but those who were questioned first were able to warn the others what to expect. There were about 47 of us altogether in the ward, where there were four naval guards and perhaps four carabinieri constantly on duty inside. The guards had orders to stop us from talking in groups and, as they were at the extremities of the ward and did not mingle with us, it seemed improbable that any of them was there as a stool-pigeon. The ward was also so large that I think it unlikely that conversations could have been picked up by microphones.

Venice, Sulmona
From Taranto we were moved to the island of Poveglia, Venice, and from there to Sulmona. We were not subjected to any further interrogation. We were in Venice for two months, leaving on 10 October, 1940.

Plans for escape
I first began planning my escape whilst at the Sulmona Camp in conjunction with Pilot Officer Boatman, Pilot Officer Stockwell, Lieutenant Pope and some other officers whose names I do not remember. We were making compasses, maps, etc. The officers were digging a tunnel and secretly making Army badges by melting down toothpaste tubes, etc. Unfortunately, the tunnel was discovered just before its completion, and we began to suspect the existence of a "stool-pigeon" in the camp.

Various unsuccessful escapes convinced me that it was next to impossible to get away from Sulmona so that it remained for me to get transferred to another camp. Ever since my arrival I had been acting as the camp barber. We now had a professional barber, and I arranged to learn all about the trade and so get a transfer to another camp in that capacity. At the same time, I began learning Italian with a view to gathering information at the next camp.

1 July 1942 – Transfer to Vetralla
In June, 1942, working parties were formed to build new prison camps; I volunteered to go with one of these parties as the barber and was accepted. On 1 July, 200 of us were taken to a new camp near Vetralla, north of Rome. Here I found that, as all the men were

working during the day, I had plenty of free time to do much as I cared, so I started learning Italian in real earnest. At Sulmona it was not possible to practise conversation in Italian, but here the position was reversed.

On arrival at this camp, I found plumbers working and immediately made contact with them. Before long we were on good terms, and I was able to go into the outer camp with them when I liked for some exercise doing pipe laying and other heavy work. In this way I believed I should learn the language, get myself toughened up, and gradually gather all the information I should require by judicious questioning of the plumbers. I had also to find some sort of clothing with which to disguise myself as a workman and which could not be obtained in our camp.

For two months I studied Italian, keeping it along the lines required for gathering information about roadblocks, carabinieri, searching of working men, etc. Most of my information I got by getting into arguments with workmen. By this means I found that very rarely was any person stopped when he was empty-handed during the day, but any person was likely to be stopped who carried a bag or case. Persons out of doors after dark, especially in the country, were usually stopped by the carabinieri. This information was rather disturbing, as at that time my plans were to head for Switzerland, which meant carrying food and being about the country at night. I therefore decided that my plans must be altered, and suddenly I thought of the Vatican City State.

I knew very little about the Vatican City State but decided that it might be worth while making enquiries. For the legal side I thought that the Italian priest would be the best source to tap. So, I guided my habitual conversations with him long these channels, taking great pains to doubt the independence of the Vatican City so that he would be inclined to give more details in order to convince me.

In this way I learned of the Lateran Treaty of 1929 in which the Pope was declared Sovereign Pontiff. At the same time, I learned that outside the Vatican the frontier was guarded by Italian soldiers, carabinieri, and plain-clothes police, while inside there were Swiss Guards and gendarmerie; that there was a British Minister to the Holy See; and that workmen lived outside and went home for meals. I also discovered that trains entered the Vatican with goods and that there was also road transport through the gates.

Here was my first problem solved. I had found a Neutral State, 75 kilometres distant, which, though so strongly guarded and surrounded by high, unscalable walls, might still with a well-thought-out plan not prove quite so impregnable as it appeared.

Each evening I had made copious notes of the information gleaned during the day, and my friend and I went over these, sorting out such as would apply for a trip from the camp to Rome, his job being to pull each individual idea to pieces and put up such difficulties as road-blocks, English appearance, suddenly confronting the Italian general foreman as I walked across the outer camp, impossibility of reaching Rome on foot in a day. Literally hundreds of snags were found, overhauled and tested again. I travelled over the whole route on train and cycle dozens of times in my mind, and in the end the cycle idea won, owing to the language difficulty.

During all this research I had become very friendly with one of the plumbers who, seeing that I always worked in a civilian shirt persistently suggested that I should escape. Eventually I decided that if he were trustworthy, he would be a very valuable ally, as he had an old cycle that I might perhaps be able to buy with my watch which he was always coveting. With this end in view, I pretended to bend under his persuasion until I decided that he was as reliable as he seemed.

After consulting an English friend of mine I took the risk of openly 'pumping' him, not forgetting to mention the obstacle of the cycle. Through him I found out that workmen enter the Vatican in overalls, which are usually of a one-piece variety in blue or brown. I was able to make plans of the lanes and by-ways to the main Rome road. I had a small souvenir map of Rome, which I studied until I could draw all the main roads, squares, palaces, etc., from memory.

One day I was fortunate enough to find a blue one-piece overall almost in shreds. This I took with me to the inner camp and had it repaired. Although large patches were required, the result was quite in keeping with the condition of the average workman's clothing. Next, I procured an old cap, covered in mud. This I washed. Later I splashed both the cap and the overall with dirty oil, as few workmen could afford to wash working clothes owing to the lack of soap, and I wished to be meticulous in my disguise.

I took every opportunity of going to the station at La Cura with working parties so as to acquaint myself with the directions to the main Rome road.

With the exception of the bicycle, I was now ready to make the attempt. I at last got my Italian accomplice to agree to exchange the bicycle for my watch and arranged to go on Monday, 5 October. During the remaining working hours, I instructed him as to his part in the programme. I gave him my watch in payment for the bicycle, which he agreed to turn over to me on Monday. This took place on Saturday, 3 October. So, I had one day in which to make the final preparations and arrange for scouts for watching the movements of the Italian general foreman. Bearing in mind the leakages that had taken place at Sulmona I divulged my plans to only a few trusted friends.

On Sunday night I warned Sergeant Rolf, the English Sergeant in charge of the camp, of my plans. I informed him that my second lookout would convey the information to him of my successful exit, so that he could warn my fellow prisoners of forth-coming searches, etc., and could himself try to cover me at the noon roll call – although, if my plans ran smoothly, this should not be necessary.

5 October
Escaped from Vetralla.

Escape and journey to Vatican City

On Monday morning (5 October), I darkened my hair with soot and oil, pencilled my eyebrows, and put on my overall and cap. In came my English accomplice to tell me that the bicycle I was expecting was not there, but that a strange one was standing in the place arranged. We concluded that the Italian had funked selling his own cycle but had produced another. He had gone, and all I hoped was that I should not meet the rightful owner on the way out of the camp or while passing through La Cura.

Receiving the sign from my friend that all was clear I slipped out of the hut into the bathroom where the cycle had been left and just walked off with my cap well down over my eyes and the collar of my overall turned up. At first, I felt very nervous, as my face was well known to all the workmen and soldiers. After I had passed within two or three feet of people who had associated with me for the past two months my confidence returned slightly, and I approached my first lookout.

On seeing me he knelt down to tie his shoelace, which was the all-clear signal, meaning that the general foreman was not on the route that I had to take. I passed on to my second lookout, and the performance was repeated. My confidence was now complete. I walked nonchalantly to the outer gate, which was in reality a small gap in the outer triple perimeter, and, without so much as a nod to the sentry, passed through a gap in the hedge and so into the lane. Mounting my cycle, I was off.

A string of people was stretched across the road just before I reached the last sentry in the roadway. I had no bell and was not able to shout because my accent would immediately have betrayed me. I then found that the brakes were poor, which meant leaping off the moving bicycle. This I did, but the patches in the overall caught on the pommel of the saddle, and I and the bicycle finished in a heap, with the sentry and Italian peasants laughing at my discomfort. I managed to mumble unintelligently and rode away. Three hundred yards further on I had to get off, as the lane rose steeply and I was not sure of the chain, which was badly in need of oil, as were the bearings in general.

Since I had first entered the lane, I had passed numerous soldiers returning to the camp, and on the hill, I found they were even more numerous but I reached the top undetected and remounted my machine. Once I was under way, my confidence returned, and as soon as I had passed the majority of the soldiers, I stopped to light an Italian cigarette.

La Cura

On reaching La Cura I tore along as fast as I could pedal.

Several roadblocks had to be encountered, but I had formulated a plan which worked admirably. Making certain that I saw them first, I dismounted on some pretext or other – such as to attend to some defect in the brakes – and waited till a cyclist or preferably a group of cyclists, came along. There was one spot between La Cura and Sutri where the road narrowed, and I was almost forced into the ditch by a motorist. He was the camp engineer on his way to Vetralla.

Sutri

After I had got past Sutri and passed through a small village and climbed up a steepish hill, I heard cheering from children from the village and the sound of a powerful motor running. I thought the cheering might be for soldiers who might be chasing me. I slung the bicycle into the ditch, pulled branches over it, and got behind it. The powerful motor turned out to be a lorry full of bricks. (The cheering must have been school children coming out at playtime.) The lorry was going slowly. I was able to hang on to it for a while, until I could see the next roadblock. Then I waited for the next bunch of cyclists to mix with.

Campagnano

From there to Campagnano the road winds downhill, zig-zig fashion, and before I could spot the roadblock, I was actually on it. The corner house seemed to be the local H.Q. for the soldiers guarding the roadblocks. The soldiers were all seated around and there was barely room to pass. I should estimate the number between 30 and 50, all out of doors. I continued cycling and was not stopped.

Rome

I saw two signposts, both directing me to different parts of Rome, and I took the left-hand one which led me over the Ponte Milvio. Having crossed the bridge, I found I was on the wrong side of the Tiber. I cycled on until I came to the Ponte di Duca d'Aosta, which brought me to the gates of the Foro di Mussolini. Here I followed a cyclist in order to be able to fulfil the traffic regulations.

In doing this I rather missed my road and found I had passed the Vatican without seeing the dome of St. Peter's which I was looking for as a landmark. I recrossed the Tiber and came down the Via Vittorio Emanuele, the Ponte Vittorio Emanuele, then up the Via Borgo Santo Spirito. I had a look at the clock on St. Peter's and it was twenty to twelve. I went up to the gate of Santa Marta but found that most of the workmen were leaving the Vatican, and I decided that it was no time for me to enter as a workman, especially as a very obvious plain-clothes policeman was eyeing me rather suspiciously. I decided that it was best to keep on the move.

I returned about 1315 hours, but still did not like the look of the Santa Marta gate, and decided to tour round the walls of the Vatican and see if there was a better entrance. The only gate that looked to me to be really busy was Santa Anna, but this was guarded on the outside by two carabinieri, one plain-clothes constable, and two Italian soldiers who were patrolling the walls.

I stood on the opposite side of the road for about twenty minutes watching the behaviour of all who entered, taking special note of those on bicycles. All, I found, dismounted before they entered the gate, passed the time of day with the guard, and (with the exception of a few who turned to the right) walked to the next gate. Considering that I had learned all that could be gathered from an outside view, I decided to take the risk. I rode off again and returned at full speed, passing the carabinieri and guard, and turned to the right. This led me to the garage, where I hid my bicycle in case I required it again, took off my safety-pin clips, walked round with a little notebook in my hand, and, busily writing in the notebook, passed the sentries. They absolutely ignored me. For about an hour afterwards I was walking round the Vatican searching for a Union Jack or a brass plate indicating the residence of the British Minister. In this I failed miserably, so I decided to ask my way. Pretending to be a deaf mute, I approached the dullest-looking Italian workman I could find working alone, and wrote on my notebook, "*Dove e Legazione Inglese*?" He showed me to the Legation, where I turned myself over to the gendarme guarding the place whom it was impossible to pass. He telephoned to the head of his department

(Commendatore Belado) who instructed him to turn me over to the British Minister pending enquiries.

Stay in Vatican City

The British Minister made me his guest for the duration of my stay in the Vatican. For the first twenty-four hours my position was very insecure, as nobody could decide whether the Vatican was powerful enough to withstand Italian pressure, but upon, I think, the Minister's suggestion of an exchange, negotiations became much easier, and to strengthen my position I wrote a personal letter to the Pope, as one of his disciples.

The British agreed immediately to the proposal of an exchange and sometime after the Italians agreed verbally. It was two months before they agreed officially. During this time, I was almost a prisoner in the British Legation, but eventually I was able to walk around the Vatican when accompanied by somebody else. It was only a week or two before my release that I was given an identity card pronouncing me a member of the British Legation, which allowed me to wander around as I wished.

I had a private audience with His Holiness Pope Pius XII on Monday, 28 December. I waited for him in the Sala di Tronetto, where he gave me his Benediction. Conversing in English, which he did reasonably well, he said he was very pleased to be able to meet me and give me his blessing. He also gave me a rosary. He asked me a few questions about my wife and family, and then personally went back to bring another rosary for my wife. Two days later I received a signed photograph of him.

3 January 1943, Left Rome. 6 January, arrived Lisbon

I left Rome by air on 3 January, 1943. Owing to a break in a petrol joint, the aircraft had to land at Palma, Majorca, where we stayed the night. We were again delayed for a night at Seville by fog and arrived at Lisbon on 6 January.

Suspected stool-pigeon in Sulmona

Penny made the following written statement regarding a suspected stool-pigeon in Sulmona:

> It was rumoured, though I do not know who the person was nor did I see the letter, that a letter was sent to a man from a non-existent relative and from a non-existent address stating in code that an Italian had been secreted among us. Everyone then started to check up on the others. The

result of this was that one man could not be accounted for. We therefore kept a careful watch on him but could get nothing to confirm our suspicions. Shortly afterwards he was transferred to another compound. While he was in this compound another good attempt was disclosed and frustrated, so that he again came under suspicion. Here is an example of the type of escape that was attempted but frustrated whilst this man was in my compound: A New Zealander named Clarence Roderick had planned to go out in a sack with the refuse which was normally placed outside the camp confines and emptied some hours later. This plan was to be carried out on the Saturday evening. On the day before this, however, an order was issued that all sacks were to be searched before they left the compound, which seemed to indicate that information had been given to the camp authorities.

On interrogation Penny stated:

The man referred to in my written statement was Petty Officer Alfred Marsh (F.A.A.). He was a Rating Observer who was believed to have been captured in September or October 1940, in Sicily or Southern Italy. He was about 27 or 28 years of age. Various people in the camp tried to find out where his home was but failed. I did not tackle him myself.

Attempted escapes

We were on the island of Poveglia (Venice) for two months until 10 October, 1940. When we heard we were going, three men decided to try escaping. They were Leading Seaman Hunt, A.B. Jamieson, and A.B. Tooes. They swam across to Malamocco, and were heading for a small fishing village when they fell into the hands of some Italian sailors. This happened on the night of 8 October.

The next day (9 October) four more decided to carry out a well thought out plan. As far as I remember it was briefly as follows. On the night of 9 October, they sank a small white yacht by putting heavy rocks into it so that when the rocks were removed it would refloat. This was proved. Then they hid for the night with their stores which they seemed to have in plenty. All was thought out in great detail and was rehearsed nightly, as far as circumstances would permit. The Italians really thought that they had gone on 9 October, and were in a great panic and searched the seas very thoroughly. These men also were extremely unfortunate. They had decided to lie low in the loft over the offices. This they did, but a piece of plaster fell upon the desk in the Comandante's office. Unfortunately, he had temporarily returned to the island, and was (I think) in his office when the plaster fell. They were knocked about and beaten when caught.

FLIGHT SERGEANT (NOW WARRANT OFFICER) 628366 CYRIL BRUCE FLOCKHART

76 Squadron, R.A.F.

Left: Stockholm, 10 March, 1944.
Arrived: Leuchars, 10 March, 1944.

Date of birth: 12 April, 1916.
R.A.F. Service: Since 2 December, 1938.
O.T.U.: No. 19 Kinloss.
Conversion Unit: Nil.
Post in crew: Second pilot.

Peacetime profession: Commercial traveller.
Private address: 155 Stranmillis Road, Belfast, Northern
  Ireland.

Other members of crew:
Sergeant Byrne (Captain and First Pilot) (Prisoner of war)
Sergeant Thomson (Observer) (Prisoner of war)
Sergeant Pitt (Flight Engineer) (Prisoner of war)
Sergeant Leigh (Tail Gunner) (Prisoner of war)
Sergeant Taylor (First Wireless Operator) (Prisoner of war)
Sergeant Brown (Second Wireless Operator) (Missing).

Capture
I was a member of the crew of a Halifax Mark I aircraft which took off from Middleton St. George about 2145 hours, on 4 August, 1941. We reached approximately the target area – Karlsruhe – and bombed

the larger of two fires, possibly at Mannheim. We were coned badly and shot up by flak, one half of the tail unit being destroyed. Sergeant Byrne put the aircraft into a steep dive and gave the order to bale out about 0200 hours, (5 August).

5 August, 1941. Baled out near Worms.

I baled at 500 or 600 feet and was only in the air for about two seconds. The aircraft went on, and I learned later that Sergeant Byrne had flown it alone as far as the Belgian coast, where he had been shot down by a fighter.

I reached the ground on a new road between Worms and Lampertheim. I sprained my knee in touching down. Two searchlights were operating along the ground near me. I lay still for a few minutes and then gathered in my parachute, took off my harness, and hid both in a ditch. The fire at Mannheim was pretty big, and I decided it would be inadvisable to make in that direction and that it would be better to head for France.

I was on the eastern bank of the Rhine, and, as I did not feel able to swim the river, I walked north in search of a bridge. I went along the uncompleted road, which was camouflaged with grass matting. At the junction of the road with the Autobahn, I turned along the Autobahn towards Worms. When cars passed me, I got into the ditch at the roadside. Before I reached the bridge I got into a wood. There was bright moonlight and good visibility, and after observing the bridge for some time, I decided to cross it, skirt the town on the south, and lie up for the day in another small wood which I could see.

Barracks at Worms

I got about a third of the way across the bridge, when a guard came out of a room in the wall of the bridge. He challenged me. I tried to bluff him, but without success. He took me into the guardroom, and I was then marched, with an escort of two with rifles at the ready, to the military barracks at the north side of Worms. I was searched in the barracks guardroom. I gave my name, rank and number, and about 0400 hours was put into a cell.

Interrogation

After two or three hours the first of a number of Army and Luftwaffe Officers came in, all spoke English and were very polite. I got off my bed for the first, sat up for the second, and ignored the remainder. They wanted to know where I had come down, where the aircraft was, what my target had been, and where the rest of the crew were. I did not answer any of these questions, merely repeating my name, rank and number.

About a dozen officers came in between 0630 and 0900 hours. I got very fed up and treated them with contempt. I was given bread and Ersatz coffee, and later was taken to see the commanding officer, who spoke no English. He tried to question me through an interpreter, asking me the same type of question the others had put. I refused to answer. I was taken back to my cell, where I remained for two days. There was no further interrogation during that time.

Dulag Luft
Two Feldwebel of the Luftwaffe took me to Dulag Luft (Oberursel, near Frankfurt). I was accompanied by Sergeant Leigh, of my crew, who had been caught near Worms about 0700 hours on the day on which we baled out. We arrived in Frankfurt in the evening. We were politely received at Dulag by a Feldwebel who had lived for many years in the United States. I was taken alone into a room outside the general compound, and a meal was brought. I was asked to change into an old Polish uniform while my own, which actually had not been "prepared", was being examined. My collar-stud, nailfile, fountain pen, and ring were all carefully examined.

Interrogation, Dulag Luft
Next morning an Oberleutnant came in. He spoke excellent English and was very charming at first. He produced a new packet of Capstans, offered me one, and put the cigarettes and matches on the table. After asking after my comfort and saying I would be well treated, he said there was one formality – the completion of the Red Cross form. I looked at the form and saw that it contained a number of operational questions. I filled in my name, rank and number, and my mother's address, putting my pen through the other questions.

After I had signed the form at his request, the Oberleutnant said I had forgotten to fill in some of the replies. I said I did not think the Red Cross particularly wanted the other information. He said I could not tell him anything he did not already know. I replied that, in that case, there was little point in his asking me. He showed me other completed forms, and said I was being very foolish in not doing what everyone else did. I got a bit rattled and told him to get the hell out of it. He became very angry and tried to bluster and bluff, but I was as angry as he was. He collected his cigarettes and matches and went away. No further attempt was made to interrogate me.

8 or 9 August, 1941. Main compound
Next day (8 or 9 August, 1941) I was put into the main compound, and was there for seven or eight days. I was keen to get away and

approached Squadron Leader Elliott about food and a pair of shoes for my journey. He sent me to see the Man of Confidence (Gardiner), who told me they were "pushed for stuff" and to see Slowey, the senior N.C.O. Slowey could not do anything for me. There was an Irishman on the camp staff (name uncertain) who gave me a copy of a map, but this was all the assistance I received. In Dulag Luft there were large stocks of food controlled by the British permanent staff, who gave us very little when we left for Stalag III E. They gave us a few tins of sardines and German sausage.

Stalag III E (Doberlug-Kirchhain)

When I arrived at Stalag III E (Doberlug-Kirchhain) in a party there were already about 50 R.A.F. prisoners of war there. Sergeant Deans, who had previously been camp leader at Barth, had been appointed camp leader here also. He was very efficient and diplomatic with the Germans. After some time, an Escape Committee was formed in the N.C.O.s compound. The members were: Sergeant Alexander, R.A.F., who had been camp leader at Stalag III E, from which we had just come; Sergeant Gibson, R.A.F., who was also on the committee at Stalag III E; and Sergeant Seymour, R.A.A.F.

During the next few weeks two more batches came in till the total strength was about 190. Food parcels did not begin to arrive there till two months later – about October, 1941.

Reprisal on Camp after escape.

Just before this 12 Sergeants got out by making a hole in the wall of their barrack. All were recaptured within four or five days. I was not in this party, as I was living in another barrack. As a reprisal for this escape about 50 or 60 guards were sent into the camp. All our boots were taken away and put into sacks, and we were issued with wooden-soled sandals. I was at the end of the first row and was the first when we were marched round a field at the bottom of the compound. There was a guard about every twenty paces.

An officer, probably a Leutnant, stood in the centre, brandishing his revolver and screaming threats in German, the import of which was that I should go faster. This I was partly unable and partly unwilling to do. I was aided by one of the guards, who had been ordered to make me march faster. He put a hand on each of my shoulders, kicked my knees forward with his knees, and trod on my heels. I still bear the marks of this. I tried to march on my bare feet but was compelled by the officer to wear my sandals. The marching round the compound continued for two and three-quarter hours.

Threats were made with rifle butts. At least a dozen of the prisoners of war fainted and were made to rise. Where they could not walk, two of their comrades were made to assist them. During this time other guards were searching our living quarters. Food which had been saved – such as bread crusts for making puddings – was thrown about. Next morning my bungalow was punished with a further hour of marching round the field, again in sandals – this time as a punishment for having been late for parade the previous evening. There were no incidents this time, as the marching was rather easier than on the day before, though most of us were in an exhausted condition.

On recapture the 12 escapers were put in a partly underground cellar. Two others who tried to escape by hiding in a latrine were also put here for five days. There was no light in the cellar, in which there were as many as five or six at one time. Except for a hot meal every fourth day they were fed bread and water. Complaint was made to the Protecting Power, and later offenders were sent to the local police station cells.

In October, 1942, Sergeant G. Gibson, R.A.F., walked out of Stalag Luft III in daylight as an Unteroffizier on a pass forged by Sergeant Harrison, wearing German working uniform made in the camp. He got out through the German compound. He was recaptured after five days.

On 26 or 27 December, 1942, Sergeant Grimson and Sergeant A. Morris, R.A.F., walked out through the gate at night in uniforms. They pretended to be Unteroffiziere who had been at a concert in the camp. They had faked passes, made by Harrison, and intended making for Switzerland. They were caught four or five days later.

The passes which I had for my journey to Poland – one for use in Germany and the other for use in Poland – were also forged by Harrison.

While I was detained in Fort Columb, Posen, in May, 1943, after my arrest in Poland, I was put into a cell in which there were 16 male German civilians. After a time one of them spoke to me in English. He said his name was MacFarlane and that he had been born in America, where his father still lived, of a Scots father and a German mother. He had come to Germany, where his mother lived, before the war. He had been doing work for the U.S. Government and had previously been caught and charged with espionage.

The charge was not proven, but he was sentenced to a year in a concentration camp. On his release the police had tracked him down and kept him under constant surveillance. He had got some important stuff through before his capture. He asked me if, on my return to the camp, I would inform Mr. ??? of the Swedish Y.M.C.A., who visited the camps, of his whereabouts. I told him that at some time it might be possible to inform my Government about him. When I got to the camp, I had a code message sent through about him.

January, 1942. Tunnel scheme

In January, 1942, we began to make a tunnel, with practically everyone in the camp assisting. There were several searches during its construction. One of the searches coincided with the visit of a General, who actually stood on the brick covering one of the ventilation holes. The General said the camp was not good enough for British prisoners of war and that we would be transferred.

On 1 May, 1942, we discovered unofficially through an interpreter that the first party of 100 was to be moved in a week's time. We redoubled our efforts to finish the tunnel, but when I left the camp in the first party there were still 20 metres to go. I learned later that on the night before the departure of the second party they broke the tunnel and 52 men got out. After a considerable search the Germans found the exit of the tunnel but did not find the entrance under a bungalow floor, till they had sent in a man through the tunnel. The engineering of the tunnel was done by Sergeant Prior, R.A.F., a Welsh miner.

Stalag Luft III (Sagan)

8 May, 1942. Arrival at Sagan.

I arrived in Stalag Luft III (Sagan) on 8 May, 1942. An escape committee was organised, but escape was difficult because of the activities of the Abwehr officers. They had seismographs to detect tunnels. Several tunnels were made – none successful – from our compound. I took no part in these schemes, as I was in hospital with abscesses in the groin during the summer.

Attempted escape by "Blitz" tunnel.

In the early part of the winter the Germans were making large holes between the warning wire and the main wire, filling the holes with rubbish, and spreading yellow sand on top. I discussed with Sergeant Chantler, R.A.F., the possibility of getting into one of the holes and building a "Blitz" tunnel under the main wire. At the last moment Chantler asked me to take him with me.

We were allowed to walk till 2100 hours along a "red line" between the barracks. My scheme was to crawl from between two of the barracks to a hole, about 100 metres away, carrying a spade head which I had stolen. On the night of 18 December, 1942, Chantler and I did this. It took us two hours to crawl, literally inch by inch, over the 100 metres.

I got into the hole beside the warning wire and between two machine-gun posts on which searchlights were mounted. There was also a guard on the outside wire between the posts.

The hole was about 4 feet deep. I started working. Chantler joined me, and we took the digging in turns. We made the first part of the tunnel large enough to hold both of us. I was then to go ahead, and pass the earth back to Chantler, who was to block the entrance. We had dug about two and a half metres and I was coming out with the last lot of soil before sealing of the entrance, when Chantler signalled for silence. There was a dog on the edge of the hole looking down at us. The dog went away without making a sound. We lay quiet. Two minutes later the dog returned to the opposite side of the hole. We heard footsteps, and a terrific shouting began. A *Hundmeister* (one of the men in charge of the dogs) appeared. The searchlights came on to the spot.

At first, I refused to come out of the hole, insisting that the *Hundmeister* stand beside me as I came out. When we came out, we were marched with hands up down to the gate, the searchlights following us. There were one or two "blind-spots" on the way, and we got rid of our maps and compasses. The *Abwehroffizier* (Major Peschel) interrogated us as to where we were going. I decided to make a joke of the whole business, including the discovery of a 100 Reichsmark note sewn into my jacket, and succeeded. We got 14 days' cells in the camp. We had intended to jump a coal train for France in the morning, having heard of two Frenchmen from a neighbouring camp who had got on a similar train bound for Lyon.

21 May, 1943. Second attempted escape

On 21 May, 1943, I succeeded in escaping from the camp. I joined a party of prisoners of war going to the camp dentist. Sergeant Hale, R.A.F., who was also in the party, had made a key for the dentist's waiting-room. He opened the door for me, and I locked it behind me. I went out into the corridor, dressed as a German. I was wearing well-worn R.A.F. trousers dyed to look like German working trousers, a white working jacket and an R.A.F. cap made to look like a German cap and with badges embroidered by a Pole. I carried a towel and a piece of German soap. I walked 80 or 100 yards to the showers in the Vorlager. Here I joined a party of about 70 Germans which was forming up and marched with them, after counting, into the square in the German camp. Here we were dismissed, and the party dispersed to the living quarters.

I walked into one barracks and wandered round for a little. Then I got a rake and started to rake the pathway. I did this for about an hour. I then got a plank and carried it on my shoulders to the stables, where a number of Germans were doing odd jobs. I started tidying the cart shed. The others drifted away for lunch. I went up the ladder to the hayloft and lay down in the back of the loft till dusk. During this time, I saw a signal from my compound that I had been "covered" on the dental party (by Sergeant Menzies, R.C.A.F., a Red Cross parcels orderly who had got into the Vorlager as an extra man and had joined the dental parade as it was returning to the camp) – and on parades. I was being covered on parades by Sergeant Eyles, my double in appearance, and by Sergeant Wilkie.

After dark I came out of the hayloft, made my way through the German camp, and found a bus outside the Sergeant's Mess, where a concert was in progress. I thought of hiding under the back seat of the bus but considered this impracticable. I spent the next two hours in lavatories in the German camp. At midnight I put my cap and jacket into the pit in one of the lavatories. This left me with a jacket of Harris tweed appearance made from a blanket, my R.A.F. trousers, a cap made from a duster, a pair of German Army boots, which had been given in Belgium to a Sergeant who had no footwear.

I went round the back of the lavatory, through trees close to the dog kennels, over a single strand barbed-wire fence and into a wood on the south side of the camp.

I had an address in the Warsaw area (since forgotten). I made my way on foot from Sagan to Sprottau and then by train to Glogau and Fraustadt, intending to make for Lissa. On the train I travelled as a Polish workman on a false *Ausweis*. I had another for use in Poland. Both were forged in the camp.

Fraustadt

From Fraustadt I walked across the Polish frontier, being unaware that there is no control on the frontier. I entered a small village a few kilometres inside Poland. A party of boys (German) in the street asked me where I was going. (It was then about 2200 hours). I said I was going to Lissa. They asked for my *Ausweis*, and I showed them the appropriate one, which had, instead of the photograph, a pencil sketch done in the camp. The sketch was good enough to pass in poor light. One of the boys was dissatisfied, but I was allowed to go. As soon as I got clear of the village I started to run along the road. A few minutes later two bicycles came along behind me. I hid in a field of barley beside the road. The cyclists were two of the boys, so I decided to cut across country.

I by-passed Lissa, walking by night and hiding by day. Two mornings later I met a barefooted boy in overalls leading a horse. I spoke to him in German, which he did not understand, so I asked him for shelter in Polish of which I had learned a few words before leaving the camp and told him I was British. He took me back about a quarter of a mile to a middle-aged man working in a field.

This man who spoke a little German said he would be glad to help. I waited with him till 0700 hours, when the man took me to a large farmhouse. He explained to three or four middle-aged Polish women there that I was British, and I was given a meal. While I was eating, a thin shrewish Polish woman came in, and got most upset at my being there. As a result of this woman's agitation, I had to leave immediately.

I went off about 0900 hours. The man said there was a wood a few kilometres further on, and I went there. On my way through the wood, I encountered parties of wood-cutters working under German gang bosses whom I recognised by the eagle badge on their caps. I passed several of these parties and saluted each with "Heil Hitler". They generally asked where I was going, and I said I was on my way to Reisen a village which I knew to be in the direction in which I was going.

I came out of the wood into heavily cultivated country where there were large numbers of workers in the fields. They also asked me where I was going, and I always gave the same answer.

A few yards outside Reisen a farmer wearing the Nazi party badge approached me and asked where I was going. I told him I was on my way to Reisen. He was a Volksdeutscher. He said he did not know me and asked for my *Ausweis*. I said I had been sent from Lissa. (My pass had been made out as from Lissa.) He looked at the *Ausweis* and, seeing that I was supposed to be Polish, spoke to me in Polish. I said that now I only spoke German. He said that there was something funny about me and that he had better tell the police. I could not break away because of the large number of people in the fields, and also because I was lame and suffering from thirst.

Arrested

The farmer kept my *Ausweis* and sent for the police. A Feldwebel of the Gendarmerie came along and asked me the details which were contained on my *Ausweis*. I answered these questions without difficulty. He said I must consider myself under arrest. Handing his rifle to the farmer, he searched me and found a tin of Horlicks tablets.

He asked me if the tin contained explosives. I said they were tablets to eat. He then noticed that the writing on the box was in English.

Realising that the game was up, I declared myself a British prisoner of war. The Feldwebel's attitude changed completely to one of sympathy. On the way to the police station, he bought me a bottle of beer and then gave me his bicycle to ride, telling me not to try to escape because he was a good shot. I rode to the police station with the Feldwebel walking alongside. He reported my arrest to his headquarters by telephone, and then allowed me to wash and shave. When I had finished, he brought me three bottles of beer in his office, and also gave me cigarettes. The two other policemen there were also very polite and at midday took me to lunch in a café in the town.

Gestapo H.Q., Lissa At 1700 hours I was taken by horse-wagon, accompanied by the Feldwebel, to the headquarters of the Gestapo in a large private house in Lissa. I was taken into a room where I was confronted by the film conception of a Gestapo agent – a pale middle-aged man with cropped hair and glasses. He sat looking at me for several minutes, and then gave an order.

Civil prison

The Feldwebel took me to the civil prison in the castle of Lissa. I was handed over to an S.S. Feldwebel in the guardroom, thoroughly searched by him, and conducted to a cell. I was given a very small meal, and all my clothing was taken away.

At 0600 hours next day the Feldwebel wakened me, giving me my clothing, a slice of bread, and a cup of mint tea. At 0700 hours the warder returned with a Pole who carried a large hamper of hens' feathers and lengths of twine. The warder said I would have to do some work. I explained I was a Feldwebel of the British Luftwaffe and did not work. He explained what I had to do – peel the feathers and tie the stalks into bundles of 100. I refused. The warder said that if I could not work, I could not eat. I insisted on seeing the Kommandant of the prison. Half an hour later the warder took me to the Kommandant, a Hauptmann. After some discussion the Hauptmann said I would not have to work, and I was sent back to my cell.

Posen

At 0700 hours next day I was put into a private car with two civilians, one of whom was the first person I had seen at the Gestapo headquarters. Two young boys in uniform, whom I discovered to be Ukrainians who had escaped en route to Germany, were in the car. By watching the signposts, I saw we were going to Posen. At the Gestapo *Hauptstelle* I was taken into a room with several S.S. men and a woman interpreter, who was interrogating two men in Russian. On learning who I was, the woman spoke very charmingly in English. I was then taken downstairs to the cells.

In the office of the cells all my possessions were taken and put into an envelope. One of the S.S. people began to talk to me in German on general matters. During our talk a middle-aged Polish woman was brought in. While her possessions were being taken, she fumbled and was struck on the face. She was then taken to a cell. Two Polish youths were brought in. One was rather nervous and not quick enough in handing over his possessions. He also received a blow on the face. Both Poles were taken to the cells. The officials who had ill-treated them were very nice to me.

I was taken to a cell which was crowded with civilians. I said to the official that I preferred to be in a cell by myself. He said I must go in beside the civilians. I went in. The cell was 12 feet long, 6 feet wide, and about 10 feet high, with one open window about 3 feet by 2 feet. There were already 20 men in this cell. Some sat on a wooden bed in the centre of the floor, and the rest on the floor itself. There was a latrine bucket in the corner.

I spoke to a young Pole in German. He said all the civilians were Poles. I said I was British and, in a few seconds, found that all the Poles spoke German. They crowded round, shook hands with me, and patted me on the shoulder. I found that they were there for questioning, but they would not tell me about what. They said that after questioning people were taken to a Gestapo prison where conditions were very bad. At intervals individuals were taken from the room. At midday all the men were filed out. I was told to stay in the cell. A Pole then brought me a plate of soup and vegetables. I got at least double the quantity given to the Poles, and also a second helping which I gave to some of the Poles.

In the afternoon some of the people taken for questioning were brought back looking very nervous and shaken. One seemed to be in great pain. Both his thumbs were badly swollen and blue, and he seemed to be in pain with his back, being unable to lie on it. Some of the others helped him off with his jacket, and I saw that his shirt was cut to ribbons and that there were large weals on his back. The Poles seemed to be fatalistic about this treatment.

About 1800 hours we all filed out into the passage, faces to the wall. Names were called out. The Poles were made to run to the office to collect their belongings. When my name was called, I walked to the office. I was told to return to my place in the line after I had got my belongings. A few minutes later names were called out again and we were marched upstairs into a courtyard between a file of S.S. guards with sub-machine guns. We were put into a flat, canvas-covered Ford 30-cwt. truck. There were about 60 or 70 in the truck, both men and women. The truck was closed, and guards were put on the back. I got to the side of the truck and managed to see out of a slit in the canvas. We went through Posen to a suburb and stopped at a Fort.

Fort Columb, Posen

We alighted inside the gate. Names were called and we were divided into parties. I was in a party of three Polish women and four Polish men. I noted the name over the entrance to the Fort, Fort Columb. We were marched inside the Fort and made to stand in a passage with our faces to the wall. Names were called. Our personal belongings were taken away and I was searched by the S.S. guards.

An Unteroffizier was in charge. I told him I was a British prisoner of war and must be treated as such, that I objected to being placed with Polish civilians, and that it was my right to have a cell to myself. He consulted someone on the telephone and said I would be taken to a room with German civilians, this being the best accommodation they could offer me. I was taken downstairs to a room on a level with the bottom of the moat. On entering this room, I found 16 German civilians – all men.

When the door closed, they gathered round asking who I was, where I came from, and why I was there. I told them I was a British prisoner of war. They were very friendly. They gave me bread, butter, jam, and Ersatz coffee. I talked with several of them on general matters – mostly why they were there. I won the confidence of some of them and found that they were there for sabotage – that is, careless workmanship or inefficiency – several others for having been intimate with Polish women. I did a fair amount of propaganda amongst these Germans who seemed to be quite impressed.

I was two days in this cell, and at 0700 hours one morning was taken out and conveyed with 60 or 70 others back to the Gestapo Headquarters where I was put back into the cell in which I had previously been, with about 20 other Poles.

Interrogation by Gestapo.

After two hours my name was called and I was taken to a room where there were three S.S. guards. One of the S.S. guards (possibly the Leutnant) attempted to interrogate me, but I said that I understood very little German. I insisted on having an interpreter. My object in doing this was to give me time, because I understood the questions and wanted an opportunity to prepare my answers. I was made to stand at attention during the interrogation which lasted about four hours.

The whole of the interrogation was taken down direct on the typewriter by one of the guards. The interpreter was also an S.S. guard who spoke imperfect English. They first asked my name. I said it was Flockhart. They said this was a lie and that my name was Wilkie. (Wilkie was one of the men who covered my absence from the camp.) I said I had never heard of anyone called by that name, except Wendell Wilkie. They did not like my answer and threatened to strike me. They continued to accuse me of lying, but eventually let this point drop.

They asked me which camp I was from. I told them. They asked me how I escaped. I told them a long story of how one gets tired of prison life, and how, in desperation, I jumped over the wire and got away. They wanted to know if the guards fired on me. I made an evasive answer that I was not wounded.

They then asked many questions about the names of my parents, my birth place, and my profession. Some of the questions I answered truthfully, and others untruthfully. They accepted all this, and then said, "Your name is Wilkie, and you killed a policemen, for which you are to be shot". I maintained that my name was Flockhart, that I had not killed anyone, and that, if they telephoned my camp, someone could be sent from the German staff to identify me positively. Their reply was that of course they would do as I suggested.

They again became threatening and said that I was in their hands and that no-one knew anything about me. They said they did not believe my story about escaping or anything I had told them, and that I was in a very dangerous position. They wanted the names of those who had helped me to escape, and again threatened me when I said I had jumped over the wire.

They also wanted to know how I had become a prisoner, how I had been shot down, what target I had bombed, and where the rest of my crew were. I volunteered no information beyond the fact that I had been taken prisoner at Worms.

At this stage an Unteroffizier of the Luftwaffe from the camp came into the room and recognised me. He was accompanied by a Gefreiter also from the camp. Both carried revolvers. They were told to sit in a corner.

The S.S. guard who had been acting as interpreter stuck his face close to mine and said "So you are a *Terrerflieger* who has come to bomb our women and children". I told this guard in German exactly what I thought of him and his methods. The other S.S. guards were at first shocked that I could speak German. They then became very threatening and told me I was much too clever, and not to try to play monkey tricks with them. There was no further questioning, and I was asked to sign the last of the sheets which were written in German. At first, I refused to do so, but finally agreed, maintaining that I did not know what I was signing.

I was again taken to the cells for about an hour. The civilian warder asked if I was hungry and brought me sandwiches. They looked very attractive, but I did not eat them in case they were drugged. A little later the Unteroffizier and Gefreiter escorted me to the railway station in Posen and took me back to camp. On the train I ate the sandwiches, which were quite nice.

As soon as I got back to camp (about 29 May, 1943) I was met by Oberfeldwebel Glemnitz of the Abwehr Department, a big, tough type of man who had lived for many years in the United States. He was very pleasant and gave me English cigarettes, asking how I got out of the camp. I said he could not expect me to answer that. He then talked about other things, but came back, at intervals during the next hour and a half, to my escape. I was in the cells, and when he left, he gave me cigarettes, contrary to orders.

The following morning Hauptmann Brody (?), of the Abwehr Department, and Unteroffizier Flokowski, of the Lagerfuhrung (administration), tried to interrogate me. Flokowski spoke very good English. They were anxious to find out how I left the camp. My statement to the Gestapo of the date on which I had left the camp changed to coincide with the date on which the "cover" on me in the camp was lifted.

This was about five days after I had got out, and during that period Eyles and Wilkie had covered up my absence. Flokowski said he was on duty at the office on this date and that he was in trouble, being suspected of having helped me to get out. Flokowski had for some months tried to be friendly with me and others in the camp. He traded on that friendliness now, asking me not to get him into trouble. I told the Hauptmann it was absurd to suggest that Flokowski had assisted me, but still did not say how I had got out. They then gave up the interrogation as a bad job. I believe they thought that I went out of the camp dressed as a Russian.

I got fourteen days in the cells with bread and water. Wilkie and Eyles who had covered me got seven days each. Eyles had been discovered because he could not speak German. I was already recaptured by that time.

Stalag Luft VI (Heydekrug)

I arrived in Stalag Luft VI (Heydekrug) on 30 June or 1 July, 1943. This was a new camp with a new German staff. The camp strength when I left on 18 February, 1944, was a little over 3,000, and the intention was to make it up to 6,000 by transfers from other camps. There are three compounds, and the camp will be overcrowded when there are 6,000 there.

On arrival there a group of us decided that it was useless to get out without perfect papers and that we would do nothing till we could procure or produce such papers. Another big item was clothing and equipment. We decided that clothing made from blankets was useless, and framed a policy that only people authorised by the Escape Committee would be allowed to talk to or trade with the Germans. An instruction to this effect was issued by Sergeant Alexander, chief of the Committee, and an order was given by Sergeant Deans, the camp captain. A number of German-speakers and people interested in escaping were chosen to converse with Germans with various objectives – to distract the Germans from any part of the camp at any time, to obtain information, and to get the goods we wanted for escape.

Not all German-speakers were authorised to trade. As a result of this policy, between July 1943 and February 1944, we obtained all we wanted to the extent to which it was available, including two cameras – a miniature and a larger one (full-plate size). Though not a member of the Committee, I became responsible for organising the production of all papers. The Escape Committee was enlarged to five by the addition of Sergeants Grimson and Morris. Alexander was the chief. Grimson looked after the trading; Morris, intelligence; Gibson, miscellaneous; and Seymour, clothing.

Our purpose was not merely to get people outside, but to get them home. There were certain people who wanted to get out, but who lacked the ability to get home. Our policy was to help such people as far as possible, but we did not give them our best papers. It took till January 1944, to get all our preparations completed.

German and Polish helpers

Unteroffizier Munkart:	This Luftwaffe N.C.O. is an interpreter. He is an anti-Nazi, being a member of the former Centre Party and probably a Roman Catholic. He belongs to Weimar, but was born in U.S.A. (A code report about him

has been sent from the camp.) Through Munkart we got several suits of good civilian clothing. Sergeant Morris, who for the purpose of trading with German guards and Polish workers has assumed the rank of Major, has sworn Munkart in to work for us till the overthrow of the Nazi Government in Germany. (Morris is aged 24 and is the cleverest lad I have ever met.) Munkart also supplied us with shirts, ties, and information, and typed for us in the office of the Kommandantur the letters and temporary *Ausweise* we needed. He also allowed us to have his gate pass and Soldbuch for copying. Though Morris later dealt with Munkart, the initial stages were in the hands of Sergeant Lehman, R.A.F. Munkart was responsible for the conduct of some *Appels* and was willing to cover any escapers if our own system of covering broke down.

Feldwebel Schröder: Schröder, employed as an interpreter in the camp, is a teacher of languages by profession. I formed a friendship with him, and he helped me to improve my German. I told him frankly I intended to escape, and he expressed willingness to help, bringing me large-scale maps, inks, gaiters, and a Luftwaffe belt.

We paid Munkart and Schröder, as well as the others with whom we traded, in cigarettes, tobacco, chocolate, tinned meat and butter, and tea and coffee. Our policy at first was to obtain small articles – lighters, flints, pencils, and pen nibs – which we distributed in the camp. Later, when we had sorted the Germans out into the helpful and unhelpful, we asked them to bring in bigger stuff. At first, we had to trade goods from Red Cross parcels, but after a time we got a few bottles of wine and Schnapps from the Germans. We raffled these bottles, and this gave us a large amount of cigarettes and tobacco for use as trading capital, though we still had to draw to some extent on the Red Cross parcels.

Untergefreiter Sommers

I formed a contact with the camp photographer, Untergefreiter Sommers. He was born in Łódź of Polish parents, had been in a Polish Army officer-cadet school at the outbreak of war, and was taken prisoner by the Russians, and handed over to the Germans. After considerable pressure in a German camp, he agreed to join the German Army, becoming Germanised (*einge-deutscht*: third class). He hated the Germans very much, and I asked him to prove it by bringing me in a belt buckle and cap. Eventually he supplied us with all the photographic chemicals we needed, as well as film for the miniature camera, reproduction plates, civilian clothing, and a false *Volksliste* third class (the *Ausweis* used by the *eingedeutschte* Polish civilians). Through Sommers we also got in touch with the Litzmannstadt (Łódź) branch of the Polish organisation, who said they could not route prisoners of war out of the country, but that if a prisoner of war came into their hands, they would cover him. In view of this answer, we did not pursue the contact further. It was probably through this organisation that Sommers got the goods with which he supplied us. Sommers said he was anxious to come to England with me to fight against the Germans and would do that if I could organise the journey for him. I agreed to bring him (or arrange for him to come) if my Government would agree. Sommers was expecting to be posted on active service. Just before I left the camp, he was informed that he would remain there for one or two months. He agreed that after I had gone, he would

Gefreiter Stetskowski

work for the Escape Committee till I had sent instructions about him.

Stetskowski (phonetic spelling), a Pole, was a guard at the camp. (A detailed report on him is being sent through in code.) He was operated on by Sergeant J. Gilbert, R.A.F., a Polish Jew who joined our forces in Jerusalem. He speaks Polish. Grimson, Morris, and myself later worked on him. He was suffering from stomach trouble, and we gave him food which he could not get otherwise. At first, he was very nervous of bringing in stuff, but eventually did so. Finally, he offered us a hide-out in his home and in the homes of friends and colleagues in the vicinity of his home. He is a member of a Polish organisation.

There were two *eingedeutschte* Polish civilian workmen who came into the camp to repair water pumps, etc., once or twice a week. First Gilbert and then Morris worked on them. They brought us tools and civilian clothes and allowed us to have their papers for copying. From the point of view of papers, they were the most valuable people we had. I do not know their names. They will be mentioned in the report from the camp.

Civilian Surveyor:

The camp was also visited by a civilian surveyor or engineer (no name). I am not certain whether he was Polish or German, but think he came from Breslau. We discovered he was a member of a German organisation which is being built up by the Centre (Catholic) Party. It was he who brought us in the two cameras, as well as photographic plates and papers. He was first dealt with by Sergeant Moyle and then by Sergeant Morris. Morris arranged with him to get in touch with the chief of the organisation for the district, saying that if the organisation needed gold, we would be able to supply it.

Morris asked me to arrange to send him, for a start, £100 worth of gold in pieces worth about £5 each. This will probably also be mentioned in the report being sent in code. The first letter of the series was sent off on 16 February.

Codes

All code messages are being arranged by the camp leader. Those sending letters are all registered. Deans sent home a message to disregard letters from everyone except those named on a list which he sent.

Forging of papers

Our method of making paper was this: We photographed the originals, and Sergeant Harrison and three assistants made free-hand enlargements. These were photographed on reproduction plates by Sergeant Sands, working under my direction. From these plates we made full-size contact prints. It took months of experiments to do this satisfactorily. We could reproduce on photographic paper, but that was not good enough, the surface being different from what we needed. Sands worked hard for months to sensitise ordinary paper, and had some, but not complete, success. We sent home a code message about September 1943, for PAC emulsion, but had had no notification of the despatch of the emulsion up to the time I left the camp. We succeeded in making a number of *Ausweise* of various kinds but were unable to reproduce the *Volksliste* (pass of Germanised Polish civilian) photographically. The *Volksliste* which I later used was made by Sergeant Beck by free-hand drawing.

Plan for organising escapes

Our scheme was that Sergeant Grimson was to leave the camp and go to the house appointed by Stetskowski near Rübenau and use it as a base from which to get in touch with a Swedish ship's captain and arrange for my passage to Sweden. He would also build up the Polish organisation and would control departures from the camp, working in co-operation with me – I to be in Sweden.

Grimson left the camp on 18 January, 1944. He went out as a guard in uniform, following the other guards after an *Appel*, and carrying a beautiful dummy rifle made by an Australian. He was covered at *Appel*s by the Escape Committee, one man always answering twice, and his absence had not been discovered when I left the camp a month later.

Grimson went to the house arranged for him by Stetskowski. We had two messages from him sent in code in ordinary letters, written in German, addressed to Munkart. He said he was comfortable, required certain things, and had the nucleus of a good organisation already in being. He had not as yet already got in touch with a Swedish sea captain. (He was looking for a specific Swedish captain as a result of a letter sent to Sergeant Harrison from Mrs. Morton (English) in Stockholm. Her message had been misunderstood, and I found later there was no such captain as she had mentioned.)

After the second message from Grimson there was a lapse of two weeks, and Stetskowski went home on leave. It was decided that I should leave the camp.

Own departure from camp

I walked out of the camp on the morning of Friday, 18 February, 1944. The previous day Feldwebel Schröder had taken me from my own compound to another compound which was nearing completion and partly occupied. My absence from my own compound was covered by the Escape Committee, and the Germans did not know I was in the unfinished compound. I met Schröder by arrangement in the wash barrack of the unfinished compound about 0830 hours on 18 February. While he conversed with the Feldwebel in charge of the guard in the guardroom outside the gate of the compound, I left the wash barrack and later left the compound.

Scheme arranged by Escape Committee

The scheme arranged by the Escape Committee was that Grimson should work from Kosten or a similar place and organise the route from the camp to the selected port. He is in communication with the camp by code and would control departures from the camp. I was to be in Sweden in code communication with him and was to arrange the shipping angle by getting in touch with members of ships' crews and officers, so that I could inform Grimson or the camp that a certain ship would be in a certain port on a certain date. I was also to control from Sweden the supply of equipment for the camp and meet any of Grimson's requirements which were unobtainable in Germany. It was hoped that I could obtain authority to remain in Sweden without coming to London, or that I could get authority in London for our scheme. Grimson is to get in contact with R.S.M. Grainger in Thorn.

Requirements in Stalag Luft VI

i.   Luftwaffe cloth in the form of blankets overdyed with a dye which would wash out at a given temperature. This was asked in a code letter at least a year ago, or Luftwaffe uniforms.

ii. Two portable typewriters – one for Grimson and one for the camp. The typewriters in the camp are "on parole" and cannot be used for forgery. We tried to make a typewriter, but the result was not satisfactory.

iii. The essentials of a sewing machine.

iv. There is a wireless receiver in the camp. The original parts were obtained three years ago, and replacements have since been obtained by trading with Germans. The Escape Committee are most anxious to have a wireless transmitter which would not be used till a break-down begins in Germany or until they have information of vital military importance. The operation of the receiver is controlled by Sergeant Deans (Camp Captain) and the Camp Secretary (Sergeant Mogg).

v.   About six automatic pistols (32s or 38s) and a few clips of ammunition.

vi. Food ration cards and genuinely printed papers. (The latter were asked for a year ago.) The cards and papers are asked for in case of the confiscation of the forgery equipment at present in use.

vii. Supplies of photographic chemicals are available in the camp. PAC emulsion (asked for in a code letter in August or September 1943) is immediately required. [PAC emulsion is a bromide emulsion which will sensitise any type of paper.] Printed papers, however, are preferable to photographic reproductions.

Material received in the camp

The last parcel received in the camp was one sent to Sergeant Callander without advice. It arrived about 12 February, 1944, and contained a suit of pyjamas and small items, as well as maps, compasses, and wire-cutters. Because we had had no advice of the parcel, no special watch was kept for a parcel for Callander, who had not previously received a parcel of this kind, and it was found by the Abwehr Department.

I believe the parcel had been sent to Callander as a result of a conversation he had with Corporal Byrne, who made a successful escape on the journey from Sagan to Heydekrug in July or August 1943. This was the first time the Germans had found anything in parcels in Heydekrug. On another occasion, however, a special parcel arrived addressed to someone in another compound, also without notification. It was spotted by chance and retrieved by the Escape Committee. I do not know to whom it was addressed.

The Germans were very keen on censoring the 12-inch gramophone records, which were taken away every three weeks (the same records) for re-censoring. I got the impression that they were looking for concealed recorded messages, which would appear when the original tune had worn down. They also used to bore holes in the centre of the discs.

Book censorship is fairly severe, but it is possible to get books through if advance information is received by the Escape Committee. No maps were received in books.

Special request

Authority is required by the camp captain (Sergeant Deans) and the Escape Committee to deal with the few people in the camp who, in spite of repeated warnings, continue to trade with Germans for purely selfish ends to the detriment of the escape organisation. They want a definite order sent out in code letter. Sergeant Deans, who has controlled the camp since the end of 1941, holds his position by his great diplomacy and by popular vote.

Additional notes of Stalag Luft VI.

On our arrival at Stalag Luft VI, the Germans made a black list of escapers and known anti-Nazis. We were taken out of our living rooms and put into a barrack room, where we were supposed to be under special surveillance. Those on the list were:

Warrant Officer Snowden
Sergeant Jack Gilbert
Sergeant Fancy
Sergeant Wilkie
Sergeant Lascelles
Sergeant Pavey
Sergeant Grimson
Sergeant Liggatt (or Leggett)
Sergeant Stanford
Sergeant Murton
Sergeant Morris
Sergeant Parsons and myself.

There were two others on the list, one of whom was Sergeant Flynn, who were later taken off.

The over-crowding of the camp and the human element destroyed this plan and the strength of the barrack room was later made up to 26 by the inclusion of new prisoners of war. This room was known to the Germans as the "black room". In the event of mis-conduct in the Camp, the Germans dashed immediately to our barracks, where they also had snap searches at night. After a few months they gave up these special precautions.

Tunnel scheme

In September 1943, a tunnel was completed in the camp, by which eight people got out. Some of them were out for over a week and got across the Lithuanian frontier, where they revealed themselves to farmers as British escapers and were given help.

Most of the construction and engineering of the tunnel was done by Sergeant Fancy and Sergeant Flynn. Sergeant Fancy and Sergeant Street got to the neighbourhood of Pilau, where they hid in a fisherman's hut for three days, intending to try to steal a fishing yawl, and reach Gotland. Lithuanian peasants, however, thinking they had discovered Russian parachutists, informed the Germans.

There were 52 people in the tunnel, but the ninth man was seen by the Germans and the alarm given. All the 52 had various types of forged papers, mostly those of foreign workers. All the people left in the tunnel managed to get rid of their papers. The Germans could not find the entrance of the tunnel, which was through the fire-box of a boiler.

I escaped alone from the camp on the morning of 18 February, 1944. The previous day I had obtained entrance to another unfinished and partly occupied compound. About 0830 hours on 18 February, I left the wash barracks in this compound dressed in a green tweed jacket, riding breeches made from Italian pantaloons, top boots (Stiefel), a soft hat, an R.A.F. officer's mackintosh. I was carrying a canvas briefcase (made in the camp) under my arm and in my hand a rolled-up plan of the compound and environs which had been made for me in the camp by architects among the prisoners of war. I had my hair cropped and had shaved off my moustache, and looked so like a German that one of the prisoners of war in my compound had actually taken me for a member of the Kriminalpolizei who sometimes visited the camp.

I walked to the warning wire, indicated to the guard that I was going to the unfinished wash barracks, inspected the wash barracks outside, and made some notes on my plan. I then went inside for a few moments. Coming out again, I walked slowly to the gate, presented my pass (a forgery) to the guard, and was accepted by him as one of the architects who had been working in the compound. I walked through the gate without being questioned.

I then proceeded to the camp sewage farm which is under construction near the river, about 200 metres from the camp. I was within full view of the watch towers. I spent about ten minutes at the sewage farm, examining the excavations, on which there was no one working, and pretending to take notes and pace distances. I then walked back towards the camp, diagonally towards one corner, and went round the outside wire. This brought me to a road which leads to the main administrative buildings. Before reaching them, I turned off on to another dirt track through a wood. This brought me to the main road leading to Heydekrug. Before leaving the sewage farm I had put my plan into my briefcase which also contained clothing, toilet gear, and sandwiches. The pass I carried was forged and made out in the name of a Germanised (*eingedeutscht*) Pole.

Journey to Sweden
On arrival at the railway station in Heydekrug I bought a single third-class ticket for Königsberg, and waited in the waiting-room. Just before the arrival of the train, an hour and a half later, several men came into the waiting-room, one or two of whom I recognised as members of the Kriminalpolizei who had taken part in a search of the camp some time before. To avoid any control of papers, I went to the lavatory till the train came in. I boarded the train and found two of the policemen in the compartment. Fortunately, an old farmer sitting beside me was very talkative about general subjects and wanted to do most of the talking. The policemen took no interest in me. They disappeared at Insterburg, where I had to change.

At Insterburg I waited about an hour in the waiting-room over a glass of beer, and then went on to Königsberg. On arrival I found I would have to wait four hours for a Personenzug to Marienburg. To avoid a possible control at the station I walked about the town in the evening. I got the train after 2300 hours and arrived at Marienburg about 0245 hours (19 February). I had to wait till 0515 hours. I feigned sleep in the waiting-room and was not disturbed by two *Bahnhofpolizei* (in green uniforms) who woke several other people to inspect their papers. Probably my respectable middle-class appearance was responsible for my not being roused.

At 0515 hours I boarded the train for Rübenau (Rybno), arriving at 0930 hours. I made my way on foot through the town to the Forest of Kosten, which is west of Rübenau.

I was making for the house of a man named Galinski (or Galinsky) (a friend of Stetskowski) with whom Grimson had been staying. Galinski was the local chief of the Polish organisation. I had trouble in finding the house. My instructions were to go to the *Forstamt* (forestry office), where, we believed in the camp, Galinski's house also was. In the office I was told that Galinski was at his own house up the road. I inquired for him at the first house but could get no information regarding him. I returned to the *Forstamt*, and the civilian whom I had previously seen – I found later that he also was in the organisation – sent me to the second house up the road.

At this house I met Galinski's wife, who seemed very nervous. She said he was not at home but invited me in to wait. She asked who I was. I said I was a friend of the gentleman who came there a month ago (Grimson). She said he was not there, that he had gone on a journey, and that she did not think he would be returning.

After about half an hour Galinski came in. When I had satisfied him as to my identity, he told me Grimson had gone to Danzig and Memel two days previously, and that as far as he knew he was not returning. I knew that Stetskowski was on leave at his home in Gronowo and asked to see him. I was given a meal, and before I had finished Stetskowski arrived. A few minutes later the chief district forester (a Hauptmann) arrived and said that someone had been inquiring for Galinski. As this had been a stranger, the Hauptmann wanted to know his business. Galinski told the Hauptmann, who did not enter the house, that the stranger had been looking for someone else, having mistaken the name. The Hauptmann went away.

After a consultation it was decided that I should go to the house of Galinski's brother, also a forester, at Straszewo (Strassen). Stetskowski took me by haulage roads through the forest to the vicinity of the house at Straszewo. He went to the house alone first, returning to inform me that the second Galinski would come for me in a few minutes. This Galinski did, taking me through the forest to his home. I was fed and given a bed.

About 0200 hours on 21 February, I was wakened and told my friend had arrived. This was Grimson. Stetskowski was with him. Grimson told me that Stetskowski had brought him from his home, that my arrival at Kosten had aroused a certain amount of suspicion, and that the Galinski at Kosten was believed to be under observation. Grimson had been to Danzig and Memel and had discovered from the Swedish pastor in Danzig that there was no Swedish captain named Karl Morton. He had not succeeded in arranging a passage for me. He had sent instructions to the camp in a code letter addressed to Munkart that I must await further instructions at the camp. I explained the position when I left the camp, and he decided that we ought to travel that day to Danzig and that I must make some attempt to get away without pre-arrangement.

That day (21 February) we travelled to Danzig by different train routes. I went via Deutscheylau. We travelled separately because our papers were similar.

I arrived in Danzig about 1900 hours (21 February) and awaited Grimson by arrangement in the waiting room, having first bought a second-class ticket for Marienburg. (It is important to purchase a ticket before going into a station waiting room, as those without tickets are not allowed to sit there.) Grimson arrived about 2200 hours. He took me to the dock area, with which he was familiar and showed me a Swedish ship which was loading coal on the east side of the Kaiserhaven. Before entering the prohibited dock area, I gave my money, papers, and raincoat to Grimson, and arranged that if I could not get aboard, I would return to the waiting room before daylight.

It was part of our scheme, when I left the camp, that if I were captured, I would not reveal my true identity, but would assume a false name and state that I had been shot down in Germany recently and had been helped by people whom I could not identify. The object of this was to safeguard the identity papers which we had in the camp. Grimson maintained that, as he had not succeeded in arranging transport for me, I ought not to take this risk. As, however, I hoped to evade capture, I decided to defer a decision till the moment of capture. (A list of false names, ranks, and numbers had been despatched in code. I was to have used one of the identities on this list.)

I made my way to the Kaiserhaven and got fairly close to the side of the Swedish ship. I lay in the snow beside the coal for about four hours. There was quite a lot of activity on the quayside, and there was a soldier posted on the end of the ship's gangway. I finally crawled within about 30 feet of the ship behind the loading crane but could not remain there as several workmen passed within three feet of me on the other side of the crane. I decided I could not get on board the ship by stealth that night, and went back to the Hauptbahnhof, finding my way by following the tram lines from the bridge.

I met Grimson again in the station second-class waiting room. He told me [illegible] had taken place sometime previously. We waited in different parts of the waiting-room till about 0700 hours (22 February). After buying tickets for nearby town, we went to the third-class waiting room for breakfast.

Grimson had an idea of trying to get on board the same ship from a rowing boat on the seaward side that night, he being an expert oarsman. He suggested that while he searched for a rowing boat in Danzig, I should go to Gotenhafen (Gdynia) and see what the position was there. My journey to Gotenhafen was fruitless, as I could not get into the harbour area in daylight. I returned to Danzig and met Grimson by arrangement in the town. We had a meal at a hotel (das Alte Deutsche Haus). Afterwards we walked about for a considerable time. Grimson had not found a rowing boat but had seen another Swedish vessel at Weichselmünde. He offered to conduct me there and show me a hole in the fence which he had discovered.

We went by tram to the terminus at Neufahrwasser and took the ferry across the Vistula to Weichselmünde. There are two ferries here, and we took the one further upstream. On the Weichselmünde side we went up a small lane directly opposite the landing stage. At the end of the lane, we turned right (south) and followed a street which joined the Weichselmünde Weg. Just before the point where this road is crossed by a railway there is a small grass path leading from the road up to the wire fence round the harbour. This path ended near the hole in the fence which Grimson had discovered. (The north harbour gate at the end of the street leading into the Weichselmünde Weg is to be avoided.)

I again gave Grimson my money, papers, and raincoat, and lay down at this spot near the fence. I was about 100 yards west of a Flak Battery. When Grimson had left me, I crawled 50 or 100 yards over the snow to the fence. After some searching, I found a small gap in the wire and crawled through. I then crawled over the railway tracks towards the ship. The harbour was well lit up and I could see that there were two ships flying the Swedish flag – one of about 800 tons and the other of about 3500 tons. I chose the larger and observed it from the cover of some railway trucks. There was a guard on the gangway who was walking up and down in front of the ship.

I walked some distance from the ship, keeping the railway wagons between me and the guard, and then crossed to the water's edge and approached the ship. I was helped in this by the fact that the leg of the crane was between me and the guard. The fore-hold of the ship was being filled. I succeeded in getting to within about three yards of the gangway while the guard was walking towards the stern, but he turned and saw me.

I was walking quite slowly. I stopped, had a look around, and sauntered slowly away from him. At this moment two Swedish seaman arrived to go on board, and the guard, being engaged in examining their papers, did not challenge me. I attribute this to the fact that I was reasonably smartly dressed, looking, in my breeches and top boots, like a German. I got out of the dock by climbing the fence, which was of close wire netting, about two metres high, with barbed wire on top. I climbed the fence some distance from the hole through which I had come in.

I returned to the Hauptbahnhof and saw Grimson. We did not acknowledge each other and sat in different parts of the waiting room.

About 0700 hours (23 February) Grimson came up to me and shook hands, and we went out together, again buying tickets (third-class) for local towns, and went to the third-class waiting room for breakfast. Grimson had some food coupons which he had obtained from Poles.

I think he was disappointed that I had not got away, but I disagreed with him, as I was determined not to take foolish chances. We were both suffering from lack of sleep, and I told him he should return to Kosten and get some sleep, while I would continue to try till I succeeded in finding a ship. He agreed that he felt exhausted but said we should try once more. I told him it was not necessary for him to stay, as I had another idea which was more sure but that he would help me by obtaining a suit of overalls, a Polish "P" badge (worn by Poles in Germany), and a peaked cap. He said he could get them for me, as he had a contact in Danzig, a Pole employed as a chauffeur by the Forestry Department, who had been recommended to him by Galinski.

Grimson left me about 0730 hours (27 February) and returned about three hours later with the necessary clothing. We arranged that I should go into a lavatory and put on the overalls over my clothing, and that Grimson should indicate when the lavatory was clear by knocking on the door. I changed and walked out. I then boarded a tram for Neufahrwasser, having handed over to Grimson all my papers except my *Volksliste* and an *Erlaubnisschein* for railway travel. I also gave him my raincoat. I put my soft hat into my briefcase, which I still carried.

I went by tram to Neufahrwasser and across the ferry to Weichselmünde. I went through the hole in the fence about 1200 hours quite openly. There were people on the road and the flak battery position. I crossed the sidings and went to a small hut beside a concrete mixer about 200 yards from the ship. Through a knothole I could observe the quayside. I hid my briefcase under some wood in this hut, and then walked along the docks towards the ship. Some Russians were loading the bunkers with coal. Another party of Russians was working on the quay beside the small Swedish ship. I went into a lavatory used by the Russians close by, in the hope that Russians might come there, from whom I could get help to board the ship. I waited for about half an hour, but no Russians came.

The sentry on the larger of the two ships was walking up and down the quay. I thought I would try my trick of the previous night and approach the ship along the water's edge under cover of the crane leg. Before I approached the ship, I removed my "P" badge from my overall and smudged my hands and face. I approached the ship unobserved and began to examine the ship's moorings on the quayside. I made this approach during the time the guard was walking away from the gangway, so that when he turned it would appear that I had come down the gangway. I walked to the next mooring and examined it very critically. This was closer to the gangway. When the guard was again walking away from me, I walked slowly up the gangway. I was almost at the top when the guard turned, but he did not take the slightest notice of me.

On arriving on the deck, I tidied up some ropes on the landward side of the foredeck and then walked round to the other side. There was none of the ship's crew on deck. Then I made my way into the fore-hold, which was about half full of coal, and looked for a hiding place. Finding none, I climbed out again and tried to get down into the chain locker in the fore peak, but the entrance to the locker was padlocked. I then went to the stoke-hole. The bunkers were still being filled, and one of the ship's crew was in charge of this operation. I avoided him on my way down.

While I was trying to find a hiding place in the stoke-hole I was discovered by another of the ship's crew. I told him in English I was British and asked for help. He explained in broken English that he would like to help, but that it was useless, as the police searched every part of the ship before it sailed. I asked him to keep quiet about my presence on board while I tried to find a hiding place elsewhere.

I went on deck and into the after hold. This was useless, as I could not find a hiding place except amongst the coal. I went into the paint store behind the after hold. This was also useless. I hid my remaining papers there. I then went aft into the crew's quarters and saw no one. The best hiding place was a small cupboard which, however, I considered too obvious. I went up on deck with the intention of trying the engine room. In a passage I met the ship's steward, told him in English that I was British, and asked his help. He took me into the cook's galley and said he would like to help me, but that he was married, and the risk was very great.

I offered him £100 if he could hide me so that I could arrive in Sweden. He changed immediately and said that he would consult the first mate. He asked me to wait a few minutes and returned accompanied by the first mate, who also spoke English. They decided that for the £100, which would be paid in Sweden, they would hide me. They took me to the officers' mess beside the cook's galley and gave me a meal, after which I was hidden until the following evening (24 February). During this time, they fed me immediately after the ship's officers had had their meals. The ship's cook and the cook's boy were informed of my presence on the ship.

On the evening of 24 February, the steward and the first mate told me they had prepared a place for me in the steward's pantry. They proposed to take me there immediately. In the steward's pantry packing cases and stacks of food stuffs had been so arranged that there was a space behind them against the wall. Some bedding had been placed there. I climbed into this hiding place, and they covered it with packing cases and suitcases.

The ship sailed about 1000 hours on Friday 25 February, after having been searched. The steward's pantry in which I was hiding was not searched. My helpers told me that the first mate went round with the police during the search, asking them to be quick as he wanted to be back in Stockholm by mid-day on Sunday, and promising them a drink.

I remained in the steward's pantry, being fed at meal times, till Saturday afternoon (26 February), when the first mate told me to go on deck and reveal myself to the cook, who had received instructions about taking me to the Captain. I did this. The Captain asked me where I had concealed myself, and I said I had been in the bunkers. I had taken the precaution of making myself very dirty with coal dust.

The Captain said I was now safe in Swedish waters and that we would be in Stockholm next day. A cabin was placed at my disposal, and I was given a bath and food. After this I saw the Captain in his cabin. He was very charming and asked for my particulars for entry in his log. I gave him my true name, rank, and number.

On arrival in Stockholm, at 1900 hours on Sunday 27 February, I was handed over to plain-clothes policemen and taken by car to police headquarters. I was enabled to purchase a meal and was told I should have to have a bath and have my clothing fumigated. I was kept that night in a cell, and after breakfast on Monday, 28 February, I was taken for interrogation by a plain-clothes policeman in the police headquarters. I made a simple statement of my name, rank, number, and place of birth, and said I was a British prisoner of war from Germany, and that as I had succeeded in reaching neutral territory, I expected to be returned to my own country. I asked to see the British Consul and was told this was being arranged. After about half an hour

I was taken by taxi to the British Legation, where I was received by the Air Attaché.

The name of the ship on which I travelled was the S.S. *Flora*. The sailors refused to give me their names. They said that if I sent the £100 in kroner to the first mate, steward, cook and cook's boy, respectively, care of S.S. *Flora*, A.B. Transmarine, Stockholm, they would receive it. After I had left the ship in Stockholm the Captain ran after me and asked me not to disclose the name of his ship, as he feared German reprisals.

27 February, 1944; Arrived Stockholm

From Heydekrug I made my way to Danzig, where I succeeded in boarding a Swedish vessel which sailed from Weichselmünde on 25 February. I arrived in Stockholm on 27 February.

SERGEANT 999513 D.D.W. NABARRO

10 Squadron, R.A.F.

Captured:	29 June, 1941.
Escaped:	25 November, 1941.
Left:	Gibraltar: 30 September, 1942.
Arrived:	Greenock, 5 October, 1942.
R.A.F. Service:	2½ years.
Peacetime profession:	Student.
Private address:	Royal Hotel, Waterfoot, Lancashire.

Shot down over Kiel

I was second pilot of a Whitley which took off from Leeming at 2100 hours on 28 June, 1941, to bomb Bremen. We reached the target and bombed it, but on the return journey were shot down by Flak at 0030 hours on 29 June, 1941, over Kiel. We baled out and came down in the Baltic Sea. The rest of the crew were:

Sergeant Gregory (pilot) (prisoner of war),

Pilot Officer Watson (rear gunner); and two Pilot Officers (names not known), believed prisoners of war.

We were picked up by a German minesweeper at 0630 hours and were treated very considerately. They allowed us to wash and gave us a blanket, coffee, and cigarettes, although they were rationed to three a day themselves. We were taken to army barracks in Kiel the same day and put into separate rooms. I had my head treated here. There was no interrogation or questioning. Two hours later we were moved on to a G.A.F. Station just outside the town by the side of the harbour. We were all interrogated here in a friendly manner during a meal. We were asked how we were shot down, make of aircraft, and squadron number.

We just gave our name, rank and number and said we were not allowed to say anything more. They said they knew we were a

185

Wellington crew and what bombloads our various aircraft carried. Their estimate was 1,000 lbs short, however. They did not persist in the interrogation. We were then taken to another G.A.F. Station and interrogated separately by a friendly Major. They used the rolling stone method, beginning with unimportant questions, such as father's Christian name, and gradually increasing the tempo, finally asking the number of my squadron. When I did not answer that, the interview came to an end.

In the evening we were taken by train to Frankfurt am Main. On the journey a German, who was very friendly and said he had been to Newcastle before the war, came in to talk to us. He provided a bottle of lemonade and apologised for not having any beer. Only the Army personnel were asked for papers on the train, which were strictly controlled. We left Kiel at 1800 hours on 29 June and reached Frankfurt at 1100 hours on 30 June.

30 June. Dulag Luft, Oberursel

We were taken from the station to Dulag Luft about 15 kilometres north-west of Frankfurt, just to the north of the railway going from Frankfurt to Oberursel. I was interrogated here by Eberhardt, the official interpreter who asked the type of aircraft I was flying and length of my R.A.F. service. He seemed to be more interested in my squadron number than base. When I refused to speak, he took down some particulars such as home address for Red Cross purposes, and then left after quarter of an hour. Later on, another man came in, who said he was a history professor. He tried to start a discussion, but I did not encourage him, and the conversation did not last very long.

Next day, 1 July, I was taken to hospital in a wood. We occupied the top floor with three beds to a room. I was with two other British prisoners of war, and we were very careful not to discuss service questions. I was two weeks in this hospital where the treatment was very good. While I was there, they brought in the false Red Cross form, on which I just filled in my name, rank, number and home address.

15 July. Stalag IX C Bad Sulza

I went back to the camp for two days before being taken to Stalag IX C, at Bad Sulza, about 15 July. I remained there in the main camp, till I escaped in November 1941. They took my fingerprints here, but there was no interrogation. The living conditions here were bad; 150 of us lived, ate, and slept in a room about 120 feet by 60 feet. Apart from French, Belgian, and Serb prisoners of war, there were a large number of British wounded from Dunkirk. Morale was high among all, but especially among the British wounded. There was an unofficial escape club, the nucleus of which was made up of people who had already attempted to escape.

First escape

I escaped first in September 1941, with Sergeant-Pilot Hall. We had food for a fortnight, a compass and map tracings of the route to the Italian-Swiss frontier provided by a Frenchman. There were watch towers at the four corners of the compound, but the sentries could not see each other, nor could they see immediately below the tower. In broad daylight we climbed over the wire up against one of these towers and out of sight of the sentry. Someone in the camp signalled to us when the sentry was looking the other way, and we dashed away into a ditch. Unfortunately, two Serbs saw us, and by their excitement roused the suspicions of the guard who looked in our direction and saw us crawling along the ditch. When they re-captured us, they found our map tracing, but not the compass which Hall hid between his legs with a bit of sticking plaster.

We were given 24 days in the cells but were turned out after a week to make room for other escapers. While in prison I talked to a Major in the next-door cell who had been in charge of the escape club at Oflag X C (Lübeck) and he told me about the Schaffhausen route.

Second escape

My second escape was made in October 1941. I was in the potato cart cleaning it out, when the guard, getting impatient, drove off with me still inside. When we got near a wood I jumped off and hid in it. On this occasion I happened to have with me a week's supply of vitamin tablets. I then jumped two goods trains, but three days later was caught asleep in a waggon at Apolda. This time I was sentenced to 21 days in the cells, but I only completed 15. I had by now made two dozen keys for the window of the cell and we were always able to keep anyone in them provided with food.

I then set about making preparations for escape with a Belgian, whose Christian name is Godefroi; he found out the times of the train, and I got sixty marks, a pair of slacks, and a leather jacket from a Frenchman in return for a fountain pen, a wristwatch, and an Army greatcoat. He also provided maps. I improved my French by conversation with a Corsican.

Final escape

We escaped on 25 November 1941 by going up to the guard at 0630 hours and saying we were going to clean out the Commandant's office, which was outside the main wire. He let us through without fuss, as he had been on duty for three hours and was due to be relieved. We had then only a single strand of barbed wire to negotiate, and this presented no difficulty. We went to the next village and caught a local train towards Berlin. Godefroi spoke German and throughout the journey bought the tickets without exciting comment. We changed at Naumburg and went out into the country till 1600 hours when we caught a train for Apolda arriving there at about 1730 hours. We walked about the town for an hour and then caught a train to Kassel at about 1900 hours. We did not go about together but met in the station lavatory to make our plans and decide which trains we were going to take.

I carried a lot of 10 pfennig pieces in order to be able to lock myself in the lavatories and avoid being seen hanging about stations. It was also a convenient place to shave. The train to Kassel was very crowded but we managed to get seats. There was an R.A.F. raid during the journey and the train stopped for three hours. Through this we missed our connection and had to wait 15 hours at Kassel. We walked about the town and then went into the buffet and slept the night there near some German soldiers. We bought beer and Ersatz coffee but no food. Our chocolate and vitamin tablets, provided by the Red Cross, kept us going for a week.

The following morning, we caught a train at 1100 hours to Koblenz arriving at 1700 hours. we had to wait overnight and caught a train on the morning of 30 November to Gerolstein about 50 kilometres from the Luxembourg frontier.

30 November. Recapture at Gerolstein

At Gerolstein we were caught leaving the station. It was Sunday, which is strictly observed in this Catholic part of Germany, and our unusual appearance attracted attention. The station police asked for our papers, but our forged documents purporting to belong to Belgian workers did not deceive them. We were taken to a cell underneath the police station where we found a French escaped prisoner of war.

1 December. Escape

We all escaped the following morning by going to the washing place, knocking out the guard and getting out of the window. We then ran across country due south for about 12 kilometres. At about midday we hid in some woods beside a railway and river. We started off again at night by full moon. It was very cold, and our shoes were waterlogged. We hid in a little copse, forded a river that evening, and carried on all night.

3 December

The following morning (3 December) without realising it we crossed the frontier into Luxembourg (near Trois Vierges). We went on by day to Houffalize in Belgium, where we stayed the night at a café, the proprietor of which recognised us as escaped prisoners of war. It was the first place we tried, and the people were extremely sympathetic. We saw no guard on the frontier, except the Customs Post at Trois Vierges. But we realised we had got out of Germany by the fact that people looked so much more cheerful.

Godefroi knew this part of the country and we went by tram to Bastogne and then on by train to Libramont. We stayed the night at Godefroi's home near here.

4 December. France

The next day I went on by train with the Frenchman via Namur and Charleroi to Erquelinnes on the Belgian-French frontier. We walked over the frontier to Jeumont without being stopped. Godefroi's father had given me 600 Belgian francs which enabled me to reach Paris by train. We travelled first to St Quentin, crossed the red line on foot near Montescourt without being stopped and went on by train to Paris.

I then decided to get to Rouen to see if I could find a friend of mine, Private Jim Sumner, R.A.S.C., whom I believed to be in Heilag Rouen, to see if I could help him. However, I could find no trace of him. A Frenchman in Stalag IX C had given me his home address in Rouen, and I went there, and his parents put me up for the night. The next afternoon I went to Paris and stayed the night with a gendarme, the brother of another Frenchman in Stalag IX C.

I then went to Nevers by train to find the Frenchman with whom I had escaped from Gerolstein. He told me how to get across the Demarcation Line, wrongly as it turned out. I was caught by the Germans just south of Nevers, when I was crossing back to Occupied France by mistake after having already crossed once in the other direction. I told them I was trying to get into the Occupied Zone, and they sent me back to Unoccupied France. I thought this might be a trap, and so walked down the road towards Sancoins. I thought the Germans were probably watching me and would recapture me if they saw me trying to hide. The result was that I was captured by the French.

I was sent to Toulouse and there interrogated by the Air Force. Apart from telling them what I knew about Germany I gave them no other information.

18 December. St. Hippolyte
I was then sent to St. Hippolyte on 18 December, 1941, and transferred to Fort de la Revère in March 1942.

FLIGHT LIEUTENANT OLIVER LAWRENCE SPURLING PHILPOT, D.F.C.

42 Squadron R.A.F.

Captured:	Off Norway, 13 December, 1941.
Escaped:	Stalag Luft III (Sagan) 29 October, 1943.
Left:	Stockholm, 26 December, 1943.
Arrived:	Leuchars, 26 December, 1943.

Date of Birth:	6 March, 1913.
O.T.U.:	No. 1 (Coastal) (Silloth).
Post in crew:	Pilot.
Peacetime profession:	Lever Brothers.
Private address:	7 Hollington Court, Chislehurst, Kent.

Capture

On 11 December, 1941, I took off from Leuchars in 42 Squadron Beaufort "O" at 0958 hours. We carried bombs and were detailed for an offensive anti-shipping patrol over a stretch of the Norwegian Coast. We were to start at the southern tip of Karmøy, and then to proceed south past Stavanger, and were to be about 25 minutes on the coast altogether.

Forced landing off Norwegian coast

We made a landfall at approximately 1200 hours and proceeded south. We photographed what appeared to be an R.D.F. Station. At one point we passed over the mainland and over a German parade ground which Sergeant F.J.J. Smith, the air gunner, shot up; he estimates having seen four or five Germans fall to the ground. At 1223 hours, while still over land, I saw a convoy of 18 or 20 ships coming north up the coast, in two lines with a large 10,000-ton M.V. in the centre.

I attacked immediately at top speed and did a mast-high bombing run over the 10,000-ton M.V. We were fired upon and hit in the starboard engine and tail. Still flying at 80 or 100 feet, I tried to return to base, but was compelled to force-land in the sea, out to sea away from the convoy, about 15 or 20 miles off shore. There were very heavy seas and a 48-knot wind. The aircraft immediately broke in half aft of the turret and filled with water. By the time the navigator (Pilot Officer G.M. Rackow) and myself had emerged from the roof hatch (to fall into the sea almost immediately) Pilot Officer Hester, the wireless operator, had somehow managed:

i.   to release the dinghy
ii. to hold onto the dinghy
iii. to get Sergeant Smith into the dingy. Smith, quite a large man, had fallen into the flooded well of the aircraft after hitting his head on the armour-plated bulkhead as we landed. He was unconscious for a short time and told me afterwards that he remembers nothing at all about the entry into the dinghy.
iv. to continue, despite the heavy seas, holding onto the dinghy with one hand and the aircraft with the other and avoid being washed away.

From the water I then ordered Hester into the dinghy, and after Rackow had pulled himself in I followed. Thus, the whole crew were in the dinghy. The aircraft sank 30 to 45 seconds after landing. Had Hester been at all "panicky" or even a little slow, no one of us would have survived.

We were almost immediately sea-sick and, once recovered, we tried to paddle towards the coast without the slightest success. We thought that, with reasonable luck, we should be blown to land by the high wind, but this was not the case. During the afternoon the coast receded, and we were undoubtedly drifting out to sea.

12 December
Night fell, and the next day (12 December) there was no land anywhere in sight. During that day, two He.115s came over (separately) about three-quarters of a mile away and, although we tried to operate a distress marine signal on each occasion, the release tape proved too stiff for our cold hands, and we could not fire our signal. The aircraft passed out of sight.

We ate rations from time to time but felt no great hunger. The band and fastening around each ration container carton I found very difficult to operate (without destroying the whole carton) with cold hands. We drank water from the two flasks provided. All the time we were in the dinghy we were going up and down the sides of the large waves, and now and again water slopped in over the sides. There was thus nearly always water sluicing about in the bottom of the dinghy. Luckily, we had our binocular case, and this served as a baler.

At the end of the second day, we settled down for another night. This meant we lay sideways in an endless circular chain instead of sitting.

13 December; Picked up by German convoy

On the morning of the third day (13 December), we found ourselves close to a coastline lined with high, steep cliffs and with the seas crashing hard against their base. There was no sign of a beach. A German convoy (one of whose ships was the *King Haakon II*) approached, and at 0930 hours we were picked up by one of the flak ships – our dinghy time thus having been 45 hours. We all had to be helped across the deck, were stripped nude below decks, and were then clothed, fed and well-treated generally. We were, of course, interrogated, and gave nationality, names, ranks and numbers. The Germans were later convinced (as we told them nothing of what had occurred) that we were a Hudson crew from a Thornaby Squadron, and I have seen "Hudson" on my official German card.

Kristiansand.

The convoy which picked us up took us round Lister, which we reached in about two or three hours, and to Kristiansand, where we arrived at 2000 hours that night.

Oslo

We were later taken to Oslo, whence Rackow and Hester were flown to Germany, Smith and myself being left in the Aker Sykehus, Oslo. Smith had a frostbitten hand, and I had frostbitten feet, having been wearing only ordinary shoes. Rackow and Hester both had slight trouble with their feet due to the cold, but not enough to warrant treatment.

Aalborg

On, I think, 16 January, 1943, Smith and I left Oslo in S.S. *Lauterfels* which took 48 hours to reach Aalborg (Denmark). The ship anchored the first night at the mouth of Oslo Fjord and the second off the Danish coast.

Dulag Luft
Arrived in Aalborg, we were taken to Dulag Luft, Frankfurt am Main, where, in contrast to the usual experience, the Germans knew practically nothing about us.

Imprisonment in Germany and Polan
After that I went to the following prison camps:

>22 February, 1942: Spangenberg village
>27 February, 1942: Spangenberg castle, Oflag IX / A (Germany)
>28 April, 1942: Sagan – Stalag Luft III (Germany)
>14 September, 1942: Schubin – Oflag XXI B (Poland)
>4 April, 1943: Sagan (again).

The dates are approximate.

Escape from Stalag Luft III (Sagan): German security measures
Sagan lies 102 miles south-east of Berlin and is divided as regards 3,700 Allied Air Force prisoners (approximate figure) into four self-contained compounds. Escape is exceedingly difficult as the Luftwaffe intended it should be when building the camp late in 1941 or early 1942. No one had got home direct from Sagan; and no one had succeeded in making a local break from the East Compound (where I was) for over a year. Wire schemes are suicidal, and orthodox tunnels are found (somewhere between 45 and 60 of them in summer 1942), since the Germans have an uncanny knack of finding the traps situated under our barrack blocks. There are two gates and an ever-changing pass system. The only method from the East Compound is, I think, something entirely new and original, and Lieutenant Michael Codner, Light Artillery; and Flight Lieutenant E.E. Williams were able to start such a scheme in which I eventually became the third participant.

Digging of tunnel. The Wooden Horse
A hollow vaulting horse, light but strong, was constructed by Wing Commander Maw, D.F.C., out of some stolen pieces of wood and the three-ply from Canadian Red Cross boxes. This was carried by four men and used to be placed quite openly close to the wire. Vaulting then took place and, when the vaulting finished, the horse was taken back to the canteen building, where it was housed.

The horse itself was, in fact, quite a good athletic horse, and the Germans accepted it as such. The real object was to have the horse to conceal the entrance to a tunnel, the advantages being twofold; firstly, it was near the wire; secondly, the entrance of the tunnel was thus in a highly original spot – out in the open flat ground in full view of everybody, British and German alike, except that there was nothing to see, since after work was completed, the hole was boarded over and carefully covered with sand to resemble the adjacent surface. It could be, and was frequently, walked over, by British and Germans alike.

The method of work was as follows. When the horse was taken out for a vaulting session one of us would be inside in its belly. This person would then open up the trap, work at the tunnel, fill with sand 12 bags (consisting of trousers legs cut-off below the knee), and hang these bags inside the horse. He would then close the trap, taking a long time to cover it over carefully, squeeze himself into one end of the horse, and be carried off.

Disposal of the sand was the usual nightmare difficulty, and in all about ten methods were used, two of which were found by the Germans who felt there was something going on but did not know what. We settled down to using chiefly the canteen roof and the space under the barber's shop in the canteen.

8 July. Tunnel scheme begun

The scheme began on 8 July, 1943, and was, of course, very slow, due to the limited amount of sand which could be removed at any one time. Codner and Williams did the first 40 feet alone, going down in turns, working entirely naked, and "side stroking" the sand down the tunnel to the entrance. Later we had an improved system with a basin and string. Two people went down, one at the face and one at the entrance, and the latter pulled down basins of sand from the former. Thirty-six bags of sand would be produced in this way and left down there. On each of the next three occasions one man would come out and collect twelve bags.

The work was tiring, and the air was poor. Flight Lieutenant Williams went sick with some type of anus trouble, and the doctors wanted him to have an operation. He insisted, however, on carrying on the work.

All the vaulting took place in full view of a guard in a raised box nearby, who used to laugh at some of the less commendable efforts at vaulting. Previously, also, it had always been the custom to work on escape operations only when the "ferrets" or German security soldiers were out of the camp. Now, however, they were always in the camp, patrolling anywhere they fancy in numbers varying from one to seven at a time.

So, to get anything done at all caution had to be thrown to the winds and we worked while they were in the camp. Throughout we had quite extraordinary luck in evading detection. One day "Charlie", the German security Unteroffizier, walked up to within six feet of the horse when operations were proceeding and suggested that the vaulters would find it easier if they had a springboard. They agreed.

The whole scheme was only made possible by a volunteer band of extremely unselfish helpers who were called on to come and vault time and time again, and who knew they never had any chance of escaping themselves. Members of the Escape Committee were among those who went out of their way not only to give general help, but to come and vault themselves.

Escape through tunnel

Breaking date was 29 October, and at 1300 hours on that date Codner went down with the luggage. He still had the final touches to put to the end of the tunnel, and at 1400 hours we sealed him in and took the horse away. He breathed through two small air holes. An R.A.F. officer assisted in falsifying the count at the parade at 1545 hours and at 1615 hours Williams, Flight Lieutenant McKay and I were all three carried out in the horse, closely squashed together.

Williams and I went down, and McKay sealed us in at 1650 hours. Once in the tunnel, we continued work, the sand being passed back to me in the basin, and I spreading it about the already rather small tunnel. Each man then dragged his kit behind him, and after Codner had broken the tunnel at 1800 hours we started to creep out one by one, with our kit. Codner was first, Williams second, and myself last.

The tunnel's total length was 95 to 100 feet, and the exit was in the open, about 15 to 18 feet outside the wire. Luckily the outside guards patrolling on foot had not yet appeared, due to some German oversight, and the sentry-box guards failed altogether to see us. We were dressed in clothes covered by a suit of dyed combinations each and a mask. Our parcels also were camouflaged so as not to be seen in the boundary lights or the searchlights.

Journey from Sagan

According to plan we went our ways independently. Codner and Williams had originally intended to walk but, owing to the cold at night, they had altered this plan and were intending to take the train to Stettin and catch a boat.

I had decided immediately after the R.A.F. Schubin break of 33 on 5/6 March, 1943, that train travel was the best escape method, especially if one remembered the trip of Flight Lieutenant Crawley to somewhere near Munich, Squadron Leader Calnan and Flight Lieutenant Kee almost to Cologne, and Flight Lieutenant Stevens to Hanover via Berlin, all using indifferent papers. Accordingly, I had since April been preparing such a trip, and I hoped that some opportunity or a break would come.

My story was that I was Herr Jon Jörgensen, a Quisling Norwegian (hoping I would never meet a Norwegian as I was ignorant of the language) on an exchange from Denofa A/K, Fredrikstad, to the Margarine Verkaufs Union, Berlin, and doing a tour of all branches, factories, etc., anywhere in Grossdeutschland. A very fine set of papers were provided in the camp. The papers were:

1. *Vorläufige Ausweis* – an original, and the first time we have used one of these.
2. Two *polizeiliche Erlaubnisse*. One original.
3. One *Bescheinigung*.
4. *Arbeitskarte*.
5. *Bestätigung* (Certificate of Issue of *Arbeitsbuch*).
6. Typed letter from the Margarine Verkaufs Union, introducing me.
7. Typed letter from the National Samling, asking me in Norwegian to go and hear Quisling speak about the reconstruction of Europe.
8. Membership card of the National Samling.
9. A very bogus Swedish sailor's pass added for the dock part of the journey.

My outfit was essentially respectable. Once I started looking like a tramp, I considered I should be ruined. I had a sort of Anthony Eden hat, Hitler moustache, R.A.F. officer's greatcoat, R.A.F. gloves, a new pair of shoes, a pair of Fleet Air Arm trousers and a non-descript black civil jacket. I carried a small vulcanite suitcase with, primarily the means to keep looking well-shaved and smart in it and, secondarily, some of the camp escape food disguised as a margarine product. I had a pipe to cover any linguistic lapses and to give an excuse for not speaking clearly.

Sagan Station
Perusal of the illicit timetable in the camp had indicated that we ought all three to catch the Berlin express at 1900 hours. As I queued up for my ticket at Sagan station, I found Codner just ahead of me, and we both purchased the necessary tickets. Williams, who does not speak a word of German, then accompanied Codner on to the platform and once the train had started, I never saw them again. The train was half

an hour late and very crowded. I stood in the gangway of the third-class and no one paid me any attention.

Frankfurt-A.D.-Oder

I left the train at Frankfurt-A.D.-Oder. There was unfortunately no further connection that night, so I walked down one of the main streets of the town and slept beside a body of water, possibly the Oder. In the early morning I returned to Frankfurt and had a wash-and-brush-up in the little cabinet provided.

In the morning I left on the 0656 hours slow train for Küstrin. It started and arrived late. During this leg of the journey, I was left alone with a little man who was, quite pardonably, confused as to which station he should get out at, Küstrin Neustadt or one of the other Küstrins. He was very difficult to understand, and I soon told him I was Norwegian, whereupon he became very friendly and said his son had been in the German Navy off there for some time.

Küstrin

At Küstrin I lost him and, as usual, I went to the lavatory, which is the prisoner of war's train traveller's normal place to sort out his papers, maps, etc., and eat his escape food, as well as to clean up generally. After this I walked about in the town and sat for a time in a park. There was very little in the shops and, as at Frankfurt, practically no motor traffic.

30 October

At 1029 hours on 30 October, I caught "D 1", the Königsberg express, which was punctual, but crowded. The journey to Dirschau I spent mostly in the gangway of a third-class coach. There were few incidents, and I maintained here, as throughout, a superior, aloof attitude, which was at one stage of this stretch rather impaired by my going to sleep on my case, falling off, and saying "Damn", to the general amusement of surrounding soldiers and civilians. On this train there was one first-class grumbler who was telling those around him of how in the West there were air raid alarms day and night and nobody got very much peace.

On the whole trip, I always felt safest when mixing with dense crowds and this stage was no exception.

Past Schneidemühl I had my first and only train check. A plain clothes member of the Kriminalpolizei asked most politely for my *Ausweis*, and he studied it with very little concern. On his asking about my movements, I explained that the Dresden Police had insisted on keeping my Norwegian passport for the time being and had issued this for travelling.

He said he supposed I would be returning from Danzig soon, and I said I would. He ended by saying that if the Dresden police had stamped the photo on my *Ausweis* it would then be "*ganz richtig*", but it was sufficiently in order. The photo, incidentally, was not of me, but of Squadron Leader Wardell. He asked me for no other papers and went away.

At Dirschau I changed to a fast train going to Danzig from Breslau. I had been afraid to take this from the Sagan area, as it passes, I think, through Posen, which we regard as dangerous.

Danzig.

This train got me into Danzig Hauptbahnhof at 1700 hours, 22 hours, 55 minutes, after emerging from the tunnel. I had planned to be there in the early morning, but the connection between Frankfurt and Küstrin was worse than was the case during the validity of our timetable, which expired at the end of September. Thus, I could not get a view of the city or harbour because of the darkness.

Neufahrwasser

After a beer in the refreshment room, I caught the No. 8 tram and went to Neufahswasser to reconnoitre. It was appallingly dark, and I blundered into what looked like an open waste space, but which really led to some oil tanks. A dog barked, a car moved up, and I moved off.

Weichselmünde

Eventually I found the ferry over to Weichselmünde and I crossed (5 Pf., I think). I then walked up and down near the Swedish docks, trying to see the lie of the land, and especially which were the Swedish ships. Distinguishing the nationality of ships is not easy when they are obscured by trucks, cranes, etc. As regards local geography the flimsy of which I had a copy, proved invaluable.

My reconnaissance was perfectly open, as I merely walked about carrying my suitcase and trying to look busy. Soon, however, I ran into an elderly railway official in a blue coat who headed me off at one point. I said I was lost and where was the ferry? He escorted me to it and we parted on good terms – I then returned by tram to Danzig and had a "Stammgericht" and beer at the Hauptbahnhof.

Danzig; Night in hotel

At this point I felt very tired, and it seemed important to avoid nights in the open if I was to remain fit and, more important, efficient and of good appearance. Accordingly, I went to the Hotel Continentale almost opposite the Hauptbahnhof and asked for a room. My reception was unfriendly but I think it may have been the reception man's normal attitude. He said there were no rooms, but after reconsideration said he had a bed for me – in the same room as another man. He asked for my Reisepass, and I had to explain that my *Ausweis* was perfectly good authority. To add colour, I showed him one of my *polizeiliche Erlaubnisse,* and he was satisfied.

This occasion and the train check past Schneidemühl were the only two occasions during the whole escape when I had to show anyone any papers whatsoever. I then had to fill in a hotel pink form and state who I was, nationality, last address, etc., none of which were at all difficult questions, providing one had one's story "pat". The form, incidentally, had the sections headed in various languages, English amongst them. I then went to my room (No. 220) and had a bath in the private bathroom adjoining. I hurried to bed and was asleep before the other man arrived. Having no pyjamas (and rather odd equipment generally), I was rather afraid of him being suspicious. He came in late and, to my relief, left next morning at 0745. I got up afterwards, avoided breakfast because of lack of coupons, paid my bill (5.80 Rm., I think) and left.

On the next morning (31 October), I took a trip up and down the harbour in a "*Hafenrundfahrt*" boat, up to Neufahrwasser (Seefer's Hotel) and back to town (40 Pf. in all). On this trip I saw the S.S. *Bjorn*, Stockholm, moored in the Swedish dock and being loaded with coal. The harbour launch took me quite close, and I was able to plan the method of approaching along the dock.

Danzig Heubude

In the afternoon, 31 October, I walked out to Danzig Heubude, and in a position past the cemetery and on the opposite side of the road from the bathing lake there I buried in the leaves of a wood my greatcoat, hat, and suitcase containing nearly all my personal equipment, but nothing to identify the things with Sagan or myself.

Weichselmünde

Hatless, and simply wearing my dark suit with viyella shirt and R.A.F. black tie with a pattern of white threading in it, I then took tram No.

4 part of the way back and walked into Weichselmünde. I was thus prepared to attempt the ship, or, if this failed and I was still free, to disinter my equipment and return to my role of a fairly respectable Jon Jörgensen.

On the way I passed two groups of two oil tanks each and in each case one of the two was ruined, presumably by bombs. In addition, I saw one bomb crater and one bomb-ruined house. It seemed advisable to keep to the public road, as there were balloon positions, labour camps, etc., all with guards, in the surrounding countryside.

I went into Weichselmünde and, it still being early, I continued in the direction away from Danzig until I came to a pine forest adjoining the open sea. Here I rested until 1800 hours. I could see a lighthouse somewhere at the mouth of the river flashing two to three seconds light to four to five seconds black.

Whether the whole of this wood is empty of Germans I do not know, but it seems a possible lying-up place for escapers, and it might even form a rendezvous for sea-borne commandos. The police dock supervision all round Danzig seems poor and, although those in the dock area are meant to have a special *Ausweis* from the Harbour Police, I was never challenged and asked for this. On the naval ships, and some of the others, I saw guards walking about.

Boarding of Swedish vessel

I left the wood and walked back to Weichselmünde to attempt the ship. I went to the north-westerly part of the Swedish dock, to the round-the-harbour boat's landing stage immediately south of the Weichselmünde stage used for the shuttle service with Neufahrwasser. There was nobody about where I was, so I slipped down onto the stage and climbed along just above water-level and below the lip of the dock round past the barbed wire fence extension. I could see that the gangway of the S.S. *Bjorn* was adequately guarded by a sentry who had a beat of about 10 paces in front of it.

Eventually I got to a vertical steel ladder let into the side of the dock to facilitate entering small boats. While I was on this ladder a small boat, apparently containing harbour officials or police, and which had been hovering round, approached. I crawled swiftly up on to the dock just as one of the sentries from the gate – marked (quite rightly) on our flimsy "avoid this gate" – approached the ladder, flashing his torch. He went to one side of a large sandbox and I to the other. After he had spoken to those in the boat the disturbance died down, and I decided to proceed further.

I was aiming all this time to reach the cable mooring the ship. As I crawled towards the cables two more guards approached with torches, but I lay dead still near the railway buffers and they walked by, the width of the track away. After this I reached the cables and climbed up one. This was a bad error, as it was secured to the far side of the ship and was drawn tight round the stern plating, affording no hand-hold up by the vessel. I knocked on a port hole, with no result, and returned. After a rest I hauled myself up the next cable, which led direct through a large hole in the plating to the deck.

Boarded vessel
I scrambled through the hole and on to the deck. There was no shouting or excitement, so I am convinced I was unseen.

During the whole evening the fairly strong dock lights situated high up were on, and the coal-loading of my ship was taking place with a powerful searchlight following the grab.

I could see no promising hiding place on deck, and it seemed senseless to remain there too long. The door in the stern on the dark (starboard) side was locked, so I crawled amidships and entered a door which led to the passage off which there was a small galley. I drank a sort of cocoa-chocolate drink which I was surprised to find simmering on the fire and then called at a lighted cabin which turned out to be the Steward's.

I felt that my ignorance of where the German search party looked and where they did not look was so great that what might appear to me a wonderful hiding place might turn out to be just where they regularly searched. Hence the obvious thing was to get help.

After I approached the Steward, the Chief Mate appeared. Neither would say anything definite until the Captain was brought and then the Chief Engineer joined us and a sort of conference was held half in and half out of the cabin. I asked to stay and stressed the fact that no one had seen me get on board. The Captain said the war was going to last only another three or four months and asked why I did not return to Germany, as if I stayed he might be hanged. It was not worth his while to risk this, even for the £500 which I offered him, and he said I must leave the ship. He also recommended another Swedish ship further down the dock. I offered to disappear – meaning to hide myself on his ship – and not re-appear until later.

The Captain then slipped away without making any attempt whatsoever to remove me physically from his ship, or to report me to the Germans on the adjacent dock. The meeting then broke up and, as I went on deck to look for a likely place, a ship's officer pointed to a hatch which I entered. As I sat below, one of his subordinates came and showed me a coal bunker to hide in. The time was now about 2100 hours on 31 October, and I was in this bunker for nine hours. It is not a place that I recommend since, besides being uncomfortable, it seems practically impossible to cover oneself up properly with coal. I should imagine the stupidest German could find one there, especially if accompanied by a dog, which, the crew told me, is the custom at Stettin.

At the end of the nine hours, one of the crew took me below to B.B. Tank No. 4, which is a tank at the very bottom of the ship. The tank was entered by the unscrewing of an oval plate which had been bolted down and which was bolted down again when I was in. It obviously had been filled with oil at one time; it was possible to crawl in it and to lie down.

2 November. Ship cast off

I stayed in this tank for 28 hours, and during that time the ship cast off at 0745 hours on Tuesday, 2 November. At about 1000 hours on that day, the same member of the crew came and took me higher up in the ship to a place by some machinery, still well below deck level. He had previously given me some rolls and water, and now he produced the same again.

I remained in this place until about 2000 hours, whereupon I was taken up to a cabin where I met one of the officers. He then told me that the story to the Captain, the ship's crew, and everybody else must be that I hid unaided in the coal and when well out to sea knocked on the bulkhead, whereupon he found me and released me. At 2300 hours I was therefore taken to the Captain, who asked me where I had been. I told him our prepared story. I doubt if he believed it, but he asked no further questions. He was never abrupt or rude in his manner but was simply frightened of the Gestapo.

Voyage to Sweden

The voyage from Danzig to somewhere between what I think was Öland and the mainland took approximately 15 hours. The Steward said we had hugged the German coast to Kolberg and then gone west of Bornholm to the mainland. The Chief Engineer said we went direct to the southern tip of Öland, and in view of the time factor this seems more likely.

As far as I could gather there was, contrary to my expectation, no interception by a German patrol vessel once the ship had got clear of

Danzig. The only search party would thus seem to be that which the crew say arrived from four to six strong, with no dog, about two and a quarter hours before the ship sailed and which carried out a two-hour search.

The other German ports which Swedish ships apparently call at are Stettin and Lübeck only.

Once I had been shown to the Captain I was entertained as a guest on board in a very hospitable fashion.

3 November. Docked at Södertälje
At midnight on Wednesday, 3 November, we docked at Södertälje, where I spent the night in a police cell.

4 November. Stockholm
Next day I was allowed the freedom of the police station until I was taken to Stockholm by the train leaving at 1452 hours. I arrived at the British Legation, Stockholm, at 1642 hours on Thursday, 4 November.

The following assisted Lieutenant M. Codner, Flight Lieutenant E.E. Williams, and myself in our escape from Stalag Luft III (Sagan) in the ways specified below:

(a) Group Captain Willetts, R.A.F. falsified the parade at 1545 hours on 29 October, 1943, when we went into the tunnel.
(b) Dean and Dawson, the camp forgers, provided a very fine set of papers. Their most skilled expert is Flight Lieutenant Shore, assisted by Flight Lieutenant Hunter, and many others.

Notes
I received assistance on board ship from the following members of the crew of the Swedish S.S. *Aralizz*:

(a) Armand Monson, Chief Engineer.
(b) Gosta Johansson, engineer.

The above have received 500 Kroner, and a box of cigars each from M.A., Stockholm.

If some German food coupons as used by travellers could be sent to Sagan, this would help future escapers.

A fair disguise for an escaper once in Danzig would be that of a Swedish sailor wearing nondescript civilian clothes. For this role, however, a Swedish sailor's discharge book (with space for personal details and then a sheet for each voyage) is necessary, also a chit from the German dock authorities permitting the sailor to be on German territory. The latter is issued to members of crews going ashore, and is returned by them to the Germans under penalty of a fine of 20 Rm., if they fail to hand it in. The sailors have under these regulations to be aboard ship again by 2200 hours.

With these two documents an escaper could probably pass the sentries without trouble and board the ship quite openly. One of the officers of the S.S. *Aralizz* said the guard did not keep count of the number going on and off. I suggest that several originals of each of these documents be sent to Sagan at the earliest opportunity, and work can then be started on reproducing them in numbers.

It would also be a good thing if some indoor rendezvous could be arranged at Danzig for escapers. The same Swedish officer said Swedish sailors used years ago to congregate at the Deutsches Haus in the square in Neufahrwasser, but this may or may not be true today.

Before I left Sagan, Group Captain Kellett briefed Codner, Williams, and myself. He said he had practically nothing for us, since the repatriees had been very fully briefed. There were, however, two things:

(a) Aircrews should be warned that there are two British ex-aircrew interpreters now helping the Germans at Dulag – one as a Red Cross man, the other as a German. Their names are so far unknown, and they have never passed through an ordinary prison camp. Dulag is thus a more dangerous camp than ever from a security point of view and aircrews should be warned.

(b) A Squadron Leader Carpenter is alleged to be in the German Air Ministry. This is being confirmed. He also has never passed through a prison camp.

1st Lieutenant David Whytehead (Paratroop) now in Sagan and three or four of his troop were at Fresnes jail near Paris at the end of September, 1943. He believes there was a leakage in London and that the Germans had prior knowledge of his mission. They were taken in Paris itself.

The Senior American Officer in Sagan says that the method of signalling change of leadership in a formation is in need of revision. Recently, for example, there was a bad case of aircraft going astray by following a crippled leader.

The Senior American Officer in Sagan says that the engine settings agreed upon for some raids are in need of revision. Some of the settings are believed to have been extravagant, and the planes failed to make the round trip through over-consumption.

The Senior American Officer in Sagan mentioned that many Germans are asking what assistance the Allies will give them against Russia in the event of a German capitulation.